3rd Edition

Writing
by Doing

Learning to Write Effectively

Elaine Hughes

David A. Sohn

National Textbook Company
a division of NTC/CONTEMPORARY PUBLISHING COMPANY
Lincolnwood, Illinois USA

Credits

Photography: cover, Bradley Wilson; p. 19, Claudia Hamblin; p. 20, Pat Brennan; p. 24, Bradley Wilson; p. 26, Al Snisko; p. 28, © 1996 Six Flags Theme Parks Inc. (SIX FLAGS and IRON WOLF are registered trademarks of Six Flags Theme Parks Inc.); p. 30, Tom Firak/Marilyn Gartman Agency; p. 35, 36, Scott Dworkin; p. 37, Leo Mesina; p. 38, Steven Goldberg; p. 77, Cindy Frendreis-Placko; p. 78, James Bensdorf; p. 85, Steven Goldberg; p. 99, Heather Donald; p. 109, John Rischke. *Text:* p. 122, Heimlich Maneuver poster: From *Journal of the American Medical Association,* October 28, 1992, Vol. 268, No. 16. © 1992 American Medical Association. Illustrations 1 and 2 courtesy of the American Red Cross. All rights reserved in all countries.

Library of Congress Cataloging-in-Publication Data

Hughes, Elaine.
     Writing by doing: learning to write effectively.—3rd ed. /
Elaine Hughes, David A. Sohn.
       p. cm.
     Rev. ed. of: Writing by doing / David A. Sohn, Edward Enger. 2nd
ed. c1990.
     Includes index.
     Summary: Provides instruction in personal writing, paragraph
writing, longer compositions, and language skills, with activities
and exercises for practice and review.
     ISBN 0-8442-5909-8
     1. English language—Composition and exercises. 2. English
language—Grammar. [1. English language—Composition and
exercises. 2. English language—Grammar.] I. Sohn, David A.
II. Sohn, David A. Writing by doing. III. Title.
PE1413.S653 1996
808'.042—dc20

        96-30484
        CIP
        AC

ISBN: 0-8442-5909-8

Published by National Textbook Company,
a division of NTC/Contemporary Publishing Company,
4255 West Touhy Avenue,
Lincolnwood (Chicago), Illinois 60646-1975 U.S.A.
© 1997, 1990, 1983 by NTC/Contemporary Publishing Company

7 8 9 0 VL 9 8 7 6 5 4 3 2

CONTENTS

CHAPTER 4   THE PERSONAL LETTER   49

Part 2

PARAGRAPH POWER: DEVELOPING YOUR IDEAS STEP BY STEP   59

CHAPTER 5   WRITING EFFECTIVE PARAGRAPHS   61

CHAPTER 6   DESCRIPTIVE PARAGRAPHS   69

CHAPTER 7   NARRATIVE PARAGRAPHS   79

Part 3

LONGER COMPOSITIONS: WRITING FOR OTHERS   111

CHAPTER 18   USING CORRECT PRONOUNS   249

CHAPTER 19   SUBJECT-VERB AGREEMENT   259

CHAPTER 20   WORDS OFTEN MISUSED OR MISSPELLED   269

CHAPTER 21   PUNCTUATION   287

CHAPTER 22   USING APOSTROPHES AND QUOTATIONS   301

CHAPTER 23   CAPITALIZATION AND ABBREVIATION   309

PREFACE

When this book first appeared several years ago, the study of the writing process had become a major priority among English teachers. Great attention was given to how to teach writing better. Teacher training projects were funded throughout the country, aimed at improving writing instruction. Today, this movement has produced many teachers who are doing a much better job of teaching writing because they understand much more about how students develop writing skills and become more effective writers. Effective writing remains a top priority in schools and the business world.

The authors of this program have received many positive comments from teachers, supervisors, and administrators who have used it since the first copies came off the presses. Some of the things they liked were the short, clear activities; explanations of concepts that were written so that students could understand them; the appealing photographs, quotations, and other graphic elements that made the book pleasant to use; and the emphasis on writing *and more writing* as a central theme throughout the book.

Hemingway, Epictetus, and many others have said it in different ways: "If you want to be a good writer, you have to practice writing." No teacher is going to use magic tricks to make you a better writer. You learn by doing, which is why we created the title *Writing by Doing.* You could read a thousand books and learn many things, but if you did not practice writing during your extensive reading period, you would not improve your writing much. The point is that you study a concept, apply it, submit it to your editor (teacher), and learn from the feedback your editor-teacher gives you. You improve as you write more and more, and as you learn more and more skills.

Writing by Doing is divided into four parts:

- **Personal Writing,** which gives you encouragement and help for developing your own style
- **Paragraph Power,** which teaches you, through the development of paragraphs, step-by-step methods for writing various kinds of papers
- **Longer Compositions,** which takes you through the writing of essays, factual reports with documentation, reviews, and business communications

- **Language Skills Review,** which gives you direction and practice in using correct language in your writing.

The Language Skills Review is not meant to be a complete grammar and usage text, but is offered as a skills sharpener where review and brief instruction are needed.

There are many reasons for wanting to improve your writing skills. One of the most important is that if you become a very effective communicator of oral and written thoughts, you stand a good chance of getting a satisfying and economically rewarding job. Learning to express yourself well through writing can improve your academic work, enrich your personal life, and help you to understand and cope better with an increasingly complex society that changes rapidly with each day.

If you work seriously with this book, you can sharpen your writing skills and discover the pleasures that writing can offer to you. We wish you well as you work and grow.

Elaine Hughes
David A. Sohn

Part 1

PERSONAL WRITING

Writing for Yourself

I KEEP SIX HONEST SERVING MEN

THEY TAUGHT ME ALL I KNEW

THEIR NAMES ARE WHAT AND WHY

AND WHEN

AND HOW AND WHERE AND WHO.

RUDYARD KIPLING

There is no person who occupies your thoughts more than yourself. Because you are the most important person in your life, you can use personal writing effectively to bring problems into focus, to record your feelings, and to discover more about yourself. Personal writing can also be valuable for conveying your feelings and ideas to others in an informal way. Because it is about yourself, personal writing is enjoyable, and to you it is always interesting.

Writing is not limited to reports and book reviews for school assignments. It is a way to communicate with yourself and others. In fact, writing for yourself sometimes provides more satisfaction than getting a good grade on a composition. Like athletes, musicians, or artists, writers need to practice their skills in order to excel. By writing for yourself, you can practice what you know and experiment with what you've learned. In addition, personal writing helps you develop ideas when you are asked to write on a topic of your own choosing.

WHAT YOU WILL LEARN

In this section, you will learn how to do the following:

1. Keep a journal in order to develop confidence as a writer, capture memories, develop a writing voice, and expand your writing style.

2. Apply your powers of observation and imagination.

3. Research, write, and revise an autobiographical sketch.

4. Write personal letters.

Chapter 1

THE JOURNAL

WARM-UP

Recall as many events as you can about what you did yesterday. List any important feelings that you had about the events. Describe them in as much detail as you possibly can.

Why Keep a Journal?

A *journal* is a day-by-day personal record of your life with *you* as the subject. It is a written account of events that happen to you and your thoughts and feelings about those events. In this sense, a journal is similar to a diary that you may have kept at home. The difference, however, is that a diary usually is thought of as very private. For your journal, rather than writing about extremely private experiences or feelings, you will be asked to write about those you are willing to share in the classroom.

You will find that a journal will help you to do the following:

- Develop confidence in your ability as a writer.
- Capture important memories.
- Develop a sense of your own writing voice.

At first, most beginning writers lack confidence in their ability to write. One reason they may not feel confident is that they have not practiced writing. Although school assignments may include writing, young writers often do not write outside class. When they do, the writing is likely to consist only of notes to friends and shopping lists.

Another reason for a young writer's lack of confidence is the belief that he or she has nothing to say. It may seem easy for people who lead unusual or exciting lives to write. After all, they can describe a skydiving or mountain climbing experience. What about someone, however, whose adventures are limited to school, homework, and weekly chores at home?

The fact is that everyone has something to say. Even the most ordinary experiences can often lead to interesting writing. Describing the bus ride home after school, the band rehearsal, the gymnastics meet, or problems with the family car in careful detail and emphasizing their effects on you and on other people can lead to interesting and satisfying writing.

Keeping a journal will help you to recognize how many interesting things you have to say. Further, a journal can help you discover new writing opportunities, as well as develop your confidence in your ability to write. One way it can do this is by giving you the opportunity to practice your writing. In order to improve, you must practice, just as good runners practice running and good musicians practice their music. No magic wand can make you a better writer. The magic of writing well comes from the practice of putting words on paper.

Setting Up Your Journal

If possible, keep your journal in a separate notebook that you use only for that purpose. Part of the process of becoming a dedicated journal keeper is selecting a notebook that you like. Because you will want to keep your journals for many years so that you can go back to read them whenever you want, a sturdy notebook is essential. In general, avoid notebooks that have glued-in pages; instead, choose ones that have spiral or stitched bindings. You might prefer small notebooks over large ones, plain ones over decorated ones, college-ruled pages over legal-ruled or unlined pages. Consider your own preferences and choose the journal notebook that suits your taste and needs. Also, when you write in your journal, you might find it useful to begin each entry on a new page, add the date, and write in ink so your writing will survive the years.

A period of nonstop, timed writing in your journal every day will give you practice writing and help you to "loosen up" for other kinds of writing. If you find this activity difficult, it is probably because you are not accustomed to writing a lot of words. As you continue to write in your journal, however, you will find that, over a period of time, thoughts will come to you much more easily than they do right now.

Continuing your journal on your own, throughout the year, can help you develop your confidence as a writer. The best way to do this is to set aside a regular time each day for writing in your journal. In this way, journal writing will become a habit, and you will have made a large first step toward becoming an accomplished writer.

Getting Started

Sometimes writing about your own experience is a problem. If someone asks you, "How was your day?" you are likely to respond, "Okay." Of course, that word does not really tell anything about your day. Fortunately, there is a formula that usually helps to rescue those at a loss for words.

Newspaper writers use this formula as a simple way to discover and record concrete details and impressions. It is called the 5Ws and H. It means *Who? What? When? Where? Why?* and *How?* These are central questions you can ask yourself when you write in your journal.

Who? Who were the people involved in my day?

Who was important to me today?

Whom did I affect in some way today?

What? What happened today?

What events changed me in some way?

What do I wish had happened differently today?

When? When were important times during my day?

When was a time that made me feel good?

When was a time that I would not like to repeat?

Where? Where did I go today that was important to me?

Where did I go today that I would not like to be again?

Where would I like to have gone today but didn't?

Why? Why did I do some of the things I did today?

Why did certain things happen to me today?

Why can't I change some things that are happening?

How? How do I feel about today?

How can I repeat some of the successes I had today?

How can I avoid some of the problems I had today?

In addition, there are some questions about time that you can ask yourself. These questions help you to focus on the past *(Then)*, the present *(Now)*, and the future *(Someday)*.

Then? What did I see today that reminded me of something in the past?

What past success did I have that was similar to one I had today?

What past mistake did I make that was similar to one I made today?

Now? How do I feel right now?

How can I describe the feeling to help me understand it?

How is this feeling similar to ones I've had in the past?

Someday? What is a success I would like to have someday?

What is a problem I would like to solve someday?

How would I describe myself as I would like to be in the future?

These questions are not intended to limit your writing. Rather, they are simply "idea starters" for your journal writing. Remember to write as much as possible to answer the questions that you ask yourself.

Journal Starter Worksheet

Who?	What?	When?
Where?	Why?	How?
Then?	Now?	Someday?

Writing Activity 1   **A Journal Starter Worksheet**

Prepare a journal starter worksheet like the one above. To do this, divide a sheet of paper into nine spaces. Label each space with one of the kinds of questions that you will ask: *Who? What? When? Where? Why? How? Then? Now?* and *Someday?* Now ask yourself the questions in the previous section, as well as any new ones that you think of yourself. Jot down the answers in that space on your worksheet. The answers may be simply words or phrases that will help you to remember your experiences or thoughts. When you are ready to write in your journal, look over your worksheet for ideas.

Making a Journal Entry

When you write in your journal, you make an *entry*. Following are two journal entries, one contemporary, one from the nineteenth century.

The first journal entry was written by a student of today. Notice the impressions of the immediate environment and the expressions of the writer's thoughts.

Tuesday, October 10, 1997
8:00 P.M.

The sky is filled with moisture as the fog begins to form. The sound of rain upon the roof and the street is like the sound of clapping hands in a concert hall. Gutters and downspouts drain off the water. The rain has a fresh scent. It seems to purify the air. Cars pass by, splashing and swishing through the water-soaked road. The birds chirp happily, while the plants and trees silently absorb the moisture.

I am both happy and sad today. I enjoy listening to the rain, but I think about the future. What am I going to do with my life? School and studies go on and on, but I wonder if I am going to make a success of myself. I like the idea of being an engineer, but there is a lot of competition. Sometimes I wonder if I want to teach. Or be an accountant. I can see that I have a lot of thinking to do. I think I'll talk to some people in these jobs. Maybe they can give me some help.

The following journal entry was written by a young woman, Margaret Emily Shore, more than one hundred years ago in England. Notice how she writes in detail about subjects that were important to her.

January 31, 1833

In the afternoon there was a fall of snow, and we began to speculate what we should do if every flake was a piece of gold money. To be sure, this shower of money would break all the windows, destroy the plants, and patter furiously down the chimney; but then, we should get ten thousand times more money than would be sufficient to pay for the repairing of the damage a hundred times over.

We then began to settle what we should do with all this money. We should in the first place purchase the whole estate of Woodbury and rebuild the house on a magnificent scale. Then we should have a splendid garden, filled with all the choicest flowers in the world. And we would have a noble library, and printing presses for us children, to print all the productions of our pens. In short, there would be no end to the magnificence of our possessions and mode of living. I should also like to have a tame elephant.

Writing Activity 2	**First Entry**

For your first journal entry, put your name and date in the upper right-hand corner of the page. Look over the worksheet and carefully study each of the questions. Select the one that interests you most and write your first entry about that item on your worksheet.

Writing Activity 3	**A Five-Minute Entry**

Label this entry with today's date. For this activity, you will be timed for five minutes. When your teacher signals you to start, write whatever thoughts are in your mind that are not too private. Do not stop writing until five minutes have passed.

During the five minutes, you may write about anything you wish to share with your class—thoughts, feelings, descriptions of the classroom, memories. The important point is that you *do not stop writing.* The writing does not have to be serious. You may want to describe little green people from Mars or your idea for a soap opera plot. If you are stuck, write down one sentence and copy it over and over until your thoughts begin to flow. Write down the first sentence of a nursery rhyme if you cannot think of anything else. *Do not stop writing* until the five minutes are up.

Writing Activity 4	**Something Important to Me**

Label this entry with today's date. If you are keeping your journal in a notebook, begin each entry on a separate page, placing the date in the upper right-hand corner. Now, think of something that has been important to you today or during the last few days. It may be a problem that you need to solve, or it may be something that surprised you or disturbed you in some way. It can be anything that you think is important enough to write about, as long as it is not too private to share. Take your pen or pencil and begin to write about it. Your first sentence can be as simple as "I was so happy when _____." or "I had a lot of fun when _____."

For the next twenty minutes or so, write about the topic you selected. Try to describe your feelings in as much detail as possible. See if, through writing, you can understand *why* the experience was important to you. In what small or large way did it change you? Write as much as you can about your subject. When your time is up, stop. Reread what you have written. Think about it. If you have written about something that is honestly important to you, then you are well on your way to good writing.

Capturing Memories

Good writing is not always about the kinds of events that you read about in the newspaper. Very often, in fact, it is about something that is remembered because it is important only to the writer.

However, your memory is not completely reliable over a long time. You may take pride in your ability to remember people, places, events, and thoughts; but a year passes sooner than you think. Your memory about any specific day will fade over time. If you keep a journal, however, you can revisit your past at any time. You can take a close look at who you were then and what you were thinking a year ago, five years ago, or even longer. In addition, these memories you have captured will give you ideas for other kinds of writing.

In all kinds of writing, details are important. In journal writing, they are especially so, for without them, your journal would have the same effect as an out-of-focus photograph. You could not use it to capture experiences. Details are the small, often unnoticed parts of experience. For example, even though you have probably been in your English classroom many times, could you describe it now, without examining it first? Do you know how many desks it contains and how they are arranged? How many windows are there? Where are they located? What posters, maps, charts, or bulletins are on the walls and bulletin boards? What are the lighting fixtures like? What is the exact color of the walls? Of the floor or carpet?

You may include many different kinds of details in your writing. One important kind is what are called the *sensory details*— details of sight, sound, taste, smell, and touch. Other kinds of details include thoughts and feelings that people may have, words people may say, and actions they may perform. For a list of sense words you can use in your journal writing, see pages 23–29.

Writing Activity 5   **An Old Photograph**

Find a photograph of yourself that was taken more than a year ago. Study the photograph, trying to remember what you were like at the time. What seemed important to you then? What were you feeling when the picture was taken? Were you happy or sad? Why? How were you different then? How were you similar to the way you are now? Label this entry with today's date. Write about yourself as you were when the photograph was taken.

If you cannot find a photograph of yourself, think about an event that happened more than a year ago. Try to recreate the incident in your mind. Recall as many different kinds of details about it as you can. What was the scene like? What were you thinking and feeling? What did you say and do? Then write as accurately and completely as you can about the event. Read what you have written. How well could you picture the details of your past? Had any memories faded in a year's time? How well could you capture the details on paper?

Your Writing Voice

You probably have many friends whose voices you recognize. When they call you on the telephone, you know who they are even before they give their names. This is because a person's speaking voice is unique. A "speaking voice" means how fast or slow, high or low a person speaks. It also includes how he or she pronounces and emphasizes certain words.

In the same way, a writer has a unique writing voice. Two important parts of a writing voice are the words a writer selects and how he or she arranges them into sentences. For example, one writer may choose many descriptive words and phrases, while another may use fewer of them. One writer may use longer and more complex sentences, while another may use shorter words and simpler sentences.

As you practice writing, you will find a way of saying things that is natural for you. Some writers call this discovery "finding your own writing voice." Remember, however, that good writing is not stilted or awkward. Most good writers have a voice that is simple and direct; it "sounds" natural. When you write, do not try to use needless large words or long, complicated sentences. Concentrate on writing simply and directly, just as you might speak.

One way to find your natural writing voice is to read what you have written aloud to yourself. Listen to the rhythm of your words and the way they are arranged into sentences. Sometimes a sentence will not sound "right," and you can improve it by rearranging or changing words. When this happens, you are discovering your writing voice.

Writing Activity 6	**Trying Out My Writing Voice**

Label this entry with today's date. Then, choose a topic from the following list and write in your journal for twenty minutes or so. Practice writing simply and directly, as though you were speaking.

How I learned a lesson   A television show I'd like to change
When I was happy   After high school
A movie star I'd like to be   A book I couldn't put down
What's good about me   Important moments in my life
My favorite weather   A favorite comic strip
The best day of the week   A place I'd like to be
An animal I don't like

Writing Activity 7	**Analyzing My Writing Voice**

Read one of your journal entries aloud to yourself or to a friend. If you have a tape recorder, tape your entries and listen to yourself as the tape plays back. Answer the following questions about your writing voice:

1. What good examples of a natural writing voice did you find when you read your selection aloud?

2. Did any of the sentences or phrases sound too formal or fancy? Give examples.

3. What suggestions would you make to yourself to improve the selection by changing the choice of words, phrases, or even sentences? Should you add anything to your selection? What?

Expanding Your Writing Style

Your journal is the perfect place to experiment with different styles of writing. You can use your journal entries to practice making your writing more vivid and lively by rewriting words and sentences that seem vague or dull or do not fully capture what you want to communicate. Two easy ways to add more style to your writing are by using *concrete words* and *figures of speech*.

Concrete Words

As a writer, you use words just as a painter uses brush strokes. With brush strokes, a painter adds and adjusts until the images on the canvas become clear and focused. Similarly, you can think of sharpening your sentences as though you were looking through a telescope. You wish to see something in crisp detail, but the image is blurred and hazy. Each turn brings the scene into better focus. You continue adjusting until you have brought the scene into sharp focus.

You can begin to bring your writing into sharper focus by paying attention to the nouns and verbs that you use. Make each one of them more specific and concrete. For example, consider the nouns and verbs used in the following sentence:

The dog showed that it didn't like the person very much.

How clear is the picture that the above sentence presents to the reader?

Now, read the sentence below. How does the addition of concrete words change the sentence?

The German shepherd growled and snarled at the thief.

Notice that the second sentence gives the reader more specific information. You know that the dog is a German shepherd, not a poodle or a toy terrier. The verbs growled and snarled give the reader a sound impression that the first sentence lacks. You also know that the person is a thief, not a friend.

The second sentence is more concrete because the nouns, German shepherd and thief, and the verbs, growled and snarled, are more precise. They give energy and life to the second sentence.

Here are some other examples:

Vague: The woman walked to the store.
Effective: Nick's grandmother hurried to the supermarket.

Vague: The girls played outside.
Effective: The Girl Scouts played basketball in the park.

Vague: The boy went somewhere.
Effective: Lee Kim jogged down Arapaho Avenue.

> **Vague:** The player scored a run for the team.
> **Effective:** Maria Lopez clobbered a homer for the Wildcats.
>
> **Vague:** The plane flew through the sky.
> **Effective:** The jet soared into the sunset.

Notice how the effective sentences use nouns and verbs that are not fuzzy or unclear. They are sharp and specific. They give the reader a precise image.

Writing Activity 8	**Using Specific Nouns and Verbs**

On a separate sheet of paper, rewrite the following sentences, using specific nouns and verbs.

1. The animal ran away.
2. The girl walked into the room.
3. The people did not like the food.
4. The couple had fun at the show.
5. The man hit the tree with his car.

Now write five sentences of your own, using specific nouns and verbs.

Adjectives and adverbs can also help present a more vivid picture to the reader. They can focus the meanings of nouns and verbs. Study the following sentence:

1. The person walked along the street.

This sentence is vague. It says very little. It could refer to almost any person in the world and almost any street in the world. The first step in focusing this writing is to make the nouns and verbs more concrete and specific.

2. The <u>jogger</u> <u>bounded</u> along <u>Elmwood Avenue</u>.

Now we know the person is a jogger, but we don't know whether the jogger is male or female. We also know that the street is Elmwood Avenue.

3. The <u>male</u> jogger bounded <u>briskly</u> along the <u>hot</u>, <u>bumpy</u> sidewalk on Elmwood Avenue.

The word <u>male</u> shows us the jogger's gender. The adjectives <u>hot</u> and <u>bumpy</u> tell us the condition of the sidewalk. The adverb <u>briskly</u> tells us how the jogger is bouncing along.

4. The <u>seventeen-year-old</u> male jogger bounded briskly down the hot, <u>steaming</u>, bumpy sidewalk on Elmwood Avenue <u>in the late afternoon</u>.

The adjective <u>seventeen-year-old</u> pinpoints the jogger's age. The adjective <u>steaming</u> suggests a humid condition. The adverb phrase <u>in the late afternoon</u> tells us when he is jogging. Read sentence 1 again. The meaning is cloudy. The picture is obscure. Compare sentence 1 with sentence 4.

| Writing Activity 9 | **Adding Vivid Adjectives and Adverbs** |

Using a separate sheet of paper, rewrite the following sentences. First, make your nouns and verbs more specific. Then add adjectives and adverbs that will bring the image into sharp focus. Study this example:

Vague: The woman ate the food and liked it.

Effective: The thin, middle-aged female juggler devoured the broiled chicken and brown rice and enjoyed each mouthful.

1. The horse won the race.
2. The boy was afraid of the dark.
3. The girl liked her outfit.
4. The man drank the water.
5. The woman was sad about the weather.

Now write five sentences of your own, using specific nouns and verbs and adjectives and adverbs to focus their meanings.

As you read the following paragraph, try to picture the scene and the action being described. Can you bring the scene into sharp focus?

The man walked down the street. Along the way, he saw a dog. Then he saw a car going fast. It just missed a young boy who was crossing the street. He stepped in some water. He turned around and went home.

Now compare this paragraph with the following description of the same events:

The frail, elderly tramp hobbled down the sidewalk, his white hair waving in the breeze. Suddenly he noticed a black-and-white beagle pup waddling in the damp grass by the curb. It barked sharply at him and scampered away. He snorted at the dog in disgust. Then he froze! A blonde boy in blue overalls dashed into the street, just as a red convertible roared toward him. The horn of the automobile blared as the speeding driver swerved, narrowly missing the child. Distracted by the near accident, the tramp stepped into a large mud puddle, drowning his cracked shoe in muck. Disheartened and shaking, he turned and plodded slowly toward the musty room that he called his home.

Compare the two paragraphs about the man, the dog, and the boy. How does the first paragraph differ from the second? What does the second paragraph contain that the first one lacks? Study the expanded paragraph before writing your own.

Writing Activity 10   **Creating a Vivid Scene**

Recall an event in your life that you still remember vividly. Write one paragraph that describes the scene and the situation. Your goal is to paint a picture with words so that the reader can see and feel the event.

Reread your paragraph. Underline all words that help to paint the picture for the reader. Make any word changes that will make your picture sharper. Then read your paragraph aloud to another student and ask for suggestions on how to make the picture more vivid.

Figures of Speech

A second method for expanding your writing so that it is specific and memorable is to incorporate figures of speech into your descriptions. Indeed, without them writing can be dull and ordinary, like the basic recipe for beef stew. Beef, vegetables, and water are the major ingredients. When the cook adds herbs and seasonings however, various flavors combine to create a delicious meal rather than a bland recipe. Figures of speech can add flavor, focus, and clarity to your writing.

There are two main types of figures of speech that writers use, the *simile* and the *metaphor*. Simile is from a Latin word meaning "similar." Metaphor is from a Greek word meaning "to bear change."

Using Similes.   A simile compares two things that are not actually the same, but suggest an interesting similarity. For instance, Robert Burns, the poet, once wrote,

My love is like a red, red rose.

He knew that his love was not a red rose, but she had qualities that reminded him of the beauty of the rose. Here is another simile:

He was as slippery as a greased, struggling catfish in your hand.

We know that the person is not a catfish, but the similarity makes the picture more colorful. It illustrates the person's character.

Similes state that something is *like* something else or *as* something else is. Although you usually use *like* or *as* to make a simile, some other words, such as *than,* can also make a simile.

The typist was faster <u>than</u> a Triple Crown winner.

The batter's average was lower <u>than</u> the price of a hot dog.

Here are some other examples of similes used by experts. All these are examples of the fresh, striking use of similes to paint a sharp picture for the reader. What two things are being compared in each of these similes?

Vachel Lindsay described the wind:

The hot wind came down like a sledge-hammer stroke.

Carl Sandburg described the whistle of a boat that

calls and cries unendingly,
like some lost child.

William Wordsworth described the evening:

The holy time is quiet as a nun breathless with adoration.

Stephen Crane wrote of a mother's grief at her son's death:

[her] heart hung humble as a button.

| Writing Activity 11 | **Completing Similes** |

On a separate sheet of paper, complete the following phrases to make a simile.
1. She smiled like _____.
2. He walked like _____.
3. She was smarter than _____.
4. The owner was as mean as _____.
5. He was as quiet as _____.

Using Metaphors. A *metaphor,* like a simile, sees one thing in terms of something else. It compares two different things in order to stimulate the imagination and to make a feeling clearer to the reader. Good metaphors, like good similes, are striking and fresh comparisons. They add spice to writing.

Her laughter was a soothing lullaby to his anger.

His anger turned his eyes into deadly flame-throwers.

Her dark eyes seemed bottomless lakes of mystery.

A metaphor does not say that something is *like* or *as* something else, as a simile does. A metaphor pretends that something *is* something else, even though the reader knows that it is not. Read the following selection:

> When John was invited to dinner, he did not realize that Harry was not a good cook. The roast was tough and overdone. The broccoli and the mashed potatoes were also cooked too long and lacked flavor. The pie crust was hard and difficult to eat, and the lemon filling was mushy and had little taste at all. The dinner was a disappointment.

The paragraph sends the reader a message, but it is a rather dull one. It lacks originality and striking language. In the following revised version, notice how metaphors strengthen the writing.

> When John was invited to dinner, he did not realize that Harry was a greenhorn in the kitchen. John's tongue told him that the roast was a boiled basketball. Harry had turned beautiful broccoli into skunk cabbage. The mashed potatoes had become steaming lumps of flavorless globs surrounded by white, melted glue. The pie crust was baked cardboard, filled with melted yellow silly-putty. John felt that the dinner was a punishment for his sins.

The following sentences show how professional writers have used metaphors effectively:

> Hope is the thing with feathers.
> Emily Dickinson

> Life's but a walking shadow . . .
> William Shakespeare

> The white mares of the moon rush along the sky.
> Amy Lowell

> The fog comes in on little cat feet.
> Carl Sandburg

> Wit is the salt of conversation, not the food.
> William Hazlitt

> Courage is grace under pressure.
> Ernest Hemingway

Writing Activity 12   Identifying Metaphors

In the following sentences, identify the two things being compared. Write your answers on a separate sheet of paper. Here is a completed example:

Darnell was a crazy Brahman bull on the football field.

Subject: Darnell   Comparison: crazy Brahman bull

1. The campers were frisky lambs on the playground.
   Subject: _____   Comparison: _____

2. The winning horse was a hurtling cannonball in the stretch.
   Subject: _____   Comparison: _____

3. Tia's face turned into a withered bouquet of sneers and frowns.
   Subject: _____   Comparison: _____

4. When she caught the robber, the police officer became a tower of fury.
   Subject: _____   Comparison: _____

5. The obedient group seemed to be frightened, spineless puppets.
   Subject: _____   Comparison: _____

Avoiding Clichés. There are many figures of speech in our language that are dull, weary, and worn out from too much usage. Here are some examples:

He eats like a horse.

Roberto is thin as a rail.

Shayna is pretty as a picture.

The sun made Angela red as a beet.

The first person in the world who used the simile "sharp as a tack" was being original and inventive. However, millions of people have used it over and over again, stealing its freshness and wearing it out.

A withered, worn-out expression such as "quick as a wink" is called a cliché (pronounced klē shā´). The French word *cliché* is the name of an implement that printed the same image over and over again. A cliché is a lazy writer's tool because it demands little thought. One will pop into your mind often when you are searching for a good image. Because it slips into your thinking so easily, it is a dangerous trap.

Clichés such as "strong as an ox" should be avoided by the writer who wants to be effective. A cliché may say what the writer wants to say, but it does not say it in a striking, fresh way. It is better to say, "strong as a champion iron-pumper" or "strong as a giant gorilla." These expressions show fresher relationships and some creative thought.

Metaphors can have the same cliché problems that similes can have. An effective metaphor is fresh imagery for the mind, but stale metaphors are old, familiar pictures. For example:

He is a bad apple in the class barrel.

She was the Rock of Gibraltar during the crisis.

In his new suit, Michael was a proud peacock.

Josef was a stubborn mule when the teacher told him to sit down.

She tried to solve the problem, but she hit a brick wall.

| Writing Activity 13 | **Rewriting Clichés** |

On a separate sheet of paper, rewrite the following five clichés so they send the same message to the reader in an original way:

1. She looked like death warmed over.
2. He yelled like a stuck pig.
3. She had a mind like a steel trap.
4. He was as tough as nails.
5. She was as light as a feather.

Next, rewrite the following five cliché metaphors so they strike the reader with a fresh comparison.

1. Gabriel was a chicken on the soccer field.
2. Calvin was a jewel when it came to helping people.
3. Her silly chatter was a pain in the neck.
4. Dimitri's smile was a ray of sunshine to Elena.
5. Antonio thinks he is hot stuff.

Writing Activity 14   **Writing Similes and Metaphors**

Closely study the scene in the photograph. What do you see that you could bring into focus with words? First write three similes and then write three metaphors that will describe what you want the reader to see.

Writing Activity 15 **Writing Similes and Metaphors**

Study the scene in the photo and decide what feature stands out most vividly for you. First write three similes to describe what you see and then write three metaphors. Or, if you prefer, you can closely examine three kinds of fruits and three kinds of vegetables in a market or at home and write your similes and metaphors about your observation.

Chapter 2

USING YOUR POWERS OF OBSERVATION AND IMAGINATION

WARM-UP

Think of an object that you are familiar with, perhaps something small that you use often. If possible, hold the object in your hands and look at it closely. Otherwise, examine the object in your imagination. Study the physical characteristics of this object from every angle; notice all its parts and how they are put together. Next, speculate on how this object came into being, why it is important to people, and how it might be improved upon. Write down your observations and imaginings about this object in your journal.

Now ask yourself: Did I observe anything unusual or unexpected about the object that I hadn't noticed before? Was I able to focus my concentration on the task for an extended period of time? To conclude your observation, you might try drawing the object.

The warm-up exercise you just completed was an active experience in using your powers of observation and imagination. These skills are essential to good writing. This chapter will give you further opportunities to develop these skills.

Indeed, observing and imagining are part of every writer's stock-in-trade—and a great part of what makes writing so pleasurable. Like an artist painting a canvas, a writer paints a world with words. Sometimes the world a writer paints is the real world and sometimes the world is an imagined one. As you continue to develop as a writer, think of your observations and imaginations as bank accounts that you can make small deposits in every day. Soon you will find that they have become valuable accounts that you can draw from for the rest of your life.

Using Your Powers of Observation

Without even thinking about it, you use your powers of observation every day as you go about activities such as driving, eating, and simply moving around a room. You've probably learned from experience that *not* being observant can sometimes cause you many headaches. So, your powers of observation already are intact and at work. The activities in this section will help you learn to observe your environment carefully; to notice details about people, places, objects, events, weather, and other aspects of your surroundings; to be alert for many kinds of details, not just those you can see; to practice touching, tasting, smelling, hearing, and looking closely at whatever you experience. You will find that the more you observe and write about your environment, the more you will improve your writing. *Remember that you learn to write by doing.* In fact, you may soon discover that writing down your observations has become a pleasure.

For your first observation, you will practice using specific nouns, verbs, adjectives, and adverbs. Here are some examples of observations that might appear in your notebook:

Scene: The park.

1. The frail, gray-haired old lady hobbled along the gravel path. She leaned on her cane with each difficult step, while she muttered to herself.

2. The short, curly-haired boy scampered across the grass, laughing loudly. He suddenly screeched to a halt and sailed his yellow Frisbee far into the air.

3. The tall, smiling policeman, dressed in a neatly pressed blue uniform, ambled along the path. His brown eyes darted everywhere, seeming to notice everybody and everything.

4. The bearded balloon-man walked slowly down the path, singing a song about stardust. About thirty balloons— red, yellow, blue, and green—danced on strings looped over his arm. He wore a black top hat, a purple T-shirt, blue jeans, and brown boots. Suddenly he released the balloons, laughed, and watched them float upward into the sky. He watched them for a long time as he continued to sing.

| Writing Activity 1 | **Observing a Scene** |

Go to a place where several people or animals are engaged in some sort of activity. It should be a place where you can observe the scene comfortably and write your observations. Some suggestions are a cafeteria, a park bench, a bus station, a zoo, or a library.

Look carefully for about twenty minutes. Notice the differences among people and observe their actions. Pay attention to objects also.

Write at least ten good observations during this twenty-minute period.

Using Your Five Senses

Expanding your powers of observation depends primarily on becoming more aware of your five senses: *hearing, touching, tasting, smelling,* and *seeing.* Words are your tools as a writer. The more words you are able to command, the better the writing can be. Some of the most important tools for writers are sense words that help to focus images and actions. For example, the following description of a lake shore is from a book by Marilynne Robinson titled *Housekeeping.* Notice how the writer uses a combination of sound, touch, smell, and sight words to help the reader imagine the scene.

> Some of these stones were a mossy and vegetable green, and some were as white as bits of tooth, and some of them were hazel, and some of them looked like rock candy. Farther up the beach were tufts of grasses from the year before, and leafless vines, and sodden leaves and broken ferns, and the black, dull, musky, dormant woods. The lake was full of quiet waves, and smelled cold, and smelled of fish.

As you read over the lists of sense words that follow, note the ones that are unfamiliar to you. List these words in your notebook and concentrate on making them a part of your vocabulary. Also, as you practice writing, refer to these lists for words that will help you to create a vivid image in your reader's mind.

The Sense of Sound. *Sound words* appeal mainly to the sense of hearing. Notice that many of the sound words in the following list are verb forms that end in *-ing.* In such a form, words usually function as adjectives, adverbs, or parts of verbs. For more information on participles (*-ing* verbs), see page 201.

banging	chattering	coughing	fizzing
barking	chiming	crackling	gagging
bawling	chirping	crashing	gasping
belching	clanging	croaking	giggling
blaring	clapping	crunching	grating
booming	clicking	crying	growling
burping	clinking	dripping	grunting
buzzing	cooing	exploding	gurgling

(Continued)

hissing	piercing	scratching	tapping
honking	pinging	screaming	tearing
hushing	plopping	screeching	tinkling
jangling	popping	singing	thudding
jingling	quacking	slamming	thumping
laughing	quiet	shouting	ticking
moaning	rapping	silent	twittering
mooing	rasping	splashing	warbling
mumbling	rattling	squawking	wheezing
murmuring	ringing	snapping	whimpering
muttering	ripping	snarling	whining
noisy	rumbling	snoring	whispering
peeping	rustling	stuttering	whizzing

Writing Activity 2   The Sounds of a Band

Imagine that you are part of the photograph shown below. Write a paragraph using at least ten good sound words to describe what is happening. Try to catch the spirit of the photograph in your writing.

Writing Activity 3   The Sounds in a Dark Room

Imagine that you enter a dark room in an unfamiliar place. Describe what happens, using several sound words from the list.

The Sense of Touch. *Touch words* suggest the sense of touch or texture. Read over the list of touch words, noting the ones you don't know.

abrasive	furry	oily	soft
biting	fuzzy	piercing	sopping
boiling	glassy	plastic	soupy
bubbly	gluey	pocked	spiky
bulky	grainy	pointed	splintered
bumpy	greasy	prickly	spongy
burning	gritty	pulpy	steamy
bushy	gushy	rocky	steely
clammy	hairy	rough	sticky
coarse	hard	rubbery	stifled
cool	heavy	sandy	stinging
cottony	hot	scalding	stony
crisp	humid	scorching	stubby
cushioned	icy	scratchy	tangled
damp	keen	scummy	tender
downy	knobbed	shaggy	tepid
drenched	lacy	sharp	thick
dripping	leathery	silky	tickling
dry	light	slick	tough
dusty	lukewarm	slimy	velvety
feathery	matted	slippery	warm
fine	metallic	sloppy	waxy
fluffy	moist	smooth	wet
foamy	mushy	smothering	wiry
freezing	numbing	soapy	woolly

Writing Activity 4   **An Unfamiliar Dark House**

Imagine that you enter an unfamiliar house that is completely dark. In a short piece of writing about the experience, use five good touch words to describe what you feel and what happens.

Writing Activity 5   **The Texture of Old Wood**

Study the photograph shown below. Imagine that you run your fingers over the object in this picture. Write a paragraph about the experience, using at least five good touch words.

The Sense of Sight. *Sight words* relate mainly to seeing. Read over the list of sight words, noting the words with which you are unfamiliar.

angular	flat	long	slick
ashen	fluffy	lopsided	slimy
attractive	flushed	lovely	small
beautiful	foamy	matted	smooth
boiling	foggy	messy	sooty
bright	fragile	metallic	sparkling
brilliant	furry	muddy	spiky
bubbling	fuzzy	muscular	splintered
bulky	gigantic	mushy	spongy
bumpy	glassy	narrow	spotted
burning	glimmering	neat	square
bushy	gorgeous	nondescript	steamy
clean	grainy	oily	stubbly
clear	graceful	pale	stunning
cluttered	greasy	pocked	swollen
coarse	hairy	pointed	tall
colorless	handsome	powdered	tangled
curved	hard	prickly	thick
dark	hazy	pulpy	thin
dazzling	hideous	rocky	tidy
dim	huge	rough	translucent
dotted	immense	round	transparent
downy	jutting	ruffled	twinkling
drenched	keen	sandy	ugly
dripping	knobbed	scummy	wavy
dull	lacy	shaggy	waxy
dusty	large	sharp	wet
elegant	lean	shimmering	wide
feathery	leathery	shiny	wiry
fiery	light	short	wrinkled
fine	lit	silky	woolly

Writing Activity 6   **A Tour of the Town**

You visit a big city or a small town where you see interesting new sights. Describe your tour of the city or town, using several sight words from the list.

Writing Activity 7   **Amusement Park**

In a short piece of writing, describe what you see in the photograph that follows. Use at least five good sight words in your writing.

The Senses of Taste and Smell. Words relating to taste and smell often can apply to both senses. For this reason, they are combined here. Read over the list, noting the words that you don't know.

acid	fishy	musky	scented
acidic	floury	musty	sharp
acrid	flowery	oily	sour
alkaline	fresh	perfumed	spicy
aromatic	fruity	pickled	spoiled
biting	gamey	piney	stagnant
bitter	garlicky	plastic	stale
bland	hearty	pungent	sugary
burnt	hot	putrid	sweaty
buttery	lemony	rancid	sweet
cold	medicinal	rank	tangy
crisp	mellow	raw	tasteless
crusty	mildewed	rich	tough
doughy	minty	rotten	vile
earthy	moist	rubbery	vinegary
	moldy	salty	

Writing Activity 8   **Life on a Deserted Island**

You are among the first group of outsiders to land on an isolated tropical island. Using at least six of the taste and smell words in the list, describe your experiences.

Writing Activity 9   **The Pleasures of a Picnic**

Study the photograph shown on page 30. Imagine that you have just arrived for a picnic lunch. Describe your experience in a short piece of writing. Use at least five taste words and five smell words in your writing.

Writing Activity 10   In a Restaurant

This activity will give you an opportunity to incorporate all five senses into one piece of longer writing. Study the following directions and the model exercise carefully. Then, write an observation exercise in a restaurant (or your school lunchroom). Follow these instructions:

1. Sit where you can observe and write without attracting attention.

2. Select one interesting person to describe in detail. Discuss age, height, build, hair, face, clothes, posture, movements, expression, voice, and any other features that you notice.

3. Describe the various smells.

4. Describe the tastes, if there are any.

5. Listen carefully to all the sounds around you, such as conversation, music, or noises.

6. Describe any touch sensations that you have.

The following sample entry will help you with this activity.

PLACE: PJ'S DINER

Sight

One person

A man, about six feet tall

Brown, curly hair—thinning on top

About forty-five years old

Flattened nose, probably broken somehow

Scar on cheek

Unshaven

Wearing worn red lightweight jacket. Has gymnasium name on back in yellow.

Muscular, large sloping shoulders

Dirty fingernails and hands

Alone, speaks politely to server

Thin lips

Says very little—stares into space

Wrinkles forehead and seems to be thinking

Drinks orange juice quickly

Drums the table with fingers

Slouches over table

Deep voice when he speaks in short phrases

Smell

Smell of freshly brewed coffee

Oniony smell

Lots of smoke

Hamburgers cooking on grill

Soapy smell from cleaning solution

Taste

Sweet chocolate taste of hot chocolate

Hot, spicy taste of taco sauce

Cheesy, onion taste of hamburgers

Salty taste of crackers

Sound

Country-western music playing love song

Solid beat

Gym bags and books dropped on tables and booths
Lots of voice noise from customers
Cash register ringing
Kind of a moaning, gravelly sound of singer's voice
Clattering dishes, laughing
Sound of siren
Cars and motorcycles starting in parking lot
Sizzle of food on grill

Parts of Conversations
"Some game last night!"
"Two cheeseburgers with everything!"
"They lost again."
"So, what else is new?"
"How are you today?"
"Another day, another dollar."
"More than I make these days."
"What'll you have?"
"Pancakes and coffee."
"Where you headed?"
"Atlanta. I hate the heat, though."
"Sugar and cream?"
"No thanks. Coffee still terrible?"
"Best in the Midwest."
"I'd hate to taste some of the others that are worse."
"Now, now. That's no way to start a day."
"You're right. The food here is pretty good."

Touch (Textures)
Oilcloth tablecloth smooth and cool
Taco shell crisp, crunchy
Cheese smooth and melted
Napkins are cheap and fall apart in your hand
Hot chocolate warm and rich
Salt shaker is greasy to the touch
Booth springy and patched

Label your journal with today's date. Review the observations you listed. Describe, in your journal, your overall impression of the place. If it is an appealing place, tell why through examples. What kind of people are there? What is the feeling you get from the place?

Here is a brief example of an overall impression based on the restaurant observation. The impression you will be asked to write will be much longer, though.

Overall Impression

Most of the customers seem to be truck drivers who have stopped for a quick meal, some conversation, and some bad coffee. A few of them look as though they are recovering from a bad night. One man, who might be the owner, leans against the counter reading a newspaper and chewing a toothpick.

The tone of the place is rough but friendly, and the loud country music contributes to that tone. This isn't the kind of place where I would like to spend my life, but it provides a quick meal.

Using Your Powers of Imagination

Think back to the way you played as a child. Already, you had an extremely active imagination. Daydreams, make-believe, and fantasies probably played a vivid part in your life. You still have that same vivid imagination, although you may have pushed it aside as you've become a young adult with practical daily concerns and responsibilities. Once you begin writing regularly, however, you'll find that your imagination can be a wellspring of creative ideas that you can convert into written pieces. Like a growing plant, your imagination benefits from regular feedings. The writing activities in this section will give you practice in expanding the powers of your imagination.

Writing Activity 11   **Making Up a Story**

Go to a public place such as a park, a restaurant, or a movie and listen in on two people who are having a conversation. Write down the things they say that particularly interest you. Make notes on their physical characteristics and jot down your fantasies about who they are and what their relationship is. Later, at home, make up a story about these two people and write a scene depicting them conversing in a public place. Include some dialogue from your notes and use your imagination to fill in the rest.

| Writing Activity 12 | **Turning a Dream into a Story** |

Think of a dream you had recently, or one that you still remember vividly. Close your eyes and watch the dream unfold like a movie. Stop each frame and look closely at the surroundings, the people involved, and the action. Where are you in this dream? Frame by frame, run through the dream several times with your eyes closed, watching each frame for new details. Now write down the dream as if it were a story or a movie.

| Writing Activity 13 | **Creating a New Ending** |

Make a list of books or stories that you still remember. Add some movies or television shows also, if you like. Select one and write it down just as you remember it. Pay close attention to how it ends. Then, after you've written down the whole story, close your eyes and imagine a different ending. How would you have liked it to end? How would you have ended it if you had been the author? Now rewrite the story's ending.

| Writing Activity 14 | **Imagining a Perfect Place** |

Close your eyes and imagine yourself walking through a perfect place that only you know about. You come to this place whenever you want to feel creative or peaceful. See yourself walking and stopping at different spots to closely observe the physical characteristics of this secret retreat. How is this place different from others you know? What special features keep you coming back to it? Take time to record all the sensory details of your place—the sights, the sounds, the textures, the smells. After you have a vivid picture in your mind of your place, write down a full description of it. Now you have a place you can visit whenever you feel the need for creative inspiration.

The next four writing activities ask you to study a picture and write about it. Write as much about these unusual pictures as you can. This will help you become more fluent as a writer. The word "fluency" means the act of flowing. Let your words flow onto the paper in an imaginative way.

Writing Activity 15   **The Faces in the Windows**

Study the photograph shown below carefully. There is something very unusual about it. Who are the characters in the windows? What feelings do you have when you see the picture? What would it be like to live in this apartment building? Think, then write as much as you can. Use your imagination and let your ideas flow as you write.

Writing Activity 16   **A Guy on the Beach**

Study the picture shown below. Pretend that you are the person in the picture. How did you get in this situation? Why did you bring your dog?

If you do not want to be the person in the picture, pretend that you have just met this person on the beach. He wants to tell you his story. Write down what he says.

Use your imagination and write as much as you can about this picture.

Writing Activity 17   **A Strange Collection of Objects**

Study the picture below. What might these objects be used for? Who gathered all of these objects? Use your imagination. Write as much as you can about the objects and why they were gathered.

Writing Activity 18   Who Are You?

Study this picture carefully. Is the person male or female? What has happened to the person? Where is he or she, and how did the person get there? Discuss the person's thoughts. Write as much as you can about this picture, letting your imagination run free.

Chapter 3

YOUR AUTOBIOGRAPHY

WARM-UP

Recall an important time in your life. Write several paragraphs describing your experience. It might be one of the following:

1. An embarrassing moment
2. A very happy experience
3. I thought I had failed, but I learned something.
4. A strange and frightening experience
5. An exciting scene

What Is an Autobiography?

The word *autobiography* comes from the Greek language. *Auto* means "self." *Bio* means "life." *Graphy* means "writing." Writing an autobiography means writing about your life yourself. When you write your autobiography, you write the story of your life as you remember it.

Writing your autobiography is important for several reasons:

1. You are writing about what you know. Nobody knows more about yourself than you do. Most professional writers advise beginners to "write about what you know."
2. You learn more about yourself by examining your past.
3. Other people will learn more about you as an individual.

The Autobiography and the Journal

The autobiography and the journal are similar in one main way. When you write either an autobiography or a journal entry, you write about yourself. Here are some differences between an autobiography and a journal.

Autobiography	Journal
1. You write mainly about your past life.	1. You write mainly about the present.
2. You tell the story of your whole life up to now.	2. You write about a small part of your recent life.
3. You write for other people to read what you have written.	3. You write mainly for yourself.
4. You give your story shape and form.	4. You usually write informally, in bits and pieces.
5. You revise and correct your writing carefully for others to read.	5. Your journal is material that you rarely revise. You are the main reader of it.

Sample Autobiography: Helen Keller's *The Story of My Life*

Read the following excerpt from Helen Keller's autobiography, *The Story of My Life*. Keller was blind, deaf, and as a child did not speak. Notice how she uses specific description to share her experiences with the reader. Review the elements of the autobiography and those of the journal. Identify the features of an autobiography that this excerpt contains. Does Keller's autobiography seem to have any journal characteristics?

The Story of My Life

The most important day I remember in all my life is the one on which my teacher, Anne Mansfield Sullivan, came to me. I am filled with wonder when I consider the immeasurable contrasts between the two lives which it connects. It was the third of March, 1887, three months before I was seven years old.

On the afternoon of that eventful day, I stood on the porch, dumb, expectant. I guessed vaguely from my mother's signs and from the hurrying to and fro in the house that something unusual was about to happen, so I went to the door and waited on the steps. The afternoon sun penetrated the mass of honeysuckle that covered the porch, and fell on my upturned face. My fingers lingered almost unconsciously on the familiar leaves and blossoms which had just come forth to greet the sweet southern spring. I did not know what the future held of marvel or surprise for me. Anger and bitterness had preyed upon me continually for weeks and a deep languor had succeeded this passionate struggle.

Have you ever been at sea in a dense fog, when it seemed as if a tangible white darkness shut you in, and the great ship, tense and anxious, groped her way toward the shore with plummet and sounding-line, and you waited with beating heart for something to happen? I was like that ship before my education began, only I was without compass or sounding-line, and had no way of knowing how near the harbour was. "Light! give me light!" was the wordless cry of my soul, and the light of love shone on me in that very hour.

I felt approaching footsteps. I stretched out my hand as I supposed to my mother. Someone took it, and I was caught up and held close in the arms of her who had come to reveal all things to me, and, more than all things else, to love me.

The morning after my teacher came she led me into her room and gave me a doll. The little blind children at the Perkins Institution had sent it and Laura Bridgman had dressed it; but I did not know this until afterward. When I had played with it a little while, Miss Sullivan slowly spelled into my hand the word "d-o-l-l." I was at once interested in this finger play and tried to imitate it. When I finally succeeded in making the letters correctly I was flushed with childish pleasure and pride. Running downstairs to my mother I held up my hand and made the letters for doll. I did not know that I was spelling a word or even that words existed; I was simply making my fingers go in monkey-like imitation. In the days that followed I learned to spell in this uncomprehending way a great many words, among them *pin, hat, cup* and a few verbs like *sit, stand* and *walk*. But my teacher had been with me several weeks before I understood that everything has a name.

One day, while I was playing with my new doll, Miss Sullivan put my big rag doll into my lap also, spelled "d-o-l-l" and tried to make me understand that "d-o-l-l" applied to both. Earlier in the day we had had a tussle over the words "m-u-g" and "w-a-t-e-r." Miss Sullivan had tried to impress it upon me that "m-u-g" is *mug* and that "w-a-t-e-r" is *water*, but I persisted in confounding the two. In despair she had dropped the subject for the time, only to renew it at the first opportunity. I became impatient at her repeated attempts and, seizing the new doll, I dashed it upon the floor. I was keenly delighted when I felt the fragments of the broken doll at my feet. Neither sorrow nor regent followed my passionate outburst. I had not loved the doll. In the still, dark world in which I lived there was no strong sentiment or tenderness. I felt my teacher sweep up the fragments to one side of the hearth, and I had a sense of satisfaction that the cause of my discomfort was removed. She brought me my hat, and I knew I was going out into the warm sunshine. This thought, if a wordless sensation may be called a thought, made me hop and skip with pleasure.

We walked down the path to the well-house, attracted by the fragrance of the honeysuckle with which it was covered. Someone was drawing water and my teacher placed my hand under the spout. As the cool stream gushed over one hand she spelled into my other the word *water*, first slowly, then rapidly. I stood still, my whole attention fixed upon the motions of her fingers. Suddenly I felt a misty consciousness as of something forgotten—a thrill of returning thought; and somehow the mystery of language was revealed to me. I knew then that "w-a-t-e-r" meant the wonderful cool something that was flowing over my hand. That living word awakened my soul, gave it light, hope, joy, set it free! There were barriers still, it is true, but barriers that could in time be swept away.

I left the well-house eager to learn. Everything had a name, and each name gave birth to a new thought. As we returned to the house every object which I touched seemed to quiver with life. That was because I saw everything with the strange, new sight that had come to me. On entering the door I remembered the doll I had broken. I felt my way to the hearth and picked up the pieces. I tried vainly to put them together. Then my eyes filled with tears; for I realized what I had done, and for the first time I felt repentance and sorrow.

I learned a great many new words that day. I do not remember what they all were; but I do know that *mother, father, sister, teacher* were among them—words that were to make the world blossom for me, "like Aaron's rod, with flowers." It would have been difficult to find a happier child than I was as I lay in my crib at the close of that eventful day and lived over the joys it had brought me, and for the first time longed for a new day to come.

Researching Your Life Story

Since you are going to write the story of yourself, you will need to do some research. Searching for something means looking carefully for it. The Latin prefix, *re*, means "again." Research means *searching again* or taking another look to find important and interesting parts of your life to write about. You can think about your research as a treasure hunt. You are looking for those details in your past that will be valuable to the reader of your story.

Planning how you will write your autobiography is very important. It would not be very interesting if you sat down and wrote one page about yourself. On the other hand, it would be impossible to write an entire book in a short time. Some autobiographies contain 800 printed pages or more! The length of your story will depend on your research and how you present it. It will not be as difficult to do as you may think. The secret is to plan it well and to do good research.

You will need to use a separate notebook or your journal for your research. It will be helpful to record your notes when you talk to people about your past or when you find things that remind you of the past. Be sure to record in your notebook any ideas of stories about your past in as much detail as possible. You will probably not use all of your notes, but you will need this "raw material" to sift through for your autobiography.

Using the 5Ws and H Technique

The 5Ws and H technique will help your autobiographical research. Answer the following checklist of questions in your journal or a separate notebook.

Who?

What people can help you by talking with you about your past life? List them in your notebook. Be certain you consider parents or guardians, other family members, relatives, friends, teachers, employers, and others who might have shared past experiences with you.

What?

Make a list of things that will bring back memories of your past. Be sure to include photographs, albums and scrapbooks, collections, diaries, favorite toys, clothes, and any other items you may remember.

When?

When did certain important events happen? Include events such as your birth, entering school, meeting your first friend, reading your first book, winning a race, attending your first birthday party, your first trip away from home, and other important events.

Where?

Thinking about where you have lived and where you have visited will bring back memories. Tell about different places you have lived, places you have visited, favorite places in your town or city, places where important things happened to you, and so on.

Why?

Some events stand out in your memory as important. Try to think about and to analyze why they are important to you. They might be happy, sad, or exciting events. Perhaps they changed your life in some way. Think of at least three events. Record them in detail in your notebook.

How?

How did you form your likes and dislikes? What things did you learn to do well? How did your talents reveal themselves? Record the answers to these questions in your notebook. Record your likes, dislikes, hobbies and other interests, and the things you do well.

Study the answers to your questions. Talk to the people you have selected. Discuss your past with them, taking complete notes when you do. Write down any stories or incidents in as much detail as possible.

Take complete notes on your reactions to photographs, toys, and other objects you have recorded as sources for your research. Do not forget any memories and observations that pop into your mind unexpectedly.

Writing Your Life Story

When you have thoroughly gathered your notes, you are ready to study them and to select material to use for your autobiography. You will use the material that you select to write a brief autobiography, which we will call an autobiographical sketch. You will not write the complete story of your life; that would take too much time and paper. Instead, you will create a *sketch* of your life in words.

You will write your autobiographical sketch in steps, one at a time:

> Step 1: Basic facts about your life
>
> Step 2: People
>
> Step 3: Places
>
> Step 4: Events
>
> Step 5: Things
>
> Step 6: Who I am today

One way to approach this is to find one or more pictures of yourself that have been taken recently. Study the picture or pictures carefully. Doing this will help you to describe yourself. As you look at the photograph, think of adjectives that would describe you. Many should occur to you as you study each photograph.

Writing Activity 1   **Writing Your Autobiography**

Write your autobiographical sketch by answering the questions listed under the following six steps:

1. Basic facts about your life

This is the section that introduces you to the reader. Begin by telling the reader some basic facts about yourself. You should answer some or all of the following questions in this section:

When and where were you born?

Who were the members of your family when you were born?

What physical characteristics did you have? Weight? Color of hair and eyes?

Where did you live?

What were you like as a baby?

When did you enter school?

What other basic facts can you use to introduce yourself?

How would you describe yourself physically now?

Answer these questions and include any other basic information about yourself in this first section.

2. People

Who have been the most important people in your life up to now? In your answer, include relatives, friends, and any other people who have made an important difference. You may want to include a teacher or some teachers. Do not list too many people, however, and be sure to explain why each is important. Decide which people you will include in this section after studying your notes. You may tell stories to show why a particular person was important to you.

3. Places

What places have been important in your life? You may wish to describe your home or the homes in which you have lived. Certain other places may have been important to you as well. You may have visited some places near your home or far away from it. If these were important to you, tell why. Always explain why any place has been an important part of your life. After you have studied your notes, decide which places you wish to describe and explain in this section.

4. Events

This is a very important section. In this part of your sketch, you should describe those situations that had important influence upon your life. Here is the place to include some of the stories that will describe why some of the things that happened were important. Do not use too many events, however. Choose your events carefully and be sure that they were significant. Describe the events in as much detail as possible. Try to help the reader see and understand why these events were important. Describe your feelings at the time.

5. Things

In this section, you will select things that have interested you or have become important to you during your life. These may include hobbies, things you like to do in your leisure time, objects that have a special meaning for you, pets, foods, and any other things you may wish to include. Here is where you may also discuss your likes and dislikes.

6. Who I am today

This is the final step in your sketch, where you sum up how you see yourself now. You may want to describe how you feel about the world you live in today. You may want to write about what interests you. You may also want to write about what you would like to do in the future and how you will try to accomplish what you want to do. This section is the one in which you write about yourself at this moment and your hopes for the future.

Many students feel that once they have written words on paper, their job is over. However, the writer who wants to write well is not satisfied with the first try.

Just as *research* means to "search again" through material for writing, *revision* also comes from the Latin language, and it means to "look again." When you revise, you take another look at your material. You go over the first draft and notice changes you can make to improve the first try. Rewriting is work, but good writing comes from good work. You will want to form the habit of revising your first writing attempt each time you write something for other people to read. You want to write the best piece of work you possibly can. After all, you want other people to read your best writing.

Writing Activity 2 | **Revising Your Autobiography**

Revise your sketch by following these steps:

Revising Step 1: **Basic facts about your life**

- Read this section of your sketch aloud.
- Place an *x* where you think a word might need changing or where a group of words sounds awkward.
- Are your thoughts in the correct time sequence? Do the events move from the earliest event through to the most recent event?
- Notice your punctuation marks and your spelling. If a word seems misspelled, check the dictionary. Correct errors.
- Rewrite the section.

Revising Step 2: **People**

- Read this section of your sketch aloud.
- Place an *x* where a word or a group of words needs changing.
- Have the people you wrote about been described clearly? Can the reader form a picture of these people in his or her mind? Have you explained their importance?
- Notice your punctuation marks and your spelling. Correct errors.
- Rewrite the section.

Revising Step 3: **Places**

- Read this section of your sketch aloud.
- Place an *x* where a word or a group of words needs changing.
- Have you described the important places clearly? Have you explained why they are important?
- Notice your punctuation marks and your spelling. Correct errors.
- Rewrite the section.

Revising Step 4: **Events**

- Read this section of your sketch.
- Place an *x* where a group of words needs changing.
- Have you written about each event in detail? Have you provided enough information to make the reader understand why the event is important to you? Have you written about each event so it will interest the reader?
- Check your punctuation marks and your spelling. Correct errors.
- Rewrite the section.

Revising Step 5: **Things**

- Read this section of your sketch aloud.
- Place an *x* where a word or a group of words needs changing.
- Have you described each thing that matters to you in detail? Have you explained why the thing or things have meaning for you? Have you explained your likes and dislikes well? Your strengths and interests?
- Check your punctuation and spelling. Correct errors.
- Rewrite the section.

Revising Step 6: **Who I am today**

- Read this section of your sketch.
- Place an *x* where a word or group of words needs changing.
- Have you thoroughly presented your thoughts about your world and your life today? Have you explained your thoughts about the future?
- Check your spelling and punctuation. Correct errors.
- Rewrite the section.

When you have carefully revised each section to your satisfaction, then put the sections in order. You have completed your autobiographical sketch, except for one important part of it. You will need to give it a good title. An effective title both interests the reader and vividly expresses the main subject. Think of several titles that would interest a reader. Select the one you feel will best fit the contents of your sketch.

Chapter 4

THE PERSONAL LETTER

WARM-UP

Try to remember the phone calls you made in the past two weeks. List them and the people to whom you talked. Make another list of the personal letters you wrote or received in the past two weeks. Finally, make a list of people to whom you owe letters or to whom you feel you could and should write. Think hard and be honest. Save the lists for future reference.

The Advantages of Personal Letters

A personal letter is written to someone you know well. Writing a personal letter to a friend or relative says that you care about him or her. You are taking the time and giving the necessary energy and thought to communicating with your reader.

Why not use the telephone instead of writing a letter? Phoning a person often seems easier, and you get an immediate response. The telephone is a useful part of our lives, but there are several reasons writing a personal letter to a friend may sometimes be a better way of communicating:

1. The fact that you are willing to devote time and energy to a letter is a compliment to your friend or relative.

2. You can say exactly what your thoughts are in an *organized* way. Telephone conversations usually are disorganized. Sometimes you leave out important information in a phone call.

3. You can read a letter more than once. Even years later, a letter will bring back an important memory. Unless a telephone conversation is recorded, it cannot be reviewed for accuracy or pleasure.

4. You can control your feelings when you write a letter. If you write angry words or words that can be misunderstood, you

can revise your letter. Damaging words in a phone call cannot be recalled or changed.

5. Letters cost less than long-distance calls. Most personal letters are written to friends or relatives who live some distance from you. Stationery, an envelope, and a stamp cost much less than a long-distance call.

Here is what one student says about writing personal letters.

I have decided to become a prolific letter writer. Writing a letter to someone is one of the most complimentary things you can do for that person. It shows real concern to take the time and trouble to write a letter. Letter writing comes close to being the perfect method of communication between two people. In daily life, it is impossible to say exactly what you mean in exactly the right way, one hundred percent of the time in conversation. When you write a letter, however, you can take time to compose your message and be thoughtful, thus making the communication say what you want in the way that you want.

Personal contact adds a great deal, of course, but with a little practice you can develop a flair for expressing love, or tenderness, or affection, or any other emotion you feel. Writing well is just like playing an instrument. Practice is the key.

Planning a Personal Letter

When you write a personal letter to a friend or relative, there are three points to remember:

1. You want the letter to continue and to enrich your friendship.
2. You want the letter to reflect your true personality.
3. You want the letter to interest your friend as much as possible.

To bring out the true "you" in your letter, you want to use your natural writing voice as much as possible. The tone of your letter should be as close to your purpose as you can make it. Certainly, it should be friendly, and your words should come across as sincere and genuine.

To make your letter interesting, write about people and events that will have meaning for your reader. Use the 5Ws and H worksheet method to help you plan your personal letters. You may want to add the *Then, Now,* and *Someday* questions as well. The following suggestions should help:

Who?

Who will receive your letter? (Take some time to think about your reader's qualities.)

What do you admire about your friend?

What common interests do you have?

What caused you to become friends?

How does this friend differ from other close friends that you have?

What?

What would your friend like to know about you in the letter?

What recent events would interest your friend?

What would you like to know about your friend in his or her letter back to you?

What recent interests would you want to share with your friend?

When?

When was the last time you saw your friend?

When did you have good times together?

Where?

Where have you visited lately that would interest your friend?

What places did you visit in the past that you could recall?

Where would you like to go with your friend that would interest both of you?

Why?

Why are you writing this letter?

Do you have any purpose in writing this letter other than to maintain and continue the friendship?

How?

How do you normally speak to this person when you are together? (You would speak differently to your favorite aunt than you would to a friend.)

Then?

What from the past do you want to recall with your friend?

Now?

What are some of the things that are happening to you now that would interest your friend?

Someday?

Are there some future plans that you would like to make with your friend?

Are there any things about to happen to you that would interest your friend?

5Ws and H Worksheet

Who? My friend, Vijay Patel. Vijay has done well in sports. He has a great sense of humor. We both like to fish and listen to music. He met Janet the last time he was here. He is always fun to be around, but he has a serious side as well. He wants to be a doctor.

What? I want to congratulate him on his success in football. I want to tell him about my new motorcycle. I also want to invite him to visit.

When? I haven't seen Vijay in two years. I want to ask him to visit me in June. We might go fishing again.

Where? He liked fishing on the lake. We might also go into Chicago and catch a movie. I think he would enjoy the Museum of Science and Industry. Maybe we can go to Wrigley Field for a Cubs game.

Why? I'm writing to renew our friendship, congratulate him, and ask him to visit.

Then? We played touch football and fished when he was here. Also, we went on a double date. He was with Janet.

Now? I passed all my subjects and got an A in English. I have a new dog named Sultan. He'd also like to hear some of my new compact discs. I still am going with Marcia.

Someday? Ask him about medicine. Does he still want to be a doctor? I want to go into forestry. My dad got a promotion at the agency.

Writing Activity 1 **Answering the 5Ws and H Questions**

Select a friend or relative to whom you would like to write a letter. (If you can't think of a real friend or relative you want to choose for this activity, use an imaginary one.) Read through the 5Ws and H, plus *Then? Now? Someday?* that are listed. Answer as many of the questions as you can in preparation for writing a letter to the person you selected. Put your answers to these questions on a sheet of paper. This list of answers is the raw material for ideas for writing your letter. Save it to use when you actually write the letter. Read the list of questions and your answers again. Check to see whether any other ideas occur to you. If so, add them to your list.

Personal Letter Formats

When you write to a very close friend or relative, he or she probably cares more about what you say than how you say it. There may be times, however, when you want to use the proper format, or form, for your letter.

The model that follows shows a widely accepted form for a personal letter. Study the letter to see how each of the following points applies:

1. A heading consisting of the writer's address and the date the letter is written goes in the upper right corner. The street address appears on the first line, the city, state, and ZIP code on the second, and the date on the third.

2. The salutation is about four spaces below the heading and even with the left-hand margin. The most frequent salutation is *Dear*, followed by the reader's first name. The first word and all nouns in the salutation are capitalized, and the salutation is followed by a comma.

3. The body of the letter begins a space or so below the salutation and is even with the left-hand margin. Each paragraph is indented.

4. The closing appears two spaces below the body and is even with the heading. Personal closings such as *Love* often are used in personal letters. The closing is followed with a comma.

5. The writer's signature, usually his or her first name, goes below the closing.

6. The letter should be bordered on all four sides by *margins*. Allow a margin of at least one inch all around the letter. The right-hand margin often is a little wider, usually about one and one-half inches. The left-hand margin of the letter should be even; the right-hand margin does not have to be.

7. The letter is written on good quality paper or stationery, preferably without lines.

8. The letter is written with a ball-point or fountain pen in legible handwriting. You can use a typewriter or personal computer, but typing usually seems less personal to the reader.

480 Kedvale Street
Skokie, Illinois 60077
June 7, 1997

Dear Vijay,

I haven't heard from you in a long time. I did read in the newspaper, though, that your team won the championship and you scored the winning touchdown. Great! Remember when we played touch football two years ago? Now you're a champion. Wow!

I hope you can visit me in July. I have a new motorcycle, so we can buzz around the countryside. We can also go fishing on the lake again. Remember the salmon we caught off the Waukegan pier? They were fantastic when we broiled them.

We could also go into Chicago — maybe to the Museum of Science and Industry. Do you still want to be a doctor? If so, you'd like the place. We could also catch a Cubs game.

I'm doing fine. I got an A in English this semester and a new dog named Sultan, plus some terrific new compact discs.

So come on down. Janet is still around, so we can double-date. I'm still going with Marcia. My mom is fine. She has a new job with an insurance company. Dad got a promotion at the agency. My sister is back from college and is working at a theme amusement park. She helps work the log ride.

We all want to see you. How about the week of July 4? We'll have some fun. Write soon!

Sincerely,

Bob

Writing Activity 2   **Writing a Personal Letter**

Using the list of questions and answers you prepared for Writing Activity 1, write a personal letter. Write to the friend or relative you have chosen or imagined.

   If the appearance and form of the letter are important to you, look back over the section "Personal Letter Formats." Check your letter against the list of points in that section and against the model letter. Correct any parts of your letter before mailing it. In addition, ask yourself whether your letter is written in your natural writing voice and whether it is interesting. If it is not, revise your letter.

Types of Personal Letters

Many personal letters are gifts of friendship. They contain interesting information about the writer and ask how the reader is doing. There are times, however, when you will have a more specific purpose for writing a personal letter. The following information describes specific types of personal letters and directions for writing them.

Letter of Invitation

You may want to invite your friend or relative for a party, a visit, or some other occasion that you want to share. Letters of invitation should be specific about the occasion, time, date, and place. In addition, they should give the receiver of the letter any special information.

843 Arapaho Avenue
Apartment 108C
Dallas, Texas 75952
June 18, 1997

Dear Alicia,

   I plan to have a cookout and swim party at my house on Wednesday, July 2, at 6:00 P.M. We'll grill hot dogs and hamburgers in the backyard, so be sure to wear comfortable clothes. Don't forget to bring your swimsuit and a towel.

   I hope to see you on Wednesday. Let me know if you can make it. My phone number is 555-1937.

Sincerely,

Chris

Writing Activity 3 **Writing a Letter of Invitation**

Imagine that you are planning either a birthday party or an end-of-the-year party for six close friends. Write a letter of invitation to one of those friends. From your imagination, supply the details you will need to write the letter.

Letter of Thanks

When a friend or relative has done something special for you, you will want to thank that person. Always write a thank-you letter or note for a gift, a party, or a visit you have made for any length of time. When you do, mention specific details about the gift or the event that will show it was a pleasant experience for you. If you have been given a gift, perhaps you have already used or worn it. If so, telling the giver this should make him or her especially pleased.

> 1210 Maple
> Minneapolis, MN 55440
> April 19, 1997
>
> Dear Aunt Caroline and Uncle Harry,
>
> Thank you so much for inviting me to spend spring break with you. I particularly enjoyed visiting Ocean World and going water skiing. Do you think I'll ever master skiing on one ski?
>
> All my friends here in Minneapolis are jealous of my tan. I didn't tell them I was so burned after the first two days I had to wear long sleeves and a hat. I hope you both can come and visit this summer. Then, I can return your hospitality.
>
> Love,
>
> Meghan

Writing Activity 4   **Writing a Letter of Thanks**

Think of a gift you would like to receive someday and a person who might be likely to give it to you. Write a thank-you letter to the giver, mentioning specific reasons for liking his or her gift.

Letter of Sympathy

When a friend or relative suffers a loss, injury, or an illness, a letter or note of sympathy may have special meaning. It tells your friend that you care and that you want to share the bad times as well as the good ones.

Many times, people feel awkward about writing to someone who has experienced the death of a family member or close friend. People who have experienced this kind of loss, however, say how much it helps for friends to offer written condolences.

1403 Kenwood Road
New York, New York 10011
December 16, 1997

Dear Stefan,

When your sister came to pick up your homework, she told me that you are in the hospital. I am sorry to hear that you have pneumonia. I hope you will have a speedy recovery.

We're all looking forward to seeing you back in school soon. The band won't sound the same without you on the drums. Ms. Davis asked about you the other day. She is still giving tough tests, but she cares about us as people.

We miss your jokes, so hurry up and get well! We'll go down to the mall for ice cream when you're up and around.

Sincerely,

Olivia

Writing Activity 5   **Writing a Letter of Sympathy**

Imagine a friend or relative who has suffered a loss, an injury, or an illness. Write a letter of sympathy to this person, using specific examples to express your feelings.

Letter of Congratulations

When a friend or relative enjoys good luck, you will want to write a letter to share the joy. An addition to the family, a promotion, an award, a graduation, or an achievement are examples of occasions when you would write a letter of congratulations. Remember to be specific when you write it.

1803 Second Street
San Jose, California 95121
March 4, 1997

Dear Murali,

I hear that you have been given a major part in the spring musical. I think that is wonderful!

I can't wait to see it, especially since you're playing a lead role. Maybe it's the first step toward Broadway! I'll be in the audience, cheering you on.

Congratulations!

Sincerely,

Kevin

Writing Activity 6   **Writing a Letter of Congratulations**

Imagine an occasion when you would want to write a letter of congratulations to a friend or relative. Write the letter, using specific language and examples to support the good fortune.

Part 2

PARAGRAPH POWER

Developing Your Ideas Step by Step

Writing is essentially a thinking process that converts thoughts and ideas into written words. When we write, especially if we are writing something for others to read, we try to focus and to organize our thoughts in order to communicate clearly. If we cast our ideas at a reader in an unrelated, disorganized barrage of sentences, the result is a mess of confused messages.

The accepted form for presenting written ideas is by organizing groups of sentences into paragraphs. A paragraph is a device for making an idea clear to a reader. By making the effort to master paragraph development, you will find it much easier to write essays.

One definition of a paragraph is "a group of sentences that develop or explain a single idea." Which of the following groups of sentences is a paragraph?

On April 15, 1981, the space shuttle *Columbia* glided to a perfect landing. Origami is the ancient Japanese art of paper folding. Muhammed Ali is a former heavyweight boxing champion of the world. Of all movie monsters, perhaps the most frightening is Bela Lugosi's Count Dracula.

The arrival of the Martian spaceship was a terrifying experience. The size and shape of a football field, the ship moved over the small town, almost blotting out the sun. Flickering blue lights from underneath the ship cast a strange shadow over objects and people below. And all the while, a steady clicking noise grew louder and louder.

The first group of sentences is not a paragraph because it is not about a single idea. The writer discusses the space shuttle *Columbia*, origami, Muhammed Ali, and Count Dracula. Even though the first line of the paragraph is *indented* (moved a few spaces to the right), the sentences do not meet the definition for a paragraph. The second set of sentences, however, is a paragraph. Each sentence is about one idea—the arrival of a Martian spaceship.

The beginning of a paragraph usually is shown by indenting the first line. The *block* style, in which paragraphs are separated by space rather than by indentation, is also popular, especially for printed material. You will probably need to indent the paragraphs you write, however, in order to be clear about the beginning of each new idea.

WHAT YOU WILL LEARN

In this section, you will learn how to plan and write the following:

1. Effective paragraphs
2. Descriptive paragraphs
3. Narrative paragraphs
4. Expository paragraphs
5. Persuasive paragraphs

Chapter 5

WRITING EFFECTIVE PARAGRAPHS

WARM-UP

Write a paragraph about one of the following topics:

1. A beautiful sight
2. My favorite subject in school
3. What I would buy if I had the money

Now reread your paragraph. Did you explain a single idea? Did you make this idea clear to your reader? Do you have a topic sentence? Notice the types of details you presented. Did you use examples? Reasons? Sensory words? Explanations?

A paragraph is essentially a miniature essay. Often, a single effectively written paragraph can be expanded into a full essay by developing each sentence into its own complete paragraph. In other words, the ingredients for a good essay are the same as those you need to incorporate into each paragraph that you write. This chapter will help you master the basics of writing good paragraphs.

Selecting a Topic

The first step in planning a paragraph is to select a topic. Unless your topic is assigned by your teacher, begin by thinking about topics that you know about or in which you have a special interest. You might think of topics such as the following:

model railroads	family history	training dogs	food
sports	school	gardening	careers
magic tricks	computer games	movies	books
television	spaceships	music	travel

The next step is to limit your topic so that you can discuss it in several sentences. Topics such as movies are so broad that you could not bring in specific details. Instead, you would find yourself writing such sentences as, "I enjoy going to the movies" and "Movies cost too much money." The following examples show how to limit a general topic to one suitable for a paragraph.

General Topic	Limited Topic
television	the worst commercial on television
food	the perfect hamburger
sports	developing a good soccer kick
school	the advantages of year-round schooling

Writing Activity 1   **Limiting Your Topic**

Think about your interests and hobbies. What kinds of television shows, movies, and books do you like? What outdoor sports do you most enjoy? Do you have a special skill such as woodworking, making stained glass, or sewing? Do you perhaps have a special ability to get along with people and to make friends? After thinking about your interests, write five general topics. Then limit each one so that you could write about it in a paragraph.

Topic Sentences

The *topic sentence* states the main idea of the paragraph. Find the topic sentence in the following paragraph:

> Snow is made of very small ice crystals. These crystals are formed from water vapor in clouds of moist air. When the air temperature reaches a certain point, the vapor freezes quickly and is crystallized. Single crystals may fall to the earth as very small snowflakes, or several crystals may join together to form a larger snowflake.

The first sentence of this paragraph, "Snow is made of very small ice crystals," is the topic sentence. This sentence gives a general idea of what the paragraph will be about. The other sentences in the paragraph give more detailed information about snowflakes.

Topic sentences do not always come at the beginning of the paragraph. They may come in the middle or even at the end. Sometimes experienced writers do not even put topic sentences into their paragraphs. However, they have the main idea firmly in their minds, and each sentence in the paragraph is about that main idea. As a beginning writer, you should include a topic sentence in your paragraph. Then you can focus precisely on the main idea that you want to develop.

Writing Activity 2   **Writing Topic Sentences**

Each of the following sets of sentences is missing a topic sentence. Write a topic sentence that would make each set of sentences a paragraph.

1. Every leaf and branch of every tree was in constant motion. Tall grasses in a field rippled like waves. On the nearby highway, diesel exhaust and fumes from traffic disappeared almost instantly. A single flag on a tall pole in front of the Highway Patrol station snapped in the wind.

2. Arctic icebergs look like sharp, craggy mountain peaks. A few of them get as far south as the Gulf Stream near Newfoundland, where they melt. Antarctic icebergs, on the other hand, are huge, flat "islands," hundreds of square miles in area. Most of them circle the south polar region, never leaving the Antarctic Ocean.

3. Teenagers like to drive and are usually very alert at the wheel. Most of them have taken driver training courses at school. Then, too, teenagers are accustomed to multilane driving and know the importance of side mirrors and proper signaling. Also, teenagers have faster reaction time than most adults.

4. It's cold in Antarctica, colder than in any other place on earth. In fact, the lowest temperature on record was recorded there in 1960—127 degrees Fahrenheit below zero. The wind that blows constantly, usually about fifty miles an hour, makes it seem even colder. Surprisingly, however, it rarely snows in Antarctica. The average snowfall there is only about two inches a year.

Audience and Tone

An important part of planning a paragraph is thinking about the audience who will read it. When you write a personal letter to a friend or relative, you know exactly who your reader will be. Without even thinking about it, you probably adjust your writing to this reader, writing about events that are of interest to him or her and using language that he or she understands. For a paragraph, however, your audience is a little different.

Your audience is likely to affect your writing in the following ways:

1. The topics you choose to write about
2. The amount of information you include
3. The kinds of words you use
4. The kinds of sentences you use

Writing Activity 3   **Writing for Different Audiences**

Write the first two sentences of a letter for each situation described:

1. You want your friend, Richard, to repay the $5 he borrowed from you two months ago. He seems to have forgotten about it.
2. You are inviting a friend to go to the event of the year—the school dance. You feel shy about doing so, but you really want the person to go with you.
3. You are writing a note to your teacher to explain why you have not done your assignment.
4. You are writing a note to a friend about a good movie you just saw.
5. You are writing a note of apology to your neighbor next door; you have broken the neighbor's window with a baseball.

Read your sentences. Be prepared to explain how the words you used differ with each situation and how you would describe the tone you used in each case.

Begin thinking about your audience when you select a topic. Good writing is informative; it tells readers something they don't already know. If you begin with an unusual topic, such as "learning to skydive," you have an advantage, since the topic itself is likely to be informative for most readers. However, even an ordinary topic can be made interesting if you are able to make readers see it in a fresh way.

The attitude you have toward your topic establishes a *tone*. Suppose, for example, that your topic is "the agony of dieting." Millions of Americans diet every year. The topic by itself is neither unusual nor informative. However, you can develop the topic with specific details that will help readers see the experience in an unusual light. For example, you might use a humorous tone by describing how you dream about food as you are dieting—mountains of potatoes drenched in gravy; thick, juicy hamburgers slathered in ketchup and mustard; and so on.

When writing to audiences you know very well, such as close friends or relatives, you are likely to use a casual tone or informal language that includes contractions, slang, and expressions such as "you know" and "okay." Describing a low grade on a test, for example, you might write "You know, I really goofed up on that one, didn't I?" With a very close friend or relative, you might even choose to write in all lowercase letters or to sprinkle your writing with numerous exclamation marks. You are also more likely to use shortened sentences such as "Wish you were here."

The language for a general audience, however, is more formal. Writing done for this type of audience usually does not contain slang;

and, if it is very formal, the writing may not even contain contractions. In addition, sentences are complete rather than shortened, so that "Hope they win this one" becomes "I hope the Scouts win the conference championship."

Formal language is not necessarily better than casual language. It simply is more suitable for certain occasions. Just as the appropriate style of dress changes according to the occasion, so does the style of language change.

Unless your teacher directs you otherwise, assume that the audience for your paragraph is a general audience. This means that you are writing for a large group of people of varied ages who may not have had the same experiences as you have had. Imagine that each paragraph that you write will be posted on the bulletin board and read by all the members of your class, or will be published in the school newspaper and read by all students and teachers in your school.

| Writing Activity 4 | **Using an Appropriate Tone** |

The following paragraph is written in a casual, informal tone that is not suitable for a general audience. What words and phrases make it unsuitable? Rewrite and expand the paragraph so it would be appropriate for a general audience.

> You know, somebody really messed up the lunch period at Mount Wilson High School! It's too short—not enough time! If the kids had a longer lunch, a lot of problems could be cut out. Like, this way the kids have to snarf their food, and there isn't always enough time to finish! Tons of garbage left over! Also, kids don't get enough time to clean up, so they leave junk everywhere! Empty milk cartons, crumpled napkins, and silverware. And they don't get to chill before they're back to the grind. They're wiped out by afternoon.

Unity in Paragraphs

An important quality of good paragraphs is *unity*. Unity means that every sentence in the paragraph seems to belong and to support the main idea.

To write paragraphs with unity, beginning writers should start by writing a topic sentence. Once you have written down the main idea, you can be certain that every other sentence develops or explains that idea. For example, the following paragraph lacks unity. Which sentence does not belong?

> In the northern Midwest, the first warm weather in spring instantly changes the scenery. Apple and plum trees almost explode into bloom. Leaf buds double in size in a single day.

Seed pods burst on maples and cottonwoods, filling the air with "identified" falling objects. Weather forecasters cannot always predict when this warm weather will arrive. The last thin film of ice disappears from ponds and lakes. Heavy coats or padded jackets are traded for short-sleeved shirts or sleeveless tops.

In this paragraph, the topic sentence is the first one. This sentence says that the main idea of the paragraph will be how the first warm weather of spring changes the scenery. Most of the other sentences give details explaining how the warm weather does this. The one sentence that doesn't explain this is <u>Weather forecasters cannot always predict when this warm weather will arrive</u>. Although this sentence is about warm weather, it does not explain *how* it changes the scenery.

Writing Activity 5	**Rewriting for Unity**

In each of the following paragraphs, there is one sentence that does not explain the topic. Rewrite each paragraph on a sheet of paper, leaving out the sentence that does not belong.

1. The North Star is easy to locate, even though it is not the brightest star in the sky. It is the last star in the handle of the Little Dipper. Also, it is on a straight line with the two stars that mark the outside edge of the Big Dipper. These star groups are called constellations. The North Star is always situated in the north sky, and it never sets.

2. The clearing in the woods was a cranberry bog. It was low-lying and swampy, colored a reddish purple with last year's leaves. Cranberries sell well during the holidays when they are served with turkey. On the edge of the bog was a shed for storing cranberry boxes. Birdhouses on stakes were scattered over the bog to attract birds that feed on harmful insects.

3. The videocassette recorder, or VCR, has changed our entertainment habits, just as other inventions have done before. Radio brought entertainment into the home in the 1920s and 1930s. Television replaced radio some twenty years later. Cable TV is another fairly recent innovation. Today the VCR brings a huge selection of movies and programs into the home, to be viewed at any time or as often as one wishes.

4. With the coming of night, the small, lost child gave way to his fears. Parents should not leave their small children unattended. In his imagination, the trees bending in the wind were creatures reaching out with long, leafy arms. To him, the howls and shrieks of the wind were those of wild animals on the prowl.

Effective Titles

Once you have written a group of related paragraphs, you will need to give your writing an effective title. Why? The answers to this question are simple. You want to capture the reader's interest so he or she will be eager to read more of your writing. You also want the title to indicate your subject.

Businesses invest a great deal of time and money to create unique brand names that will sell their products, whether new soap, perfume, or automobiles. Likewise, the effective writer works to find an appropriate title that will attract and sell the reader. Composing effective titles demands careful thought, however.

Suppose that you wrote a composition arguing that whales are being exterminated because of people's greed and are becoming an endangered species. Which of the following titles would be the best choice for attracting the reader while still describing the topic?

1. The Whale
2. An Outrage!
3. We Should Stop This Now!
4. Destroying Whales
5. Save the Whales!

Choice 1: This title is much too broad. The composition could be about any aspect of the whale.

Choice 2: This is also broad and vague. It could be about any outrage.

Choice 3: This title also is too vague. Nobody knows what *this* is.

Choice 4: "Destroying Whales" does state the subject, but it doesn't indicate the writer's point of view.

Choice 5: This is probably the best title. "Save the Whales!" expresses alarm about the destruction of whales. Most readers would want to know why the whales need to be saved.

Writing Activity 6   **Choosing Effective Titles**

Select the title in each group that you think would have the most appeal while describing a subject. Defend your answers in writing.

1. Subject: a book about improving writing
    A. Writing as an Educational Activity
    B. Writing
    C. Pen and Paper
    D. Snap, Crackle, and Write!

2. Subject: a composition about the uses of the horse
   A. The Horse Is a Good Animal
   B. Hay and Neigh
   C. The Horse
   D. From Pegasus to the Black Stallion: A History of Horses

3. Subject: a paragraph explaining the popularity of soccer
   A. Soccer: A Fun Game
   B. An Interesting Sport
   C. Soccer: Its Heroes and History

4. Subject: a paragraph about the value of vegetables
   A. Eating Vegetables
   B. Vegetables Are Good for You
   C. Vegetables: Your Key to Good Health

5. Subject: an article describing the advantages of stamp collecting
   A. Collecting Stamps as a Hobby
   B. The Joy of Stamp Collecting
   C. Stamps
   D. Lick and Stick

Chapter 6

DESCRIPTIVE PARAGRAPHS

WARM-UP

Read the following paragraph. After you have read it, write on a separate sheet of paper the words that helped to create pictures in the reader's mind. Then, in one sentence, give your impression of the scene. How did the author use words to paint pictures for the reader?

> The firelight gave the campsite an eerie glow. The orange flame shot up like splashing paint. Sparks burst into the air. Bold shadows, cast by the fire, seemed like giant, evil ghosts. The white bottom limbs of trees looked like coiled bones of skeletons. The tops of trees disappeared into the murky, mysterious night. It was a small, weird world in the wilderness.

Descriptive Details

A paragraph that describes is called a *descriptive paragraph*. In a descriptive paragraph, the writer describes a person, place, object, or event. Descriptive details help the reader to see, hear, touch, smell, and taste what the writer describes. What are the descriptive details in the following paragraph from the writings of Anton Chekhov?

> Before the table sat a man, unlike an ordinary human being. It was a skeleton, with tight-drawn skin, with long, curly hair like a woman's, and a shaggy beard. The color of his face was yellow, of an earthy shade; the cheeks were sunken, the back long and narrow, and the hand upon which he leaned his hairy head was so lean and skinny that it was painful to look upon. His hair was already silvering with gray, and no one who glanced at the senile emaciation of the face would have believed that he was only forty years old.

As you read the paragraph, you may have formed an image in your mind of a very sick man. If you did, the writer was successful in his purpose. The following details helped you to form this image:

tight-drawn skin	sunken cheeks
shaggy beard	lean and skinny hand
yellow color	

Details in a descriptive paragraph may be either factual or personal. *Factual* details can be measured or checked. For example, you can measure a table to show that it is 36 inches long. You can check to see that an object is round, that it weighs 16 ounces, and that it has a reddish color. Observers usually will agree about factual details. What are the factual details in the following paragraph?

> The shape and size of a soccer ball are determined by official soccer rules. To begin with, the ball must be round. The distance around the ball—its circumference—must be between 27 and 28 inches. The outer covering of the ball must be made of leather or a similar substance. As the game begins, the ball must weigh between 14 and 16 ounces.

The details in this paragraph are all factual, because they can be measured or checked. The ball can be measured and weighed, and most observers will agree when a ball is round and when its covering is made of leather.

Personal details are not as objective. Often they are influenced by the writer's feelings about a topic. Other observers may look at the topic differently and report different personal details. For example, read the following paragraph to find the personal details:

> The morning of the soccer match dawned clear and crisp. Tension filled the stands as supporters of the opposing teams filed in. Shortly before noon, the tall, capable captain of the Red team jogged confidently to the center of the field. Joining her was the less poised captain of the Blue team.

The details in this paragraph cannot be objectively measured. To the writer, the morning was clear and crisp. To another observer, however, the morning might have been uncomfortably cold. The captain who appeared tall and capable to this writer might have seemed awkward and ineffective to another.

Writing Activity 1	**Using Factual Details to Describe an Object**

Factual details that you use in a descriptive paragraph can come from your own observation. Learn to record factual details precisely. For practice, select an object that you can easily study, such as a shoe, a book, or a pencil. Then record details about the object that you can measure or check. Write labels such as *Weight, Size, Shape, Color, Material, Markings*. Now measure or weigh your object and note the results under the proper labels. Under *Markings,* make a note of any special features that set the object apart from others like it. For example, the markings on a book might be smudges of dirt on the front cover or pages turned down. For a shoe, markings might be frayed shoelaces, worn-down heels, or a hole in the sole. Then, when you have finished recording details, write a paragraph that describes the object, using all the factual details you have recorded.

Writing Activity 2	**Using Personal Details to Describe a Place**

Think about a place that you would like to describe. Next, think about the feeling that you want readers to have about your topic. Write a topic sentence, perhaps like the one below, that expresses that feeling.

> On Saturdays my house is a place of confusion as we all rush to finish our weekly chores.

Now, make a list of personal details that will help you convey that feeling to readers. Then use your topic sentence and list of details to write a descriptive paragraph of the place you have chosen to describe.

Creating a Mood

Very often, the topic sentence of a descriptive paragraph creates the mood for the sentences to come. In writing, the word *mood* means the feelings the writer wants to create. For example, as you read the following paragraph, think about the feeling that it causes you to have. Is the feeling one of happiness? Sadness? Peace? Gloom? Strangeness? In this paragraph, H. G. Wells describes some visitors from Mars:

> They were, I now saw, the most unearthly creatures it is possible to conceive. They were huge round bodies—or, rather, heads—about four feet in diameter, each body having in front of it a face. This face had no nostrils—indeed, the Martians do not seem to have any sense of smell, but it had a pair of very large dark-colored eyes, and just beneath this a kind of fleshy beak. In the back of this head or body— I scarcely know how to speak of it—was the single tight tympanic surface, since known to be anatomically an ear, though it must have been almost useless in our denser air. In a group round the mouth were sixteen slender, almost whip-like tentacles, arranged in two bunches of eight each.

The feeling most readers find in this paragraph is one of strangeness. Notice how the first sentence—the topic sentence of the paragraph—helps to set the mood. The word *unearthly* prepares readers for details about the strange creatures that follow. With a different choice of words, the mood established by the topic sentence might be different. For example, what mood would you expect from each of the following topic sentences?

They were, I now saw, the most frightening creatures it is possible to conceive.

They were, I now saw, the funniest creatures it is possible to conceive.

They were, I now saw, the most peaceful creatures it is possible to conceive.

When the topic sentence creates a mood, it is important to select specific details for the rest of the paragraph that develop the same mood. The following is a "plan" for the H. G. Wells paragraph. Notice how the details help to develop the feeling of strangeness.

Topic: Martian creatures look unearthly

Details: Round, head-like bodies

Face—large eyes, beak, no nose

Back—tympanic "ear"

Tentacles—two groups of eight, around beak

If the topic had been that Martians look humorous, what details might have been used to develop that mood? If the topic had been that the Martians look peaceful, what details might have been used?

| Writing Activity 3 | **Writing to Create a Specific Mood** |

Imagine that you are a science fiction writer about to describe visitors from another planet. First, think about the kind of creatures they will be. Do you want readers to feel that they are strange? Evil? Quiet and shy? Write one sentence that describes how you want readers to feel about the visitors. This is your topic sentence. Then, make a list of specific details about the visitors. How do they look? Smell? Sound? Finally, write a paragraph in which you describe the creatures, using your topic sentence and list of details to do so.

Good writing has precise details. Give your description of a visitor from outer space to a classmate. Ask him or her to draw the creature, using your details for guidance. If you have been specific enough in your description, your classmate should be able to draw a picture that comes close to your mental image of the alien.

| Writing Activity 4 | **Selecting Specific Details to Convey a Feeling** |

Think of a kind of day that makes you feel a certain way. For example, a dark, gloomy day might leave you feeling tired or sad; or a bright, sunshiny day might cause you to feel happy or energetic. Perhaps you think of a crisp and clear autumn afternoon as invigorating. Write down the kind of day and the feeling it gives you. Read the following example:

> A very snowy day, when I stay inside, leaves me with a sense of coziness.

Now list specific details that help to create the feeling for you. For example, the following details might help to create a feeling of coziness on a snowy day:

Sight: The heavy, white snow that blankets the garden

Sound: The hiss of steam from the radiators

Taste: The sweetness of the hot chocolate and marshmallow drink that's a special treat on snowy days

Touch: The warmth of the furry slippers you wear inside on cold days

Smell: The aroma of vegetable soup simmering in the kitchen

Concentrate on recording as many specific details as possible. Then use these details for writing a descriptive paragraph about the kind of day you chose.

Sentence Order

How sentences are ordered in paragraphs is an important part of description. To readers, the sentences "hang together" better when they are arranged in a sensible order. A sensible order for details in a descriptive paragraph is the order in which they might be seen by an observer. This order is called *spatial order*. For example, notice how the observer's eye in the following paragraph has moved from the outer edges of the scene to the center:

> The ghost town was left to dry out like a skeleton in the hot, desert sun. On either side of the street, doors hanging by rusty hinges flapped in the wind. Through large cracks in rotting wood planks, sagebrush and mesquite sprouted like mushrooms. In the street itself, two scrawny chickens pecked aimlessly at the red dusty ground.

How are details arranged in this description?

> The ghost town was left to dry out like a skeleton in the hot, desert sun. In the upper stories of the buildings, windows that once boasted brightly colored calico curtains now held only a few tattered strips of cloth. Beneath the windows, doors hanging by rusty hinges flapped in the wind.

Through large cracks in rotting wood planks, sagebrush and mesquite sprouted like mushrooms. In the street itself, scrawny chickens pecked aimlessly at the red dusty ground.

In the above paragraph, the details are arranged in an order that moves from the upper to the lower part of the scene. Of course, the order could easily be reversed, with the following result.

The ghost town was left to dry out like a skeleton in the hot, desert sun. In the street itself, scrawny chickens pecked aimlessly at the red dusty ground. Through large cracks in rotting wood planks, sagebrush and mesquite sprouted like mushrooms. In buildings along the sidewalks, doors hanging by rusty hinges flapped in the wind. In the upper stories of the buildings, windows that once boasted brightly colored calico curtains now held only a few tattered strips of cloth.

Still another kind of spatial arrangement would be near-to-far or far-to-near. How are the details arranged in this paragraph?

The ghost town was left to dry out like a skeleton in the hot, desert sun. A lone rider approaching the town saw a group of wooden buildings standing on either side of a dirt street. On closer inspection, the buildings seemed to be leaning on one another, as though they might collapse if one were taken away. Scattered throughout the length of the street were large holes, worn by wind and rain. In the street itself, scrawny chickens pecked aimlessly at the red dusty ground.

Writing Activity 5   **Using Spatial Order**

Each of the following paragraphs begins with a topic sentence. The other sentences, however, are not in an order that makes sense. Following each paragraph is a suggested spatial order, such as far-to-near. First, decide how to rearrange the sentences to fit that order. Then, rewrite the entire paragraph in the suggested spatial order.

1. The town of Plymouth, Massachusetts, is famous because it is the site of Plymouth Rock. Within its surrounding or protective structure are some beach pebbles, rocks, and one larger boulder. That boulder is Plymouth Rock. Looking down the shoreline from the town, the visitor sees a classic structure with columns, something like a small Lincoln Memorial. A closer look reveals that the ocean side of the structure is open at water level, except for a metal grating. *Suggested order:* far-to-near

2. As the final buzzer sounded, the gymnasium exploded into a wild celebration of victory. On the sidelines, cheerleaders quickly joined in a ragged victory line, made longer by fans who began to spill onto the floor. In the center of the gym, the winning team members slapped each other on the back and embraced happily. In the stands on either side, the remaining spectators began to stamp their feet and whistle, causing the bleachers to shake. *Suggested order:* inner-to-outer

3. Soil and water mixed in a glass jar and then left alone can show how topsoil forms itself. Next to the bottom will be a layer of grainy material, such as sand. At the bottom will be the largest particles, such as pebbles or small rocks. Floating on top will be any dead plant material, such as leafy parts or sticks. Above the sandy layer will be the almost solid material, such as clay or mud. *Suggested order:* lower-to-upper

4. The city of Philadelphia was planned in 1682 with an unusual arrangement. Most streets are parallel to Broad or Market streets, forming squares or "blocks." The entire plan, continuing on into the suburbs, forms a pattern of squares called a *gridiron*. The two major thoroughfares, Broad and Market, intersect at right angles in the center of the city. Most other streets are placed at regular intervals, starting at the Broad and Market intersections. *Suggested order:* inner-to-outer

| Writing Activity 6 | **Four Descriptive Paragraphs Using Spatial Order** |

The following are plans for four descriptive paragraphs. Each plan contains a topic, details, and a suggested order. The details already are arranged in that order. To use the plans, follow these steps:

- Read the topic and write a topic sentence that states it clearly.
- Read the details and write sentences describing them, but keep them in the given order.
- Arrange your sentences in paragraph form.
- Give your paragraph a title.

1. **Topic:** Ocean beach on stormy day
   Details: Waves hitting on shore
   Whitecaps forming off shore
   Order: inner-to-outer

2. **Topic:** A small sports car
   Details: Grill on front
   Retractable headlights
   Racing mirrors on either side
   Luggage carrier on trunk lid
   Order: front-to-back

3.   **Topic:** A person
     Details: Curly, natural hair
                 Sunglasses
                 Pullover sweater
                 Running shoes
     Order: upper-to-lower

4.   **Topic:** A messy closet
     Details: Shoes and sports equipment on floor
                 Tangle of clothes hanging in closet
                 Compact discs, tapes, and books on first shelf
                 Souvenirs from school on second shelf
     Order: lower-to-upper

Writing Activity 7   **Writing Your Own Spatial Order Paragraph**

For this activity, you will make up your own topic sentence, list of details, and order for details. Begin by thinking of a person, place, or object that you would like to describe. Next, make a list of all the details you want to include.

Once you have compiled your list of details, think about the main idea that you want to convey in your paragraph. State this main idea in a topic sentence. Then, select the details that support the topic sentence and write sentences about them. Finally, select an order for your sentences and write your paragraph.

Writing Activity 8   **Conveying a Mood**

Study the photograph shown below. List as many details about it as you can and arrange the details in the most effective order. When you have done this, write a paragraph that conveys the mood of this picture, using the details to build the effect of the mood.

Writing Activity 9   **Conveying a Feeling**

Think about how you *feel* about the photograph shown below. Does it seem strange to you? Funny? Sad? Make a list of personal details that will convey how you feel about the photograph and decide on the best arrangement of these details. Then write a topic sentence that sums up the details. Finally, write a paragraph that describes the photograph, using your topic sentence and list of details.

Chapter 7

NARRATIVE PARAGRAPHS

WARM-UP

Read the following paragraph:

> Jerry crouched, poised for the starting gunshot. After training for the hundred-yard dash for two years, this was the moment! The gun cracked. The runners hurtled forward. Jerry felt the rhythmic crunching of the cinders. The tape loomed ahead. His lungs filled with pain as he pumped his legs vigorously. Suddenly, he felt a light slap against his chest. It was the tape, snapped in a wink! It was over! It was worth all the torture and the time. It was victory!

In one sentence, tell exactly what happened. Look back over the paragraph and see how it is a condensed version of a longer story. In fact, each of the twelve sentences could be expanded into a full paragraph, thereby creating a long narrative paper.

Telling a Story

The following paragraph is from a story by Jack London about a man lost in the frozen Arctic. In order to survive, he must build a fire. As you read the paragraph, think about its purpose. Is the writer's purpose to describe how cold it was or to tell what the man did to get warm?

> He had hoped to get into camp with the boys at six o'clock, and this would delay him an hour, for he would have to build a fire and dry out his footgear. This was imperative at that low temperature—he knew that much; and he turned aside to the bank, which he climbed. On top, tangled in the underbrush about the trunks of several small spruce trees, was a high-water deposit of dry firewood—sticks and twigs, principally, but also larger portions of seasoned branches and fine, dry, last year's grasses. He threw down several

large pieces on top of the snow. This served for a foundation and prevented the young flame from drowning itself in the snow it would otherwise melt. The flame he got by touching a match to a small shred of birch bark that he took from his pocket. This burned even more readily than paper. Placing it on the foundation, he fed the young flame with wisps of dry grass and the tiniest of dry twigs.

The writer does mention the cold, but his main purpose is to tell what happened—what the man did in response to the cold.

Paragraphs that tell what happened are *narrative* paragraphs. Narrative means "story," thus a narrative paragraph is telling a story. While telling the story, there may be some description or some explanation included, but the main purpose is to tell what happened.

Events in a narrative are arranged in a *time* order. The easiest time order is that in which the events happen. You tell what happens first, next, and so on. To order the events in your narrative paragraph, you can use a time line, such as the following, that shows the order of events in the Jack London paragraph.

START	Needed fire to dry footgear	Climbed bank	Found wood	Prepared fire	Lit match	Fed fire with dry grass	STOP

Notice that the Jack London paragraph does not have a topic sentence. It is helpful, though, as a beginning writer, to start with a sentence that states the main idea. These are examples of topic sentences for narrative paragraphs.

Nothing I did that day worked out right.

Just as the roller skating rink was about to close, there was a terrible accident.

How could anyone so intelligent have gotten into such a mess?

Lost in the dangerous swamp, the tourists fought for their lives.

From beginning to end, the party was a failure.

Writing Activity 1   **Writing a Narrative Paragraph**

Choose one of the topic sentences above and write your own narrative paragraph.

Writing Activity 2   **Arranging the Events**

Each of the following paragraphs continues the events begun in the paragraph on pages 79–80 from "To Build a Fire," by Jack London.

The main idea is given for each paragraph. Read each paragraph and pick out the events. Then, write each event down in as few words as possible. Finally, arrange the events along a time line similar to the one shown previously.

1. **Main idea:** He worked slowly, carefully

   He worked slowly and carefully, keenly aware of his danger. Gradually, as the flame grew stronger, he increased the size of the twigs which he fed it. He squatted in the snow, pulling the twigs out from the entanglement in the brush and feeding directly to the flame. He knew there must be no failure. When it is seventy-five below zero a man must not fail in his first attempt to build a fire—that is, if his feet are wet.

2. **Main idea:** He was safe

   But he was safe. Toes and nose and cheeks would be only touched by the frost, for the fire was beginning to burn with strength. He was feeding it with twigs the size of his finger. In another minute he would be able to feed it with branches the size of his wrist, and then he could remove his wet footgear, and, while it dried, he could keep his naked feet warm by the fire, rubbing them at first, of course, with snow. The fire was a success. He was safe.

3. **Main idea:** No life in his fingers

   And he had not thought his fingers could go lifeless in so short a time. Lifeless they were, for he could scarcely make them move together to grip a twig, and they seemed remote from his body and from him. When he touched a twig he had to look to see whether or not he had hold of it. The wires were pretty well down between him and his finger ends.

4. **Main idea:** Tries to take off footgear

   He started to untie his moccasins. They were coated with ice; the thick German socks were like sheaths of iron halfway to his knees; and the moccasin strings were like rods of steel all twisted and knotted as by some conflagration. For a moment he tangled with his numb fingers, then, realizing the folly of it, he drew his sheath knife.

Writing Activity 3   **Selecting Specific Details**

Good narrative paragraphs contain details about the events that make readers feel that they are experiencing them. These details may be factual ones that can be measured or checked; or they may be personal details, especially your thoughts and feelings about the event. Sensory details—sights, sounds, smells, tastes, textures—also are important.

Write the topic for a narrative paragraph. Then, divide the page into as many sections as there are events in your narrative. Give each event a name and label the section with it. Next, jot down details that describe each event in that section. A sample entry follows:

Topic: Failure of the party

Event 1:
Guests arrive
20 guests, mostly in twos or threes
I'm nervous, hands shaking
Can't think of conversation
Guests wear suits and dresses, no jeans
Feel awkward
Same people I see at school, but could be from another planet

Event 2:
Dog loose in house
Large dog, muddy paws
Dog dragging leash and brother behind
Comes tearing through swinging door
Dog looks like small elephant
Loud screams when dog jumps up on guests
Torn dresses and muddy suits

Event 3:
Food runs out
Hours I spent making sandwiches and dip
Guests gobble food like they haven't eaten in months
Pile of sandwiches gets smaller
My mother's words: "You'll need a lot more food than that."
Potato chips and cake crumbled into rug
I wonder if we have any peanut butter?

Event 4:
Tape player stops
Dancing seems last hope
Slow song, most couples are dancing
Party seems to be going again
Elton John's voice sounds like coming from underwater
Slower and slower, then stops
Absolute silence in room, except for a few groans
Frayed cord from dog's chewing

Using the notes you made, write a narrative paragraph.

Writing Activity 4　　**Four Narrative Paragraphs**

Use the following plans to write four narrative paragraphs. Each plan contains a topic and list of events. The events already are listed in a time order. Follow these steps:

- Read the topic and write a topic sentence that clearly states it.
- Read the events and write sentences giving details about them.
- Arrange your sentences in paragraph form.
- Give your paragraph a title.

1.　　**Topic:** The bicycle race
　　Events: Bicyclists at starting line
　　　　　First few laps dominated by home team
　　　　　Contestants come in for change of riders
　　　　　Checkered flag signals winner

2.　　**Topic:** "Squeeze" play in a baseball game
　　Events: Player on third base started for home during pitch
　　　　　Batter bunted ball toward first base
　　　　　Player crossed home plate
　　　　　Batter thrown out at first
　　　　　Batter credited with "sacrifice hit"

3.　　**Topic:** Mysterious disappearance of a man
　　Events: Man last seen in town during afternoon
　　　　　Heavy fog comes in from lake at midnight
　　　　　Loud scream heard about that time
　　　　　Fog leaves next morning
　　　　　Man never heard from again

4.　　**Topic:** Getaway chase
　　Events: Ski-masked thieves leave bank
　　　　　Thieves take off in car
　　　　　Police in pursuit
　　　　　Second police car blocks thieves' escape

Using Transitions

In the following paragraph, the details are arranged in a sensible order; but that order may be difficult to follow.

On Sundays, the downtown street of office buildings and banks resembles a remote canyon in the mountains. The deserted subway entrance yawns open like a cave. An empty newsstand resembles an abandoned tool shed. Pages of newspaper tumble like dry leaves in the wind.

Notice how adding the underlined words makes the outer-to-inner order more obvious:

On Sundays, the downtown street of office buildings and banks resembles a remote canyon in the mountains. <u>On the sidewalk</u>, the deserted subway entrance yawns open like a cave. An empty newsstand <u>at the curb</u> resembles an abandoned tool shed. <u>In the street</u>, pages of newspaper tumble like dry leaves in the wind.

The underlined words in this paragraph are called *transitions*. Transition means passage from one subject to another. Transitions form a bridge from one sentence to another. In a description, transitions often tell *where*. The following words are some that might be used as transitions in a descriptive paragraph.

at the left, right	in front of
in the center	beside, behind
on the side	next, next to, nearby
along the edge, curb, walk	in the distance, beyond
on top, above	in the foreground
below, beneath, under	within sight, out of sight

In narrative paragraphs, details usually are arranged in the order they happen. Bridging words that tell *when* can help to show this order. Here are some examples of transitions that might be used in narrative paragraphs:

after	finally
before	soon
then	meanwhile
next	at the same time
at last	for a minute, hour
first, second, etc.	during the morning, day, week

You probably use transitions often in your everyday conversation. In writing, they can help to make a paragraph read smoothly and clearly. Be careful, though, not to overuse them.

Writing Activity 5   **Checking for Transitions**

For this activity, select one of the four narrative paragraphs that you wrote in Writing Activity 4. Read over the paragraph and underline the transitions you used. Then, decide whether your paragraph would be improved by adding more transitions. If so, rewrite the paragraph, adding them. Underline each.

Writing Activity 6 **The Story Behind the Photo**

Study the photograph below. In this unusual photograph, what is happening? There is a story behind this event. Think carefully about the picture and write about what happened before this picture was taken. What happened afterward? Who is the person involved in the picture? What problem needs to be solved in the story?

Chapter 8

EXPOSITORY PARAGRAPHS

WARM-UP

Read the following paragraph and write one sentence summarizing the information given.

> A trencher, as it is known today, is a wooden plate or board on which food is cut or served. In England during the Middle Ages, however, a trencher was a slice of yeast bread that acted as a plate. There were few utensils or plates available in those days. The dinner at an average home in 1450 would be eaten from a bread trencher, while the crust acted as a spoon. After dinner, the trencher would be eaten by the diner, or it might be given to poor people. For this reason, the need for a dishwasher was slight in the Middle Ages.

Informing and Explaining

Paragraphs that give information or an explanation are called *expository* paragraphs. What information do you get from the following paragraph?

In his 1927 silent film *Napoleon*, French filmmaker Abel Gance used film techniques far ahead of their time. Unlike many other films of the same period, the camera was not fixed in one spot. Instead, it was strapped to the back of a horse, suspended from overhead wires, and even placed underwater to capture the effects of a violent storm at sea. Gance had also perfected the split screen technique. At one point, the screen is separated into nine images at once. Even more surprising is the technique known as Polyvision, a forerunner of the modern CinemaScope. Toward the end of the film, the stage curtains are drawn farther apart, and a wide screen is revealed. Then three images, each the size of a normal screen, are projected at once. Unfortunately, filmmakers paid little attention to these accomplishments, for shortly after Gance completed *Napoleon*, *The Jazz Singer*, a film acclaimed as the world's first "talkie," was released. Instead of granting Gance the attention that he deserved, filmmakers turned their attention to a new form of motion picture—movies with sound.

The main purpose of this paragraph is to give information about the film techniques Abel Gance used in *Napoleon*. Although this paragraph describes these techniques, it does so in order to give information.

The topic sentence of an expository paragraph gives a general idea of the information or explanation in the paragraph. For example, the topic sentence of the preceding paragraph is the first one, "In his 1927 silent film *Napoleon*, French filmmaker Abel Gance used film techniques far ahead of their time." The other sentences give specific details about the film techniques.

Details in an expository paragraph often are *facts* and *data*. Facts are pieces of information believed to be true. Data are pieces of information containing numbers: Many facts contain data. For example, there are twelve inches in a foot; every four years, February has twenty-nine days; George Washington was the first president of the United States. In the paragraph about *Napoleon*, the details all are facts. Details about the date of the film (1927) and the number of images on the screen are data.

When including facts and data in a paragraph, consider your readers. Think about how much they already know and what you should explain. If you use facts and data that are already known to a large part of your audience, your paragraph won't be informative. If you use facts that are unfamiliar, you may need to explain some of them. For example, in the *Napoleon* paragraph, the writer mentions the technique known as Polyvision. By itself, this word probably doesn't have much meaning for many readers. Notice, however, that the writer went on to explain the term, so that readers could understand it.

It is important that facts and data be checked for accuracy. Reference books such as dictionaries, encyclopedias, and almanacs are good places to verify your information. These books also are good sources for details to develop an expository paragraph.

| Writing Activity 1 | **Developing an Expository Paragraph with Facts and Data** |

For this activity, select a topic that you can develop with facts and data. Some suggestions are given on page 89. Then, use a dictionary, encyclopedia, almanac, or other source to find facts and data about your topic. Make a list of the facts and data that you find. Save your lists to use later.

Suggested Topics

1. How meteors are formed
2. How hurricanes are formed
3. How dolphins communicate
4. Giant snakes of the world
5. Neil Armstrong's walk on the moon
6. Pitchers who have pitched perfect games
7. The legends of werewolves
8. The courage of Babe Didrickson
9. Rules for playing soccer
10. The "Bigfoot" monster

Use your list of facts and data to write a paragraph. Follow these steps:

- Write a topic sentence that gives a general idea of the information or explanation that you want to give.
- Decide which of your facts and data develop or explain the topic sentence.
- Write sentences that include your facts and data.
- Arrange your sentences in paragraph form.
- Give your paragraph a title.

Review your expository paragraph by looking first at individual sentences. Does each sentence contain details that will help readers understand your topic? If not, add those details. Is there information in your paragraph that will be new to most readers? If not, go back to your sources for more information or change your topic and start over. Are there any facts that your readers might not understand? If there are, decide whether you should explain them, give examples of them, or both.

Next, look at the paragraph as a whole. Is there a topic sentence that clearly states the main idea? Does each sentence help to develop or explain the main idea by giving details about it? Are there enough detail sentences to make the topic clear to readers? If your answer to any of these questions is no, make the necessary changes in your paragraph.

Information in Order

Many expository paragraphs give directions or explanations. In these paragraphs the information often is arranged by time. For example, the following paragraph explains how a "black hole" is formed. What is the first step in the process? The last?

The temperature at the center of a star is millions of degrees. At this temperature, hydrogen atoms fuse to form helium, and energy is released. This energy causes the gas in the star to expand. After millions of years, however, the hydrogen in the star is used up. When this happens, the gas stops expanding. The center of the star is so heavy that it pulls the gaseous material towards it. Finally, the star collapses in on itself. The dying star is so dense that no heat or light can escape from it. The star has become a "black hole."

Notice how the information in this paragraph could be arranged along a time line.

START	Hydrogen atoms fuse to form helium	Energy causes gas to expand	Hydrogen used up	Gas stops expanding	Star collapses	STOP

Writing Activity 2   **Putting Information in Order**

Each of the following paragraphs begins with a topic sentence. The other sentences, however, are not in an order that makes sense. First, read each paragraph and decide what should happen first, second, and so on. Then, rewrite the paragraph, putting the sentences in the order in which they happen.

1. Here's how to tell how far away a bolt of lightning strikes. Begin counting seconds as soon as you see a bolt of lightning. First, have on hand a watch or clock that shows the seconds. Divide the number of seconds you counted by five. Your answer is the number of miles distant that the lightning struck. Stop counting when you hear the thunder. If it is less than five seconds, it is less than a mile.

2. A jet engine works with only three basic parts: an air intake, a combustion chamber, and an exhaust outlet. Air and fuel mixed in the combustion chamber catch fire. First, air comes in through the air intake. The hot exploding gases push out at great speed through the exhaust outlet. The air and fuel mixture actually explodes in the chamber. As the gases push outward and backward, the plane moves forward.

3. Making natural dyes from flowers is not a difficult process. Boil them in about three gallons of water for 15 minutes. The first step is to collect the flowers at full bloom. After cooling the mixture, strain out the cooked flowers. You will need about two and one-half pounds of flowers to dye one pound of material. Then cut the flowers into small pieces and put them in an enamel or glass pot for cooking. What you have left is the dye.

4. "Heading" in soccer means deliberate contact between a player's head and the soccer ball. In returning the ball, use all of your upper body muscles, not just your head. Keep your eyes on the ball as it comes toward you. This is the safest spot. At the moment of contact, tighten your neck muscles to prevent the head from snapping backward. As the ball approaches, use your forehead as the contact spot.

Writing Activity 3   **Writing Paragraphs That Give Directions**

The following are plans for writing expository paragraphs. Each plan consists of a topic sentence and the steps to follow in carrying out a direction. The steps are already arranged in logical order. Using the plans, write four paragraphs. Begin by writing a topic sentence. Then write a sentence for each step, using the order already given. Use transitions where necessary.

1.   **Topic:** How to show the relative size of the sun and the earth

   Steps: Draw a circle 27 inches across (diameter)

   Draw a circle one-fourth inch in diameter

   Large circle stands for sun, small circle for earth

   Draw line straight across "sun"

   How many "earths" equal sun?

2.   **Topic:** How to cook pancakes

   Steps: Prepare batter according to package directions

   Heat the frying pan and test for correct heat

   Pan is hot enough when drops of water "dance" on surface

   Put spoonfuls of batter in pan

   Turn pancakes over when bubbles form on top

   Life cakes with spatula and brown on other side

3.   **Topic:** How to be a good babysitter

   Steps: Arrive promptly at arranged time

   Write down numbers where parents can be reached in case of emergency

   Write down information about feeding times, bedtime, etc.

   Follow schedule set up by parents

   Do not entertain friends while adults are away

   Do not leave children unattended

4.   **Topic:** How to dive from the side of a pool

   Steps: Stand straight at the side of pool

Hold arms at side in relaxed manner
Curve toes over edge of pool
Begin to fall forward toward water
Swing arms forward
Bend at knees and push off from edge
Drop head toward water
Stretch trunk and leg muscles as you hit water

Explaining a Process

Often, expository paragraphs explain the steps in a process, such as cooking a meal, assembling a bicycle, locating a star constellation, and so on. The steps in the process usually are explained in the order they are performed. When the steps are out of order, the process may be difficult to follow.

Each of the following paragraphs gives directions for the same process. Which one is easier to follow?

> Here is how to bake frozen macaroni and cheese. Preheat the oven to 425 degrees. Remove the foil pan from the package. Remove the cardboard lid from the pan. Place the pan on a middle shelf and bake for 35 to 40 minutes. Browned and bubbly, remove and serve.

> Here is how to bake frozen macaroni and cheese. <u>First</u>, preheat the oven to 425 degrees. <u>Next</u>, remove the foil pan from the package. <u>Also</u>, remove the cardboard lid from the pan. <u>Then</u>, place the pan on a middle shelf and bake for 35 to 40 minutes. <u>When</u> browned and bubbly, remove and serve.

The underlined words in the second paragraph help the sentences flow together. They bridge the gaps between sentences, making the paragraph read more smoothly. In a paragraph giving directions, use transitions such as these:

after	before	now
also	finally	once
as soon as	first, second, etc.	then
at last	next	when

A paragraph of information also can use transitions:

> The story of the English language is actually a story of many languages. <u>When</u> the Angles, Saxons, and Jutes settled in the country known today as England, they brought a Germanic language with them. <u>As a result</u>, modern-day English is related to the German language. <u>In addition</u>, England

was also invaded at different times by people from Scandinavia and France. <u>Therefore</u>, English also contains a mixture of words from these languages.

Here are some transitions that could be used in a paragraph that gives information:

also	however	moreover
as a result	in addition to	on the other hand
besides	in the same way	therefore
for example	meanwhile	when

Don't overdo it, though. Use transitions when you need them, when you think they make the paragraph read more smoothly.

Writing Activity 4	**Finding Transitions**

Read each of the following paragraphs. Some of the sentences begin with transitions, and some do not. Make a list of the transitions that you find in each paragraph.

1. A thesaurus is a very useful word-meaning book of a special kind. In it, words are listed in meaning groups. For example, the "future" word group includes *tomorrow, in time, eventual,* and *approaching.* In the same way, the "untruth" group includes *falsehood, lie, forgery,* and *myth.*

2. Although they both give words and meanings, a thesaurus is not a dictionary. In fact, the two books are just the opposite. That is, you use a dictionary to get the right meaning for a word. You use the thesaurus to get the right word for a meaning.

3. Once you catch on, a thesaurus is easy to use. First, you have a meaning or idea for which you need a word. Next, you find the indexed category for your meaning or idea. Then you turn to the page or pages of words. You try out words one by one. At last you find just the right word.

4. Some thesaurus words are informal, even slangy. For example, some words in the "untruth" group are *yarn, fib, tall tale,* and *fish story.* Even though they seem a bit out-of-date, they still are in the book. On the other hand, new informal words and expressions are added to new editions. For example, in the "transportation" group are *jet lag* and *skyjacking.* As a result, the thesaurus is a collection of old and new expressions and meanings.

Writing Activity 5	**Adding Transitions**

The sentences in the following paragraphs do not have transition words. Those sentences that could use such words begin with

"(Transition)". First, choose appropriate transitions from the lists, or select ones that you know. Then, rewrite each paragraph, adding your transitions. Underline the words that you add.

1. Has the North Pole always been in the same place? The earth is a spinning body. *(Transition)* it resembles a toy top in that it spins and wobbles at the same time. The wobble shifts the position of the pole a few feet. *(Transition)* the South Pole shifts to the same degree. *(Transition)* over millions of years, the poles appear to have shifted great distances.

2. What happens when a person's foot falls asleep? He or she usually is in an uncomfortable or awkward position. *(Transition)* the person might be sitting on one leg. *(Transition)* the blood supply to nerves in the area is slowed. *(Transition)* the nerves themselves may be compressed. *(Transition)* the person gets the "pins and needles" feeling of a sleeping foot or leg.

3. How long would it take you to count the stars in our solar group or galaxy? *(Transition)* scientists estimate that there are about 100,000 million stars in our galaxy. *(Transition)* most of them are not visible in our sky. *(Transition)* suppose you could see them and count them at the rate of 100 per minute. *(Transition)* working day and night, it would take you about 200 years.

4. What is a falling star? *(Transition)* a chunk of metal or rock from outer space enters the earth's atmosphere at high speed. *(Transition)* friction with the atmosphere slows the object's speed. *(Transition)* friction heats the object until it glows. *(Transition)* the slower-moving, glowing object is a falling star or meteorite.

The first step toward writing about a process is observing the process carefully yourself. Although you probably are involved in many processes, most likely you don't give them much thought. You might make your bed every day, for example, without stopping to think exactly how you do it. Similarly, you may ride a bicycle, pitch a baseball, play a game of backgammon, or prepare a favorite dish without stopping to think about the steps in the process.

Imagine yourself teaching a process to another person. First, select a simple process that you do often, such as performing a certain dance step or throwing a Frisbee. Next, divide the process into steps (an example follows).

Topic: Boiling an Egg

Step 1 Select a small saucepan with a cover.

Step 2 Select the egg that you wish to boil.

Step 3 Place the egg carefully in the saucepan.

Step 4 Take the pan to the sink.

Step 5 Turn on the cold water.

Step 6 Let the water run into the pan until the egg is covered by about one inch of water.

Step 7 Put the pan uncovered on the stove.

Step 8 Turn on the heat and set on "high."

Step 9 Let the water heat quickly to a boil.

Step 10 Remove the pan from the heat.

Step 11 Turn off the heat.

Step 12 Cover the pan and set it aside for twenty minutes.

Step 13 After twenty minutes, remove the cover of the pan.

Step 14 Take the pan to the sink.

Step 15 With a spoon, hold the egg in the pan while you empty the water into the sink.

Step 16 When the pan is empty, run cold water into the pan, covering the egg.

Step 17 Remove the egg from the cold water.

Step 18 Tap the egg against a hard surface, slightly cracking it in several places.

Step 19 Roll the egg in your hands to loosen the shell.

Step 20 Under running cold water, peel the shell from the egg and discard the shell.

Step 21 Shake the water from the egg.

Step 22 Halve, slice, or chop the egg and eat it.

If possible, again perform the process to be taught, thinking about each step as you complete it. How could you explain the step to someone so precisely that he or she could perform it? For example, suppose you are explaining how to stand up on water skis. How, exactly, do you hold yourself in the water? Do you stretch out or bend forward? If you bend forward, how far do you bend? How do you hold your head? Your arms? How do you hold your skis in the water? Are they held straight up in front of you or at an angle? Are the skis touching, or are they held slightly apart?

Writing Activity 6	**Writing Paragraphs to Explain a Process**

Write one or more expository paragraphs that explain a process, using your own topic sentence and list of steps. A list of suggested topics appears below. Follow these steps:

- Select a topic that is limited enough for a paragraph.
- Outline the steps that are involved.
- Write a topic sentence.
- Write sentences that give details about the steps in the process.
- Use transitions where needed.
- Give your paragraph a title.

Suggested Topics

1. How to throw a foul shot
2. How to bunt
3. How to change a bicycle tire
4. How to cook scrambled eggs (or another simple dish)
5. How to change the oil in a car
6. How to read a road map
7. How to change a fuse
8. How to perform a simple chemistry experiment
9. How to pitch a tent
10. How to apply eye shadow

Order of Importance

Sometimes you are dealing with information that makes better sense in one arrangement than another. For example, if some details are more important than others, you may want to put them in a certain order. Which is the most important detail in this paragraph?

> An incandescent light bulb is by far the most popular in the home, with about one and a half billion of the bulbs sold in the United States each year. This type of bulb is popular, most of all, because it is so inexpensive. Also, it is easy to install and gives a "warm" color. It is popular even though it is less efficient than other types of bulbs, wasting much of its energy as heat instead of light.

The topic sentence states that the incandescent bulb (the everyday light bulb you use at home) is the most popular. The other sentences give details, but they give them in order of importance. The first sentence after the topic sentence says that the bulb is inexpensive—the main reason for its popularity. The next sentence says that the bulb is convenient and attractive—also important reasons it is favored, but no so important as the cost. The last sentence explains that the bulb is popular even though it wastes energy.

The paragraph gives the most important reason first, less important reasons second, and, finally, the reason that is least important, but still supports the topic sentence. A plan of the paragraph looks like this:

Topic: Incandescent bulb most popular
Details: Low cost

Easy to use, warm color

Wastes energy

The paragraph could be arranged another way:

> An incandescent light bulb is by far the most popular in the home, with about one and a half billion of the bulbs sold in the United States each year. It is popular even though it is less efficient than other types, wasting much of its energy as heat instead of light. However, it is easy to install and gives a "warm" color. Most of all, the bulb is popular because it is low in cost.

This paragraph begins with the same topic sentence. This time, however, the paragraph builds up to the most important reason. After the topic sentence, the next sentence tells of the disadvantage. The next sentences give advantages. Then, the last sentence gives the most important reason. Here is a plan for the paragraph with this new arrangement:

Topic: Incandescent bulb most popular

Details: Wastes energy

Easy to use, warm color

Low cost

Both arrangements are effective. One paragraph begins with the most important item. The other ends with it. It is up to you to decide which way you prefer to arrange your information. Do you want the most important detail to be introduced first or last?

To arrange information by importance in a paragraph:

- State the topic clearly in a topic sentence.
- List the details.
- Decide where you want the most important detail emphasis to be (first or last) and arrange the details in that order.
- Write the detail sentences.

Writing Activity 7   Using Order of Importance

The following are sets of information with material for a topic sentence, a "most important" sentence, and "other" sentences with additional information. Begin with the topic sentence. Then write the "most important" sentence. After that, write the "other" sentences with additional information in one complete paragraph. Use transitions where necessary.

1.   **Topic:** Thomas Edison began improving the light bulb as soon as he invented it.

Most Important: Developed machinery to shape the glass part of the bulb

Other: First bulbs made by hand

Machine takes molten hot glass from furnace

Pulls molten glass over air jet, forming bulb

2.   **Topic:** Filament, the part that gives light, needed to be improved

Most Important: Filament now made of special metal—tungsten

Other: Original filaments made of cotton thread, often burned up

Others made of paper and bamboo, also burned easily

3.   **Topic:** Modern bulbs lose energy through heat

Most Important: Working on heat-saving bulb

Other: Inside of bulb coated with special substance

Coating lets light out, keeps heat in

Heat reflected back to filament

4.   **Topic:** Fluorescent tubes more efficient

Most Important: Use less electricity, a 40-watt tube same amount of light as a 150-watt bulb

Other: Tubes longer lasting than bulbs

Tubes give off very little heat

Writing Activity 8   **Describing and Explaining a Process**

Study the photograph shown below. Describe this object and explain how it is used. Break down the process of using it into steps, beginning with the first step, where material for the object is assembled, to the final step, where the user is finished with it. Describe the process of using this object in as much detail and as clearly as possible.

Chapter 9

PERSUASIVE PARAGRAPHS

WARM-UP

You have learned that your city council has recommended that the branch library near you be closed. You oppose this recommendation. List the points you would make in a paragraph that might convince the city council to change its position.

Now examine your list. Did you include all the important points that favor keeping the branch library open? If so, write a paragraph that you feel would persuade the city council to accept your position on this issue.

Persuasion

Persuasion is the act of convincing others to believe or behave in a certain way. In small ways, you probably use persuasion every day. For example, you convince a friend to lend you a video game or to go with you to a concert.

You may also use persuasion in other ways. For example, imagine that a television network is about to drop your favorite show because of its low ratings. You decide to write to the network, giving reasons the show should remain on the air. If enough viewers write letters, the show may remain. Regardless of whether you succeed at convincing the network, however, you are developing your ability to persuade.

Forming and Supporting an Opinion

In areas close to your own experience, it may be easy for you to form opinions. For example, based on your experiences at home and school, you may have formed opinions such as these:

- Teenagers should not have to pay adult prices for admission.
- Parents should pay teenagers to babysit for younger brothers and sisters.

101

- Dieting can be dangerous to a teenager's health.
- The legal driving age should be kept at sixteen.

Once you leave your immediate world of home and school, however, it may seem more difficult to form an opinion. One reason for this difficulty may be a lack of observation. How observant are you about what happens in your city or area? In your state? In the nation? In the world? Of course, it is difficult to have first-hand information about such events, so your observations must be indirect—based on what you hear in conversations, read in newspapers and magazines, and see and hear on television and radio.

| Writing Activity 1 | **Keeping a Log of Information** |

Make a special effort to keep yourself informed on regional, national, and international events. For one week, read a newspaper daily and watch both a local and a national news program. Read at least one news magazine such as *Newsweek, Time,* or *U.S. News and World Report.* Keep a log in which you record information about events of special interest to you and where and when you observed them (a sample follows). Use your log to help you form opinions about events.

Information Log

Date	Source	Event	Opinion
May 6	Chicago *Sun-Times*	Tougher drunken driver legislation passes state Senate	Laws concerning drunk drivers should be tightened.
May 9	*Sun-Times*	First couple both to graduate from Naval Academy have married	Both men and women should serve in Armed Forces.
June 1	*Time*	Heart attacks are on increase in U.S.—major reason is cigarette smoking	Cigarette smoking is dangerous to health.
June 1	*Time*	Attendance at movies is down nationwide	The quality of movies has declined over the past few years.
June 2	Channel 9 News	Gang violence is increasing in the city	Federal money should be spent to provide jobs for unemployed youth.

To add strength to an opinion, most persuasive paragraphs also include reasons to support the stated opinion. What is the opinion stated in the following paragraph? What are the reasons to support it?

> Sugar is bad for your health. When first consumed, it leaves you with a feeling of "quick energy." Very soon, however, the sugar level in your body goes down, leaving you feeling more tired than before. In addition, sugar is a leading cause of tooth decay, resulting in discomfort and expense for millions of people. Then, too, sugar is high in calories. When used in large amounts, it can lead to a weight problem.

The opinion in this paragraph is that sugar is bad for your health. The writer uses these reasons to support this opinion.

1. Sugar produces a tired feeling.
2. Sugar causes tooth decay.
3. Sugar can lead to weight problems.

Often, reasons are more persuasive if they are supported by evidence. This evidence may include facts and figures, statements by authorities, and actual incidents.

Facts and figures should be accurate, and they should be up-to-date. You can find and check facts and figures in reference books such as encyclopedias, almanacs, and atlases. Before using one of these sources, however, check the copyright page to see when it was published. Because of the rapid changes in modern society, out-of-date facts and figures can be very misleading. For example, suppose you were looking for information about America's space program. If you looked in a reference book published in 1969, you might come up with this fact: "Only one American, Neil Armstrong, has walked on the moon." What is wrong with that statement?

Further, facts and figures can be used in misleading ways. For example, suppose you write a paragraph supporting your opinion that student absence is a problem at your school. To support your opinion, you make this statement, "On January 23 of this year, 27 percent of the students were absent." While it might be true that 27 percent of the students were absent on that date, was this a typical day? Perhaps a flu epidemic accounted for the high rate, and that figure does not represent the normal absence rate for the school.

Statements by authorities can also be important pieces of evidence. An *authority* is someone who is an expert in a given field. In using statements by authorities, however, be certain that the expert does not have a selfish reason or financial motive for his or her opinion. For example, a doctor who specializes in nutrition might be a good source for a statement about the effects of sugar on the body. However, if the same doctor is employed by the sugar industry, then his or her statement might be slanted in favor of sugar. In addition, remember that a person who is an expert in one field may not qualify as an expert in another. For example, a professional football player might be an expert on the advantages or disadvantages of playing on artificial turf, but that does not make him an expert on nutrition. (See Chapter 11 for further information on documented research.)

If well chosen, an incident can be a powerful piece of evidence. However, the incident should not be an isolated one; it should fairly represent the situation. For example, in trying to persuade a student audience that your school has an attendance problem, which of the following incidents would represent the situation fairly?

> Sue was absent 63 days during the school year. Sue was absent because she was involved in a serious automobile accident and had to be hospitalized.

> John was absent 23 days during the school year. Among John's excuses for being absent were oversleeping, car trouble, bad weather, a cold, and a sick brother.

If an incident is highly unusual, as is the one involving Sue, it is not fair to use it to support a statement such as, "Worth County High School has a serious problem with student absenteeism." However, if the incident is typical and is repeated over and over, then it would not be misleading to relate it.

Organizing Reasons That Support an Opinion.   In many persuasive paragraphs, the opinion serves as the topic sentence. Reasons and other evidence follow the topic sentence. The following example shows this arrangement.

> The practice of selling junk food in this school should be stopped. For one reason, the junk food machines throughout the school contribute to unsightly litter. As far away as the football field, students have scattered potato chip packages and soft drink cans. Also, the selling of junk food contributes to poor academic performance among students. According to Ms. Muller, school dietician, students often spend their lunch money in the soft drink and snack machines. As a result, they sit in class without the energy and alertness that a more balanced diet would provide. Most important, however, this practice encourages poor eating habits that may last a lifetime.

Another way to organize a persuasive paragraph is to give the reasons first and then build up to the opinion itself. Use the same steps in planning. Then write your "reasons" sentences. Finish with your "opinion" sentence.

Regardless of the organization you select, use transitions that can help your readers follow your ideas. Transitions that can help to develop an opinion are words such as these.

another	in addition
as a result	in conclusion
best, most of all	moreover
finally	most important
for example, instance	then, also
for one reason, for another	therefore

Here is the junk food paragraph, with the "opinion" sentence placed last. The bridging words are underlined.

> The junk food machines throughout the school contribute to unsightly litter. As far away as the football field, students have scattered potato chip packages and soft drink cans. <u>Also</u>, the selling of junk food contributes to poor academic performance among students. According to Ms. Muller, school dietician, students often spend their lunch money in the soft drink and snack machines. <u>As a result</u>, they sit in class without the energy and alertness that a more balanced diet would provide. <u>Most important</u>, <u>however</u>, this practice encourages poor eating habits that may last a lifetime. The practice of selling junk food in this school should be stopped.

In this paragraph, the most important reason has been presented last. Another arrangement would be to give the most important reason first, followed by the less important reasons.

Writing Activity 2	**Deciding Where to Present an Opinion**

Each of the following paragraphs gives the reasons for an opinion. However, the opinion itself, the topic sentence, is missing. First, read each paragraph and decide what the missing opinion is. Next, decide whether the opinion should be presented at the beginning or at the end of the paragraph. Then state the opinion in a topic sentence and rewrite the paragraph to include it.

1. Staying in the sun may make you look tan and healthy. However, too much sun dries out the skin and ages it faster. As a result, wrinkles develop at an early age, and the skin may even get a leathery texture. Worst of all, skin cancers often come from too much sunlight.

2. In the first place, animals raised for food often are kept under cruel conditions and are killed in painful ways. Also, there is no food value in meat that cannot be found in equal or greater amounts in nonmeat foods. Finally, a vegetarian diet is healthier than a diet that includes meat. Increasing evidence shows the relationship between eating meat and heart disease.

3. Most important, boys who are kept back a year are being taught that sports are more important than academic subjects.

Then, too, although their larger size may give the boys an advantage on the ninth grade team, it also means that they will always be a year older than most of their classmates. Finally, the practice is unfair to the boys whose parents refuse to allow them to repeat the eighth grade for this reason.

Writing Activity 3   Organizing Supporting Reasons

Below are plans for writing persuasive paragraphs. Each plan consists of an opinion and reasons to support it. To write paragraphs using the plan, follow these steps:

- Read the plan.
- Write a topic sentence stating the opinion.
- Write sentences explaining the reasons. Use transitional words or phrases when you think they can help you build up the reasons.
- Arrange the sentences in paragraph form.

1. **Opinion:** Students should have a television lounge.

   Reasons: Keeps students with free time out of trouble

   Gives students a place to relax and unwind

   Solves problem of noise in study halls from students who have no homework

2. **Opinion:** All students should take cooking class.

   Reasons: Learn the basics of good nutrition

   Cheaper and more healthful than depending on fast-food restaurants

   Learn rewarding hobby, even vocation

3. **Opinion:** Everyone should serve in Armed Forces.

   Reasons: Shows that men and women have equal responsibility

   Helps the individual—discipline, career guidance, "settle down" period for many

   Helps the nation—a reserve of trained personnel

4. **Opinion:** "Pee Wee" football should be abolished.

   Reasons: Physically damaging to 7- to 11-year-olds whose muscles and bones have not fully developed

   Emotionally hard on young children

   Young children should concentrate on developing cooperation, not competition

Writing Activity 4   **Writing a Persuasive Paragraph**

For this activity, write a persuasive paragraph by following these steps:

- State your opinion in a topic sentence.
- Write sentences explaining the reasons and evidence to support your opinion.
- Decide whether you want to place your topic sentence at the beginning or end of the paragraph.
- Decide whether reasons should be arranged by order of most importance or least importance.
- Arrange your sentences in paragraph form, bridging with transitional words when they are helpful.
- Give your completed paragraph a title.

Building Evidence to Support Your Opinion. As you plan your persuasive paragraph, ask yourself these important questions.

1. Who are my readers?
2. What do I want my readers to think or do?
3. What evidence will help me achieve my purpose?
4. Where can I find this evidence?

Knowing your readers will help you to plan the approach you will take. For example, suppose your audience consists of your fellow classmates. With these readers, which of the following topic sentences would probably be the most effective?

Dieting is dumb.

Diets high in lipoproteins and triglycerides should be avoided.

Dieting can be dangerous to teenagers.

Before you can persuade your readers to accept your opinion, you must find a way to identify with them. If the majority of your classmates are concerned about their appearance, they probably would not relate to the "Dieting is dumb" topic sentence. Also, since it is unlikely that your classmates are experts in nutrition, they probably would not know the terms *lipoproteins* and *triglycerides*. Therefore, it would be difficult for them to identify with the second statement. The third topic sentence, however, is one that most teenagers can understand.

The second question to ask yourself concerns what you want your readers to do as a result of reading your paragraph. In a paragraph with the topic sentence, "Dieting can be dangerous for teenagers," would you want your readers to stop dieting? Probably not. More likely, you would want them to understand that certain "fad" diets can be dangerous.

The third question is about the evidence that will help convince your readers. The evidence in this case will relate to facts and figures about the dangers of fad diets, statements by authorities about these diets, and actual incidents involving those who were harmed by fad diets.

The final question to ask yourself is where you can find the evidence to support your opinion. Possible sources include reference books in your school library, textbooks or books on your general subject, newspapers and magazines, and interviews.

| Writing Activity 5 | **Stating an Opinion with Reasons** |

From your own experience, select an opinion that you can support with reasons and evidence. Then ask yourself the four evidence-building questions given on page 107 and write down the answers.

Now, write a paragraph giving your opinion and the reasons that you believe support your opinion. Make a list of information you will need to get from outside sources.

| Writing Activity 6 | **Supporting Your Opinion with Outside Information** |

Using your opinion and reasons from Writing Activity 5, find some facts and figures to support your opinion. Also, find at least one statement by an authority that supports your opinion. Finally, based on your own experience or that of friends or relatives, think of an incident to help support the opinion. List your evidence on a sheet of paper along with the sources where you found it. Then rewrite your paragraph, expanding it by adding this new information.

Writing Activity 7 **Writing to Persuade**

Study the photograph shown below. Describe the animal in the photograph. In a short piece of writing, try to persuade your reader to accept one of the following statements:

1. Animals are better off in the zoo than they are in the jungle.
2. Animals should be left in the jungle instead of being placed in a zoo.

Be sure to think about your main persuasive points before you write.

Part 3

LONGER COMPOSITIONS

Writing for Others

EASY WRITING

MAKES HARD READING.

ERNEST HEMINGWAY

Probably the word *composition* already is familiar to you.

Teachers have likely assigned compositions for you to write. Have you ever thought, however, about what the word *composition* means?

Composition is a noun that is based on the verb *compose*. To compose means to create something—to give it form—by putting together parts or elements. You are constantly composing sentences to communicate with another person through the elements of words. Artists compose music, sculpture, paintings, photographs, films, and all other forms of art. Writers compose essays, stories, poems, novels, and all other forms of writing by using words and sentences.

In previous chapters, you have learned how to write four major types of paragraphs: descriptive, narrative, expository, and persuasive. The structure of the paragraph is very much like that of a small composition. Very often, it is a one-paragraph essay—a miniature model of a larger piece of work. When an essay contains several paragraphs, it is called a multiparagraph composition (*multi* is from Latin, meaning "many"). Both a one-paragraph composition and a multiparagraph composition develop one central idea. In the one paragraph essay, the central idea is called a topic sentence. In the multiparagraph essay, the central idea is stated in a thesis statement, which appears in the introductory paragraph of the composition.

The advantage of a longer, multiparagraph composition is that it gives the writer more opportunity to develop ideas that he or she wants to express clearly and completely. Many ideas are too complex to compress into one paragraph. It is important for you to learn how to design and write multiparagraph compositions, since there will be many occasions in the future when you will be asked to write them.

111

WHAT YOU WILL LEARN

In this section you will learn the following:

1. How to write an essay
2. How to write a factual report
3. How to write a review
4. When and how to write business communications

Chapter 10

WRITING AN ESSAY

WARM-UP

Find a short (one page) article in a magazine. Count the number of paragraphs. Find the main idea. Write the main idea in one sentence.

Now review your statement of the main idea. Reread each paragraph in the article. Does each paragraph express the main idea? How? If not, identify those paragraphs you would delete if you were the author.

Prewriting

In order to understand the process of creating and composing a multiparagraph composition, a typical situation will be considered. Suppose that your teacher assigned the class a multiparagraph composition on something connected with first aid. The teacher gives you all the freedom you may want to write about all or part of the subject. What are you going to do? You don't know much about first aid. The technique to use is called *prewriting*.

Prewriting is "brainstorming" on paper. It involves thinking about a problem and writing down any thoughts and words that come to your mind concerning that problem.

The best way to state the problem is to ask questions about it. In this case, the questions might be posed like this:

1. What do I know about first aid?
2. What will I write about it?
3. Should I write about all of the subject or part of it?
4. How will I find out more about the subject?

Prewriting about the questions might look something like this:

> Band-aids. Broken arms. Drowning. Artificial respiration. Big topic, write about part of it. What part? Nosebleeds? Boy Scout manual? Mr. Perez, the health instructor. Ask him? Don't know much. Library might have good information. See Perez. He's a nice guy.

113

You have jotted down your thoughts in a stream-of-consciousness style that is informal, loose, and disorganized. These thoughts are valuable, nevertheless, because they lead you toward a solution to your problem.

Writing Activity 1	**Brainstorming a Topic**

Choose one of the broad topics listed below and list questions and thoughts about it. Then give some possible answers to questions you have listed.

Computer games	War	Animals	Work
Food	Women	Energy	Money
Sports	Men	Fear	Crime

Prewriting and Research

What you discovered in your prewriting was direction. The author preparing to write about first aid was led to Mr. Perez and the library as two possibilities for more information. Had the author been an authority on first aid, he or she probably would not have needed to brainstorm so much. When you search for information about a subject you do not know well, you are doing *research*. For further help in doing research, see Chapter 11.

Many students are not aware of the resources that are available to them. Two important resources that can be very helpful are experts and libraries. An expert who knows much about the subject will often guide you. Further, libraries quite often have the information you need in books, magazines, periodicals, or other materials.

In this situation, Mr. Perez does turn out to be a great resource. He suggests that you narrow the subject to a specific first-aid technique that is important, simple, and useful to people in real-life situations. Some of the possibilities are treating burns immediately, using the tourniquet, mouth-to-mouth resuscitation, and the Heimlich maneuver for saving choking victims. He points out that the Heimlich maneuver is a fairly recent discovery as a technique. It is easy to learn, and everybody should know about it. Most restaurants have a description and a diagram in a conspicuous place on a wall so that customers can use it if there is a choking emergency. Mr. Perez suggests that you go to the library and to a restaurant to learn more about it.

At the library, you find the topic "Heimlich maneuver" listed in the card catalog or the on-line catalog. You check out a booklet about the technique. You also study the poster in a nearby restaurant. The topic appears to be specific, easy to learn about, and useful information that could save a life. You are on your way!

Writing Activity 2   **Taking Notes**

Turn to the poster of the Heimlich maneuver on page 122. Jot down some questions about how it is performed. List some possible answers to your questions.

Prewriting means jotting down everything that might help you with your problem. As you talked with Mr. Perez, you took notes. Now, as you read the booklet on the Heimlich maneuver, you jot down the major steps and important facts about the technique. You compare your notes with the poster notes you took at the restaurant. You are zeroing in on your topic. You now have enough raw material from prewriting to think about arranging it in an order that will form the basis for writing your composition.

Thesis Statements

After you have completed your prewriting on any subject, you read over everything you have written and strike out anything that you cannot use. Then you ask yourself the most important question concerning the composition: What is the major point of the composition—the main idea? The answer to this question will be the *thesis statement*. It is the central idea that controls which information your composition will include.

In your situation, you ask yourself why the Heimlich maneuver is important. You attempt to state your answer in a specific, clear sentence. You decide to use this sentence: <u>The Heimlich maneuver is a simple, easily learned technique that everyone should know because it can save a choking victim's life.</u>

Now that you have composed your thesis statement, it becomes the master control of what you are about to write. Your next job is to design the steps of your composition by making an outline that will include what the Heimlich maneuver is, when you use it, and how you administer it.

The Outline

An outline for any project can be one of the most helpful guides a writer can use. While prewriting is gathering raw material, an outline can be called preplanning—designing the shape that your composition will take.

Designing an outline need not be difficult if you know what you want to say. Good raw material collected through research gives you a solid base to work from. You begin an outline by asking important questions that your composition will answer. For example:

1. What is the Heimlich maneuver?

2. Why is the Heimlich maneuver important?

3. When do you use it? When don't you use it?

4. How do you administer it?

The answers to these questions will form the basis for your writing.

Parts of the Composition

Any composition ordinarily follows a simple, three-part design.

I. The Introductory Paragraph

Here, the main point of the composition—the thesis statement—is presented.

II. The Body

This includes paragraphs that illustrate, support, and develop the thesis statement.

III. The Concluding Paragraph

This paragraph confirms the importance of the thesis statement. It frequently sums up what has been said and emphasizes the importance of the main idea.

In making your outline, you must include the important points about your topic—the answers to your initial questions. Consider an outline to be a skeleton, a guide that gives you direction as you write and keeps you from wandering off the subject. The following outline is a possible design for the essay on the Heimlich maneuver.

Introduction

The Heimlich maneuver is an important, simple technique that can save a choking victim's life.

I. Is the victim truly choking?

A. Symptoms

1. Victim cannot talk or breathe

2. Victim gradually turns blue

3. Victim collapses

II. How to use the Heimlich maneuver

A. Standing or seated victim

B. Collapsed victim who is lying down

III. How do you know if it worked?

  A. Victim resumes breathing

  B. Victim does not respond

Conclusion

Everyone can be prepared to help a choking victim in an emergency with the Heimlich maneuver.

This topic outline is material gathered from prewriting. For longer compositions, you may want to put your outline in sentence form and include more details. For short compositions, however, the topic outline will be useful and appropriate.

Indeed, the preplanning you do in writing an outline is time well spent. Your outline gives you guideposts to follow along the road to a successful composition.

Writing Activity 3	**Making an Outline**

Make an outline for the topic you selected in Writing Activity 1. Follow the topic outline form we have just studied.

The First Draft

Once you have completed your outline, you are ready for the first draft. A first draft is your first attempt at writing your composition. A writer should never consider the first attempt to be his or her best effort. Even though you may feel that you have been creative and have made your points well, there are always finishing touches that you can apply to your work that will improve it.

In other words, always consider your first draft to be a trial run. It is your first try, but not your best one.

The Shape of Your Composition

Many short compositions can be written in five paragraphs.

  I. The Introductory Paragraph

  One paragraph that includes the thesis statement

  II. The Body

  Three paragraphs that illustrate, support, and develop the thesis statement

  III. The Concluding Paragraph

  One paragraph that sums up and affirms the thesis statement

Here is a diagram that illustrates the shape of a five-paragraph composition:

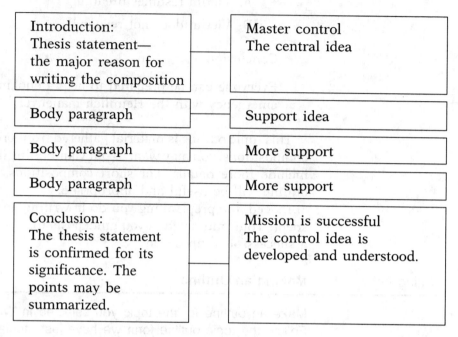

Introduction: Thesis statement— the major reason for writing the composition	Master control The central idea
Body paragraph	Support idea
Body paragraph	More support
Body paragraph	More support
Conclusion: The thesis statement is confirmed for its significance. The points may be summarized.	Mission is successful The control idea is developed and understood.

The Introduction

There are several ways to begin your composition and to interest the reader. Here are some of them:

Question–Answer:
What would you do if you saw a person choking and turning blue at your dinner table?

Would you like to learn a simple technique that could save someone's life someday?

Statistics or Facts:
Several hundred choking victims were saved last year through the use of the Heimlich maneuver.

Quotation:
"The Heimlich maneuver has saved hundreds of lives throughout the nation, thanks to Dr. Heimlich's discovery of this simple technique," said Dr. Nathan Buxby Hardcastel during a television interview.

Narrative Anecdote:
Mary Jo Botts loves to eat steak, but her love affair was shaken one evening when a piece of sirloin lodged in her throat. She found she could neither breathe nor speak. She began to gesture wildly. Because Lance Barrington, her dinner partner, knew how to use the Heimlich maneuver, Mary Jo is alive to talk about her experience.

Define an Important Term:
The Heimlich maneuver is a simple, manual technique that has saved many choking victims from death.

These are a few devices for introducing your composition and your master control idea—the thesis statement. Once you decide upon a beginning, you can follow your outline and develop your composition.

Transitions

Once the introductory paragraph has stated the central, controlling idea, the supporting paragraphs in the composition must be linked so that the reader can connect each idea to the preceding one with ease. The writer uses transitional words or phrases to make these connections between paragraphs clearly and smoothly.

Turn back to page 92 to review the use of transitions within a paragraph. Remember that transitions help to form bridges from one idea to another and from one paragraph to another. The reader crosses the bridge connecting one paragraph to another if the transitional words are good ones.

The following expanded list of transitional words and phrases may be used with success in many cases when you are writing your compositions:

Space:	Time:	Adding Information:	
at the left, right	after	also	thus
in the center	before	next	in contrast
on the side	then	another	in conclusion
along the edge	next	as a result	because
on top	at last	consequently	since
below	first, second, etc.	finally	similarly
beneath	at first	in addition to	yet
under	now	in the same way	inasmuch as
around	last	for example	in the second place
above	duration	for instance	although
over	formerly	furthermore	instead
straight ahead	rarely	however	for
at the top, bottom	usually	in fact	even though
surrounding	another	likewise	
opposite	finally	but	
at the rear, front	soon	again	
in front of	meanwhile	on the contrary	
beside	at the same time	contrariwise	
behind	for a minute, hour, day, etc.	in other words	
next	during the morning, day, week, etc.	to sum up	
next to	most important	another point	
nearby	later	moreover	
in the distance	ordinarily	nevertheless	
beyond	to begin with	on the other hand	
in the foreground	afterward	otherwise	
within sight	one thing	then	
out of sight	generally	therefore	
nearby	in order to		

Here are two first drafts about the Heimlich maneuver. Read them carefully.

The Heimlich Maneuver

When suddenly I encounter a person who is choking, this is what I should do. First, I should not panic, and I should work fast. The first four minutes or so are very critical. My first step is to approach the victim from behind if he is standing up, and I wrap my arms around his waist under his arms, slightly below the ribs. Then I place the thumb of my left fist between his navel and his rib cage. Subsequently, I cover the left fist with my right palm. At the same time, as I hold him tightly within my arms, I am powerfully flexing my muscles, pressing hard against his upper abdominal area. This would force the air from the lungs to escape forcefully through the mouth and nose, unplugging or carrying out with it food remnants, or whatever caused the laryngeal spasm. Finally, an ambulance should be called, so that the victim can be attended by a physician to further clear his air way, or possibly administer antibiotics to prevent any infection.

In case the victim is sitting on a chair, I follow the same steps. However, as I stand behind the victim, I wrap my arms around the chair as well.

Another possible position that Heimlich's maneuver could be used for is with the victim lying down. First, I extend his head backward. Second, I sit on his thighs gently, spreading my legs on each of his sides. From this position, I proceed by placing the heel of my left palm again in the area between his navel and his rib cage, with fingers pointing upward. Simultaneously, with the heel of my right hand against my left hand, I forcefully push against the upper abdominal area, forcing again the air from the lungs to work in the same way I described earlier.

It is advisable, as the head is extended, to try with the fingers to reach deep down in the throat to retrieve the causative agent before trying the Heimlich maneuver. Also, I should keep in mind that a person in such a condition might be violent or resisting help. Finally, care should be taken to avoid rib fracture or hemorrhage.

The Heimlich Maneuver

Choking victims are usually incapable of speaking or breathing while they are choking. If someone collapses while eating, the first thing you must do is to establish whether he is choking or having a heart attack. You want to rule out a heart attack, so you ask the victim if he can speak.

If he cannot, then he is probably choking. You must do something right away.

There are two ways of performing the Heimlich maneuver for choking victims. One method is for a victim who is standing. The other method is for someone who has collapsed. For a choking infant or child, perform the maneuver as usual, but reduce the amount of pressure used in the upward thrust.

Standing

When the victim is standing, stand behind him and wrap your arms around his waist. Make a fist with one hand and place it, thumbside in, against the victim's stomach, just above the navel and just below the rib cage. Grasp your fist with your other hand, and press into the victim's stomach with a quick upward thrust. Repeat several times if necessary. When the victim is sitting, stand behind him and follow the same procedure.

Collapsed

If the victim has collapsed and you are unable to lift him, place the victim on his back. Facing him, kneel astride his hips. With one hand on top of another, place the heel of the bottom of the hand on the stomach, slightly above the navel and just below the rib cage. You then press into the victim's stomach with a quick upward thrust. If the victim should vomit, quickly place him on his side and clear out his mouth.

Helping Yourself

If you are alone, you can help yourself by pressing your fist, thumbside in, against your stomach, slightly above the navel and below the rib cage. Once your fist is in place, drop down hard on your fist against the edge of a sink or chair, or just press your fist (or a firm object) into the area just below your diaphragm.

If you learn these methods for helping choking victims, you may not just save your own life. You may save the life of a loved one, friend, or a complete stranger. Any choking victim needs your help at that particular moment in life. You could make the difference between life and death.

Writing Activity 4   **Writing a First Draft**

After reading these first drafts, write a first draft of your own, using the information in the two compositions as a basis. Study also the diagram of the Heimlich maneuver on page 122.

Be certain to pay attention to your introductory paragraph and thesis statement. Also, use transitions to help your reader move from one paragraph to the next.

Emergency Care for
CHOKING

Emergency Phone Number:

——— CONSCIOUS VICTIM ———

If victim CAN breathe, cough or speak— DO NOT INTERFERE.

If victim CANNOT breathe, cough or speak— Give quick upward thrusts (grip above waist but below ribs).

Hold fist with thumb tucked in.

With thumb side inward, use other hand to give an in and upward thrust.

Repeat thrust steps until effective or until victim becomes UNCONSCIOUS.

——— UNCONSCIOUS VICTIM ———

Clear airway with finger...

...begin mouth to mouth breathing. Seal victim's mouth with your mouth. Pinch nose closed with thumb and index finger. Give victim 2 slow breaths.

Give up to 5 upward abdominal thrusts. Continue ventilation. If victim still has no pulse, perform CPR and call for help.

Illinois Department of Public Health
Division of Emergency Medical Services and
Highway Safety

525 West Jefferson
Springfield, IL 62761
(217) 785-2080

Standards for CPR and ECC is the reference for this
poster as published in JAMA, October 28, 1992,
Vol. 268, No. 16.
Printed by Authority of the State of Illinois
P.O. # 33004—25M—3/93

• Have someone call for an Ambulance, Rescue Squad or EMS.

• DO NOT PRACTICE ON PEOPLE. Abdominal thrust may cause injury. Use the back blows and chest thrust on infants. Use the chest thrust on pregnant women and obese victims.

• Learn to perform emergency care for choking and cardiopulmonary resuscitation (CPR).

• For CPR training information, call your local Heart Association or American Red Cross Chapter.

Selecting a Title

You already have practiced selecting an effective title in Chapter 5 on writing paragraphs. The title should be specific, fresh, and interesting. It should suggest the thesis statement—the controlling idea—in such a way that the reader will want to read further. Read the following title possibilities for the Heimlich maneuver composition:

Saving Lives	Life and Death
All Choked Up	The Heimlich Maneuver
A Real Lifesaver	First Aid for Chokers
Thank You, Dr. Heimlich	When You Can't Breathe or Talk
Life and Breath, or Death	What You Should Know about Choking

It is possible that none of these is a good title. Some of them, in fact, are terrible. See if you can create an excellent title for the Heimlich maneuver composition.

Writing Activity 5   **Selecting a Title**

Write a title for your revised composition. Tell why you think your title is a good one.

Revising Your Rough Draft

Revise your composition by looking first at individual sentences. Does each sentence contain details that will help readers understand your topic? If not, add those details in your revision. Is there information in each paragraph that will be new to most readers? If not, go back to your sources for more information or change your topic and start over. Are there any facts that your readers might not understand? If there are, decide whether you should explain them, give examples of them, or both.

Next, look at each paragraph as a whole. Is there a topic sentence that clearly states the main idea? Does each sentence help to develop or explain the main idea by giving details about it? Are there enough detail sentences to make the topic clear to readers? If your answer to any of these questions is no, make the necessary changes in your paragraph as you revise.

Writing Activity 6   **Writing a Second Draft**

Use the following checklist to guide you as you revise your rough draft into a final paper. At this point, while you are correcting and revising your rough draft, consult the Language Skills Review, Part 4, of this book to check for and correct any problems in your paper. After your second draft is edited, you will then be ready to prepare your final draft.

1. Does the composition develop one controlling idea?
2. Is the idea stated clearly in the first paragraph?
3. Does one paragraph lead to the next paragraph smoothly?
4. Are the transition words and phrases appropriate? Do they make good bridges for the paragraphs?
5. Is each main idea in the supporting paragraphs developed or explained sufficiently? Is all necessary information included?
6. Does the conclusion emphasize or sum up the controlling idea and form an effective ending that shows the importance of the controlling idea?
7. Are your words clear, concrete, and vivid?
8. Did you avoid clichés?
9. Did you use a natural writing voice?
10. Have you read your paper aloud to detect any errors?
11. Are your sentences varied enough to avoid boredom?
12. Have you proofread your paper for spelling and punctuation errors?
13. Is the meaning clear in all your sentences?
14. Are you satisfied that this is the best job you can do?

Writing and Proofreading Your Final Draft

Once you have revised your rough draft into a second draft and have then corrected the second draft to your satisfaction, you're now ready to complete the final draft of your paper. Unfortunately, this step is one where errors may creep into your work. After working with the same material over and over, it's natural to feel tired of a writing project and eager just to finish it. This step in essay writing is of the utmost importance, however, and ultimately determines how well you will represent yourself through your writing.

Writing Activity 7 | **Writing Your Final Paper**

Write or type the final draft of your paper, incorporating all the corrections and changes you made in your second draft. Here are a few tips on putting together a neat, readable final paper:

1. Type your paper on a computer, if possible, and double-space your work. Otherwise, write it legibly using blue or black ink. Use only one side of the paper and allow for adequate margins at the left, right, top, and bottom of each page.
2. Number each page after the first in the top right-hand corner.
3. Add a cover sheet that includes the title of your paper, your name, the assignment, and the date. Staple once in the top left-hand corner.

4. Before handing in your paper, read over it at least three different times. Leave a day, or at least an hour, between each proofreading, if possible.

5. As you read, make neat corrections in ink if you find missing punctuation, misspelled words, omitted words, and so on. Mark lightly with a pencil those spots where the wording troubles you, or where you want to add or delete something. Later, go back and decide whether you can make the corrections by hand, or if the page will need to be retyped or rewritten.

The Final Step: Proofreading

The final step in completing your paper—and one of the most important—is carefully proofreading it several times to be certain that you have said what you meant to say. A majority of errors on student papers could be caught in proofreading. In order to proofread efficiently, you need to do the following:

- Slow your rate of reading. Read carefully, looking at each word. You can even begin at the end and read each sentence backward, word by word.

- Proofread your paper several times. Expect to find errors; usually, you will.

- Pay special attention to the spelling of names and the accuracy of numbers. Double-check them several times.

Writing Activity 8	**Proofreading Your Final Paper**

Use the following checklist to help you focus on trouble spots in your paper. Refer to the Language Skills Review in Part 4 if you have any concerns about the wording you have used in your writing. This final step in writing an essay is your opportunity to make refinements so that your paper will be a good representation of the work you have put into it.

Proofreading Checklist

1. Is your paper carefully written and neat?
2. Are your sentences complete and clear? Check for run-ons, fragments, wordiness, and wandering sentences.
3. Do the subjects and verbs agree in your sentences?
4. Have you avoided double negatives?
5. Have you used pronouns with clear antecedents?
6. Have you avoided confusing shifts in pronouns, such as *I* to *you?*
7. Have you kept to a consistent tense in your writing? Check for changes in time. Have you jumped from present to past to present again without a clear reason?

8. Have you used the correct form of troublesome verbs? See pages 225–247 for the correct forms.

9. Have you used the correct ending for nouns and verbs? Check for the use of -s with the third person singular present tense, such as *She writes well.*

10. Did you avoid dangling modifiers?

11. Have you used capital letters to begin sentences? Have you capitalized proper nouns?

12. Have you spelled words correctly? Check any word you question.

13. Have you punctuated your sentences correctly? Check your use of commas, semicolons, and apostrophes.

14. Have you correctly used capitals, quotation marks, and end marks for dialogue?

15. Is slang used only when it is suitable?

Chapter 11

THE FACTUAL REPORT

WARM-UP

In an encyclopedia, look up something you would like to know more about. Read the article and list the major details of information given about the topic.

Now check that all your details are factual. Make another list of details which could be included in a nonfactual report on your topic.

Planning a Factual Report

Having studied the steps involved in writing an essay, you are ready to write papers that give specific information about a specific topic. Such papers are called factual reports.

A plan for a paragraph of information can be structured like this:

> **Topic Sentence**
> Detail Sentence
> Detail Sentence
> Detail Sentence

The same kind of plan can apply for a longer report containing several paragraphs:

> **Introductory Paragraph** (Thesis Statement)
> Body Paragraph
> Body Paragraph
> Body Paragraph
> **Summary Paragraph** (Concluding Paragraph)

The report begins with an introductory paragraph that states the topic or problem and gives enough information to get the report started. The body paragraphs tell about groups of related details. Finally, the summary paragraph repeats the topic and the main ideas.

The following is a rough plan for a five-paragraph report on the problems in converting to the metric system. Note that this is a simple listing of ideas, not a series of sentences.

Introductory Paragraph

Metric conversion in America very slow

Planned fast conversion; people not ready

Body Paragraph

Slow public acceptance

Most success in volume measure on products

Some use of Celsius

Little success with distance measures

Body Paragraph

Few school curriculum changes

Teach new terms and measures

Most success with youngest children

Body Paragraph

Changes continue in science

Scientists don't agree

Kelvin thermometer scale

Computers use binary numbers, not decimal

Concluding Paragraph

Metric conversion proceeds slowly

Give public time to accept

Give schools time to change

Continuing changes in scientific practice

The introductory paragraph will tell that metric conversion has been slow and that there are reasons for the slow pace. Each of the body paragraphs will discuss a different area of changes or problems. The paragraphs will be arranged by importance, beginning with what seems the most important or widespread and going on to the more specialized reasons. The concluding paragraph will bring the whole report together.

Here is a report based on the outline.

Slow Conversion to Metrics

It seems that America was in too much of a rush to convert to the metric system. The idea of immediate conversion has lost some of its steam. Most people were not ready for the immediate changes that the metric conversion would bring.

The public simply wasn't ready to accept quick changes. The most success was in packaging of products. On packages you will find two measures—grams or liters and ounces or quarts. Temperature readings are given in Celsius and

Fahrenheit, but most people go by Fahrenheit. Distance measures have not caught on at all. People still go by yards and miles, not meters and kilometers.

In addition, changes in the school curriculum have not been widespread. There has been some teaching of new terms—meters, liters, grams, Celsius. The most success has been with young children in the primary grades who don't have to "unlearn" the old terms and meanings.

Finally, changes in science keep happening, and some of these changes have moved away from metric measures. Scientists themselves do not agree on some changes. Many scientists, for example, prefer the Kelvin scale instead of the Celsius. Computers are the mathematicians of the future, and computers use binary numbers rather than the decimal or metric system.

As a result, conversion to the metric system is proceeding slowly and more realistically than planned. The public is taking its time in accepting the changes. Schools need more time to change the curriculum, starting with the primary grades. Changes are continuing in scientific discovery and practice, some of which are moving away from the metric system.

Notice that transitions begin some paragraphs. The transitions help one paragraph build upon another, leading to the summary. (For more information on bridging words, refer to page 119.)

Writing Activity 1	**Choosing a Topic**

Choose a topic upon which you could write a factual report with little research. Write a thesis statement and three details about the topic.

A Sample Plan and Report

A plan for a report can be written like the following one on the topic of home solar collectors.

Introductory Paragraph

Solar collector—fuel and money saver

How one is built

Body Paragraph

How a solar collector works:

Sun heats water in zigzag pipes

Water into house pipes

Radiators

Hot water tank

Body Paragraph

Solar collectors in different climates:

Sunbelt

Winter climates—storage tank for cloudy days

Concluding Paragraph

Fuel and money saver:

Simple

Uses little energy; pays for itself

Good in different climates

Notice that the introductory paragraph will emphasize savings and then will describe a solar collector. The detail paragraphs will tell how one works and in what climates. The concluding paragraph will summarize and repeat, pulling all the information together. Here is the report.

Home Solar Collectors

A solar collector for the home can save fuel and money. The typical solar collector is a glass box on the rooftop on the south side of the house. Inside the box are zigzagging pipes on top of a metal backing. The pipes are connected to the water pipes inside the house. Everything in the solar collector box is painted black to absorb the sun's heat.

A solar collector works very simply. First, the sun heats the water in the zigzagging collector pipes. Then, hot water from these pipes is pumped into the house pipes. Some water can go through the radiators to heat the house. Some of it goes into a tank for household hot water uses.

Solar collectors can work in different climates. In the sunbelt, they can be used almost every day. In winter climates, collectors are ideal on sunny days. On these days, some heated water can go into an insulated storage tank. On cloudy days, the stored hot water can be drawn from the tank.

A home solar collector is a simple and practical fuel and money saver. It is simply a heat collector that heats and distributes water. Once installed, it uses almost no energy and pays for itself in a few seasons. It is useful in both warm and cold climates.

Writing Activity 2   **Writing a Five-Paragraph Report**

Write a five-paragraph report on the topic "Conserving Energy Every Day." Use the written plan on page 131 to write your paragraphs. Be sure to use transitions.

Introductory Paragraph

Many ways to conserve in daily lives

For home heating:

Insulate roof, walls, storm windows

Heat down at night or when away

Blinds open in sunny windows

Warm clothing

Body Paragraph

Home cooling:

Insulation

Blinds shut in sunny windows

Shade trees near house

Fans more than air conditioners

Air conditioning only when needed

Body Paragraph

Transportation:

Combine shopping trips

Switch to small car

Share rides

Walk or bicycle

Public transit

Body Paragraph

Other household savings:

Cold water rinse for clothing

Sun or air dry clothes

Take short showers

Open refrigerator or freezer only when necessary

Don't preheat oven until needed

Concluding Paragraph

Everyone can conserve energy:

Home heating

Home cooling

Personal transportation

Other

Writing Activity 3 | **More Practice in Writing a Five-Paragraph Report**

Write a five-paragraph report on the topic "Earning Extra Money." Use the following written plan to write your paragraphs. Add information of your own if you want to. Use transition words to begin some paragraphs.

Introductory Paragraph

Many ways to earn extra money

Jobs hard to find

Can make your own work and get paid

Find out what people in your area need

Body Paragraph

Set up a babysitting service

Organize to provide sitters on short notice

Hourly rates; higher rate for short notice

Body Paragraph

Car washing specialists

Make "house calls"

Charge according to work done: interior cleanup, exterior wash, wax

Body Paragraph

Other special service ideas:

Give lessons on musical instrument

Pet sitting and pet care

House or apartment watching during owner's absence

Concluding Paragraph

Make money by making your own work

Babysitting service

Car washing house calls

Many other possibilities

Incorporating Research into a Factual Report

Now that you have had the experience of writing two five-paragraph reports based on minimal research, you are ready to learn the proper techniques for incorporating wider research into your papers. Most subjects on which you choose to write factual reports will require you to gather a wide variety of information from several different sources. Once you have gathered this information and added it to your paper, you then must include proper documentation that acknowledges the sources of your added information. This section will give you help with the research and documentation involved in writing a research-based factual report.

Conducting Research

You probably will conduct most of your research at either your school library or your community library. Don't overlook, however, the many other resources outside the library that could also be of great help to you. These include local organizations, people knowledgeable about your topic, pamphlets or brochures that you obtain from various institutions, informative lectures, radio and television programs, videos, and government publications.

Even if you have had experience in using library resources, the best place to start your research on a specific topic is with a staff member of the library. At the research desk, usually you will find a librarian who can help direct you and save you hours of wasted time. Before asking the librarian for help, however, be certain you have narrowed your topic so that it is very specific; otherwise, you will spend valuable research time gathering information that is not relevant to the topic you will be writing about. For example, instead of asking the librarian where he or she would suggest you start in researching the general topic of "railroads," state your specific topic, which might be "How the First Railroads in America Were Financed."

Writing Activity 4	**Brainstorming a Topic**

Brainstorm about a specific topic for ten or fifteen minutes, writing down your ideas. Begin by writing the general topic at the top of the page. Then jot down lists of questions, ideas, and any information on the topic that you already know. Determine which area of the topic interests you most. After you have narrowed your topic, write down all the sources you could check for information on the topic. If, for example, you are writing about preventing household fires, you might start at your local fire station; if you are writing about the latest treatments for high blood pressure, you might visit a doctor who specializes in such treatment and ask at his or her office for printed brochures available on the subject.

After you have checked the general research information recommended by the librarian, your next stop should be the library's card catalog, which usually is in a database you can access through a computer. Ask for help in doing a search of the database for your subject field and in selecting only those catalog items that are relevant to the subject of your paper. Be certain that you use a wide variety of sources, including the following:

- Recent sources—items published in the last year or so
- Sources that give some historical background
- A variety of sources—books, magazine articles, videos, pamphlets, etc.

Writing Activity 5	**Locating Sources of Information**

Review your notes from Writing Activity 4. By the time you begin your research in the library, you ought to be clear about the specific information you want to obtain. If you are uncertain, do some general reading on your topic for a few hours without taking notes. Then, once you have your topic sufficiently narrowed for a short research paper, select five information sources that you will use. Try, if possible, to include among them the following sources:

1. A general article from an encyclopedia
2. A book published within the last five years
3. A book published within the last year
4. A very recent magazine article
5. A pamphlet, audiotape, videotape, or some other unusual source of information

Using an index card for each of your five sources, write down all of the following pertinent information:

1. Title
2. Author (or authors)
3. Publisher
4. Publication date
5. Volume number (if shown)

Check out any library items you are permitted to take home, and photocopy important reference materials that cannot be checked out of the library. On each photocopy, be certain to write down information such as the title, authors, publisher name, and copyright date. The five sources you select will serve as the foundation for your research report, so choose them carefully.

Taking Notes. The secret to taking usable, meaningful notes lies in *writing less and thinking more*. If you write down everything that seems important to you, or everything that you think you will need at some point in your paper, you will be copying virtually every sentence you read. Instead, take notes sparingly; read slowly, think about what you're reading, and write down information that is outstanding or unusual. Your notes can be your own ideas and reactions to what you're reading, or they can be direct words from your source.

The term *plagiarism* means stealing someone else's written ideas and passing them off as one's own work. In some instances plagiarism is unintentional, such as in student papers in which passages are accidentally plagiarized. This occurs when students take down notes without crediting their source and then forget where the information was found. Or, in the process of writing, students insert words without checking their notes and discover later that the words they wrote are not actually their own. To avoid plagiarism, take notes carefully and follow these practices:

- As soon as you decide you will use a particular source, write down the pertinent data concerning the author, the publisher, and so on.

- Whenever you copy notes directly from your source, put the words that are not your own within quotation marks. Jot down the number of the page from which you took the quotation.

- If a passage is too long to take down every word, read it and condense it *in your own words*. Note the page number as well, because you must credit ideas as well as direct quotations.

Writing Activity 6   **Taking Notes from Research**

Using the five sources you selected, begin to take notes from them. Start by making a temporary informal outline of what you think you will want to include in your paper. Write a strong thesis sentence that you will keep in mind as you take notes.

Next, decide how you will organize your notes. Index cards are the easiest way to keep notes because you can easily shuffle them to rearrange the order of information. Of course, such shuffling is possible so long as you put only one idea on each card. Be sure to include both the page number and the author's last name to identify the source of the information. If you don't want to use cards for your notes, use a spiral-bound notebook. Put notes from each source in a separate section and write on one side of the paper only; this leaves the back of each page available for additional notes or for adding your own ideas or comments.

Finally, once you have compiled all the information you want to include in your paper, you're ready to begin to write.

Documenting a Report

A "documented paper" means simply that you have included three components:

1. Information from published sources
2. Parenthetical citations—acknowledgment of the source of information
3. A "Works Cited" page—an alphabetical listing of sources that appears following your paper.

How to Incorporate Parenthetical Citations into a Paper. You must give a parenthetical citation any time you use someone else's information in your paper. This information can be a direct quotation, a statistic, an idea, the author's opinion or someone else's opinion that the author of your source is quoting, concrete facts, graphics, and any other kind of information not commonly known.

The most frequently used citations are as follows:

- *author's last name and page number*
  (Harvey 527) (no comma between)

- *article title and page number*
  ("Beyond Appearance" 24) (used when there is no author)

- *page number only*
  (149) (used when you have already mentioned the author's name in the preceding sentence)

- *quoted in*
  (qtd. in Harvey 312) (used when the source author has quoted someone else whom you are now quoting)

- *author, key word in title, page number*
  (Bell, *Mirrors* 542) (Used only when you have two or more works by the same author. Note the use of *one* comma only, between the author and title.)

The following is a sample of how the parenthetical citations should be used and how they look when incorporated into the text of a paper. Notice that the period that ends the sentence comes *after* the parenthetical citation and that the citation follows directly after the closing quotation mark.

> If we ultimately agree that appearances are deceiving, then, as Michele Harvey puts it, "None of us can be certain that what appears as reality to us is the same reality perceived by the person standing next to us" (518). When we are small children, we are delighted to view the world in our own individual way; but as we grow up, we start wanting confirmation that how we see things parallels with the views of other human beings (Farris 135). We want to belong. Only after we truly mature and experience our own drive for creativity do we then desire "a different reality . . . something that sets us apart from the rest of the world" (James 138). Soon we begin to discover, through talking with others and seeing the world in different ways, that there are, in fact, a million different realities and that we are free "to create our own unique reality" (Bell, *Mirrors* 47) and not think of ourselves as insane. Constructing our individual reality is really the beginning of our ability to act creatively as adults. "Indeed," says Althea Wetmore, "any creative action, such as writing a story, composing music, or painting a picture, carries within those moments of creation a trace of insanity, being *out of our heads* for a short period of time" (qtd. in James 156).

The parenthetical citations on page 136 cover a variety of uses:

- **(518)**—a direct quotation with the author's name mentioned in the text
- **(Farris 135)**—a paraphrase of the author's idea
- **(James 138)**—a quotation with a portion omitted (shown by ellipses . . .)
- **(Bell, *Mirrors* 47)**—a quotation from an author who has written two or more of the sources used
- **(qtd. in James 156)**—a quotation originally from another source, but used by one of your sources. (In this case, always use the speaker's full name in your sentence. In this example Althea Wetmore made the statement, though you found the quotation in James.)

How to Compile a "Works Cited" Page. A Works Cited list always is added to the end of any documented paper. This page lists (alphabetically, by author) complete publishing information for each source you cited in writing your paper. Remember, do not add to your Works Cited list any sources other than those from which you actually used parenthetical citations in your paper.

Following are the most common types of entries in Works Cited lists. Closely study the spacing and punctuation. Notice that the second line is indented, that the author and title are separated by a period, and that there is a period at the end of each entry.

Book
Author. *Title*. City: Publisher, date.

Bell, Phillip. <u>Fractured Mirrors of Reality</u>. New York: Franklin, 1996.

Article
Author. "Title of Article." *Title of Periodical* Date: Page(s).

Farris, David. "Real Time, Real Places." <u>Sojourner</u> Nov. 1992: 86–87.

Encyclopedia
"Title of Article." *Encyclopedia*. Year of edition.

"Creative Reality." <u>Encyclopedia Britannica</u>. 1990 ed.

No author
Alphabetize by first main word of the title.

"Multiple Realities." <u>Logo Reports</u> Spring 1994: 316.

Following is a sample Works Cited list.

Bell, Phillip. <u>Fractured Mirrors of Reality</u>. New York:
Franklin, 1996.

Bell, Phillip, and Anne Teachworth. <u>Time After Time</u>. New
Orleans: U of New Orleans P, 1993.

"Creative Reality." <u>Encyclopedia Britannica</u>. 1990 ed.

Farris, David. "Real Time, Real Places." <u>Sojourner</u> Nov. 1992:
86–87.

Harvey, Michele. <u>Beyond Appearance</u>. Los Angeles: Alpha-
Beta, 1989.

James, Archer. "Myths and Dreams Pointing to Reality." <u>New
Voices</u>. Ed. Rachel Lockhart. Springfield: Dealer, 1978.

"Multiple Realities." <u>Logo Reports</u> Spring 1994: 316.

Writing Activity 7   **Writing a Documented Paper**

Begin by planning and writing your paper *without looking back at
the notes you have taken.* Prepare an outline and start writing your
paper accordingly. As you write, leave spaces and write yourself
notes in places where you want to expand the paper with
documented research. By adding information to your paper, you are
supplying evidence from outside sources to support your own
position.

After you've written a first draft, go back and add direct
quotations or paraphrased ideas from your sources. Don't overdo it,
however—most of the paper should be in your own words. Be
certain to credit the source of these quotations or ideas by adding
parenthetical citations.

Now, write a second draft that includes all the added material
from outside sources. Read and revise this draft as you see fit. In
particular, check all page numbers, spelling of authors' names, and
titles of the sources to be certain they are correct.

Finally, type your final draft with the parenthetical citations
added. Include a Works Cited list at the end of your paper. If your
teacher has asked for an outline and a cover sheet, include those
as well.

Writing Activity 8   **Checking Documentation Form**

Closely check your final documented report against the sample
parenthetical citation paragraph and the sample Works Cited list to
be certain that you have used the correct form for both. For more
information on documentation style, consult the Modern Language
Association of America's *MLA Handbook for Writers of Research
Papers.*

Chapter 12

THE REVIEW

WARM-UP

Write the answers that immediately come to your mind when you read the following questions.

1. What makes a book good?
2. What does a good movie need to make it effective?
3. What is a good television show? Why?
4. What is one of your favorite short stories? Why was it good?

Compare your answers with your classmates'. Did you all agree on what made a good book? A movie? A television show?

Writing Reviews

Reviewing is an important skill. To review means "to see again" and to evaluate an experience. There are many types of experiences that can be reviewed: Short stories, books, plays, movies, and television shows are some examples. The review is another type of longer composition that you may find that you enjoy writing, once you recognize the elements of a well-written review.

The purpose of a review is to give the reader your clear reaction to the subject of the review. This statement may seem simple, but a "clear reaction" includes not only opinions, but concrete reasons for your feelings about the subject. In conversation, most people give a very shallow reaction to artistic experience. The good reviewer digs deep into the experience, however, and examines why it is excellent, mediocre, or terrible.

Specific Language

In writing a review, it is very important to use specific language. Most excellent writing is clear, precise, and focused. Using words such as *like, enjoy, good,* and *excellent* is perfectly acceptable if you illustrate your judgments with specific examples.

Writing Activity 1   **Using Specific Language**

Complete the following activities. For each judgment cited, write specific reasons for your feelings with supporting examples.

1. Consider a friend you know very well. Tell why you think he or she is a good friend.
2. List specific reasons for feeling that a meal you have eaten recently was "delicious" or "awful."
3. Look out the window. Give concrete reasons for the statement, "This is a lovely day" or "The weather today is dreadful."
4. List reasons for liking or disliking a certain type of music.
5. Think of a school subject you enjoy. Give specific reasons for liking it.
6. Think of a sport you like or dislike. Tell why, and be specific.

If you thought carefully as you completed the previous writing activity, you may have discovered that it is not always easy to explain your feelings. There is, however, satisfaction to be found in creating specific explanations. To write clearly, a writer must think clearly. Clear writing involves hard work, but the focused, finished product can be a source of pleasure and pride.

Elements of a Review

To learn to review well, you need to understand the elements that make an experience effective. The good reviewer continually asks questions as the experience unfolds. The major question is, "Why?" "Why am I enjoying this?" "Why does this bore me?" The answers to these questions form the foundation of a good review. For this reason, a reviewer often has a note pad and a pencil close at hand when attending a concert, movie, or play or reading an author's work. The notes may be brief, but they store the answers to the "why" questions. They refresh the writer's memory when the time comes to "re-view" them.

The Questioning Technique

Once again, the 5Ws and the H approach can be valuable for reviewing virtually any experience. Certainly, it will lead you to basic facts that you will need for any review.

Remember that you use these questions to stimulate your thinking. Each of them can apply in some way to the subject you are evaluating and analyzing.

Who?   What?   When?   Where?   Why?   How?

Using the following updated fable by Aesop, examine how the questioning technique can work.

The Turtle and the Rabbit

One June day, a rabbit started bragging to the world of Zooland about his talents and abilities. "I am so fast," he said, "that I can beat anyone who wants to race with me. I am Mr. Hot Stuff on the track."

The turtle blazed at the rabbit through drooping eyelids.

"O.K.," said the turtle. "I'll take you up on it. I think I can beat you. Let's do it."

"You?" exclaimed the rabbit, astonished. "Why you're slower than an elephant asleep, stuck in the mud. I can beat you ten times before you go three feet."

"Insult me if you want," replied the turtle. "I have a hard shell. But hold up on the bragging and boasting until the race is over. You never know, you know."

They decided to race for a distance of a mile. The giraffe acted as the starter. "Ready? On your mark! Go!" barked the giraffe.

The rabbit took off like a tornado, rounding the bend in a few seconds. He felt that the race was such a joke, he decided to take a little nap. He fell asleep and dreamed about fields of lettuce.

The turtle chugged along at a determined, steady pace, very slowly. Eventually she lumbered past the rabbit. Sharp observers noticed a faint, odd smile on her face and a slight twinkle in the eye beneath the droopy eyelids.

Meanwhile, the snoring rabbit dreamed on about luscious lettuce. A thunderclap awoke him. The sky was cloudy, and the sun was setting.

The rabbit leaped up, rubbed the sleep out of his eyes, and zoomed down the road. When he got to the finish line, a crowd of chimpanzees was cheering the turtle on. The turtle inched over the finish line, a foot ahead of the speeding rabbit. She was victorious!

"Eat my dust, Bunny Boy!" said the turtle. "You can eat your smart words for dinner, too!"

The embarrassed rabbit blushed deeply. He slunk back to the hutch, somewhat educated in the school of experience.

Applying the 5Ws and the H approach, here are some sample notes:

Who? Who are the main characters? Who wrote the story?
Answers: The rabbit and the turtle. Aesop was the author.

What? What is the title? What happens?
Answers: "The Turtle and the Rabbit." The turtle challenges the boasting rabbit to a race. Against all odds, the turtle wins this unlikely contest.

When? When did the race take place?
Answer: In June. The year is unknown.

Where: Where does the race occur?
Answer: In Zooland, on a one-mile area.

Why? Why did the turtle win? Why did Aesop write the fable?
Answers: Because the rabbit was too confident and stopped to take a nap. Aesop probably wrote the story to show that hard work and commitment can sometimes win out over severe competition.

How? How did the turtle win?
Answer: By running the race with steady, determined effort.

Writing Activity 2   **Using the 5Ws and the H**

Read this fable by Aesop. Then, in writing, answer the 5Ws and the H for this story.

The Sun and the Wind

The wind liked to show off her power. Old Mr. Sun, however, had a large ego, too. One day, Ms. Wind said to Mr. Sun, "You're not so hot, you know. I am more powerful than you are."

"Oh, yeah?" replied Mr. Sun. "Well, I think you are just a blowhard. Let's have a contest, windbag."

"O.K., Sunny Boy," said Ms. Wind. "Let's do that. See that traveler walking down the road with his cloak on? I'll bet you that I can blow so hard, the cloak will come off him."

"I'll bet I make him take it off before you do, Windy," said Mr. Sun.

"We'll see, Bright Eyes," said Ms. Wind.

So Ms. Wind began to blow and blow, something fierce. The traveler was frightened. The stronger the wind roared, the tighter he tugged and wrapped his cloak around him. Soon the wind grew tired and out-of-air. She had blown herself out.

Mr. Sun smiled. He peeked from behind a fluffy cloud where he had been hiding and watching. Then he came out from behind the cloud, the full force of his beams striking the earth and the traveler.

"Whew!" said the traveler, "it sure is getting warm."

The traveler began to perspire. Finally, he could not stand the heat. He took off his cloak. Mr. Sun laughed a jolly laugh of victory. He watched the traveler wend his warm and weary way to an air-conditioned movie theater.

Reviewing the Short Story

Now that you have used the 5Ws and the H technique for reviewing, you will study the ingredients that make a good short story effective.

The short story form will be used as a basis for reviewing because it is manageable and can be included in this book. Later, you can apply what you learn to other forms such as the novel and the film. The following questions highlight those elements a reviewer considers when evaluating the work.

Title. What is the exact title of the story? Who is the author? Does the title have any special meaning in relation to the story?

Setting. Where does the story take place? Is the place important to the story? Why? How? Does the story take place in one area, or is there more than one place? Is the time frame in the story important? Does the story take place during a brief period, or are there several time sequences?

Characters. Who are the major characters in the short story? What are their names? If they have no names, describe them briefly. Do the characters change in any significant way during the story? Are they believable as people? Why or why not? If they are interesting, what creates the interest?

Plot. What problem does the main character face? Is there more than one problem? What is the major conflict in the story? As the action of the plot builds, where is the turning point in the story that leads to the ending? How is the problem solved? If it is not, why is it not solved? Does the story use suspense to create interest? Since the suspense arises from an unanswered question (or questions), what answer does the reader seek? Is the story believable; are there any false notes in the story?

Style. Does the author describe people and places well? Give an example. Is the dialogue effective? Does it reveal anything about the characters? Give examples. Does the author use hints, repetition, symbols, and other devices for effect? Quote an effective passage that illustrates the author's style.

Theme. Does the story attempt to say anything significant about human beings? How would you sum up what the author is trying to say through the story? Do you agree with the author's theme?

Impact. Did you like the story? Describe specifically what elements you liked in the story. Would you want to read another story by the author? Why?

Read the following story by Edgar Allan Poe carefully. Take notes as you read.

The Tell-Tale Heart

True!—nervous—very, very dreadfully nervous I had been and am; but why *will* you say that I am mad? The disease had sharpened my senses—not destroyed—not dulled them.

Above all was the sense of hearing acute. I heard all things in the heaven and in the earth. I heard many things in hell. How, then, am I mad? Hearken! and observe how healthily—how calmly I can tell you the whole story.

It is impossible to say how first the idea entered by brain; but once conceived, it haunted me day and night. Object there was none. Passion there was none. I loved the old man. He had never wronged me. He had never given me insult. For his gold I had no desire. I think it was his eye! yes, it was this! One of his eyes resembled that of a vulture—a pale blue eye, with a film over it. Whenever it fell upon me, my blood ran cold; and so by degrees—very gradually—I made up my mind to take the life of the old man, and thus rid myself of the eye forever.

Now this is the point. You fancy me mad. Madmen know nothing. But you should have seen *me*. You should have seen how wisely I proceeded—with what caution—with what foresight—with what dissimulation I went to work! I was never kinder to the old man than during the whole week before I killed him. And every night, about midnight, I turned the latch of his door and opened it—oh, so gently! And then, when I had made an opening sufficient for my head, I put in a dark lantern, all closed, closed, so that no light shone out, and then I thrust in my head. Oh, you would have laughed to see how cunningly I thrust it in! I moved it slowly—very, very slowly, so that I might not disturb the old man's sleep. It took me an hour to place my whole head within the opening so far that I could see him as he lay upon his bed. Ha!—would a madman have been so wise as this? And then, when my head was well in the room, I undid the lantern cautiously—oh, so cautiously—cautiously (for the hinges creaked)—I undid it just so much that a single thin ray fell upon the vulture eye. And this I did for seven long nights—every night just at midnight—but I found the eye always closed: and so it was impossible to do the work; for it was not the old man who vexed me, but his Evil Eye. And every morning, when the day broke, I went boldly into the chamber, and spoke courageously to him, calling him by name in a hearty tone, and inquiring how he had passed the night. So you see he would have been a very profound old man, indeed, to suspect that every night, just at twelve, I looked in upon him while he slept.

Upon the eighth night I was more than usually cautious in opening the door. A watch's minute hand moves more quickly than did mine. Never before that night had I *felt* the extent of my own powers—of my sagacity. I could scarcely contain my feelings of triumph. To think that there I was, opening the door, little by little, and he not even to dream of my secret deeds or thoughts. I fairly chuckled at the idea; and perhaps he heard me; for he moved on the bed suddenly, as if startled. Now you may think that I drew back—but no. His room was as black as pitch with the thick darkness (for the shutters were close fastened, through fear of robbers), and so I knew that he could not see the opening of the door, and I kept pushing it on steadily, steadily.

I had my head in, and was about to open the lantern, when my thumb slipped upon the tin fastening, and the old man sprang up in the bed, crying out—"Who's there?"

I kept quite still and said nothing. For a whole hour I did not move a muscle, and in the meantime I did not hear him lie down. He was still sitting up in the bed listening—just as I have done, night after night, hearkening to the death watches in the wall.

Presently I heard a slight groan, and I knew it was the groan of mortal terror. It was not a groan of pain or of grief—oh, no!—it was the low stifled sound that arises from the bottom of the soul when overcharged with awe. I knew the sound well. Many a night, just at midnight, when all the world slept, it has welled up from my own bosom, deepening, with its dreadful echo, the terrors that distracted me. I say I knew it well. I knew what the old man felt, and pitied him, although I chuckled at heart. I knew that he had been lying awake ever since the first slight noise, when he had turned in the bed. His fears had been ever since growing upon him. He had been trying to fancy them causeless, but could not. He had been saying to himself—"It is nothing but the wind in the chimney—it is only a mouse crossing the floor," or "it is merely a cricket which has made a single chirp." Yes, he has been trying to comfort himself with these suppositions; but he had found all in vain. *All in vain;* because Death, in approaching him, had stalked with his black shadow before him, and enveloped the victim. And it was the mournful influence of the unperceived shadow that caused him to feel—although he neither saw nor heard—to *feel* the presence of my head within the room.

When I had waited a long time, very patiently, without hearing him lie down, I resolved to open a little—a very, very little crevice in the lantern. So I opened it—you cannot imagine how stealthily, stealthily—until, at length, a single dim ray, like the thread of a spider, shot from out the crevice and full upon the vulture eye.

It was open—wide, wide open—and I grew furious as I gazed upon it. I saw it with perfect distinctness—all a dull blue, with a hideous veil over it that chilled the very marrow in my bones; but I could see nothing else of the old man's face or person: for I had directed the ray as if by instinct, precisely upon the damned spot.

And now have I not told you that what you mistake for madness is but over-acuteness of the senses?—now, I say, there came to my ears a low, dull, quick sound, such as a watch makes when enveloped in cotton. I knew *that* sound well too. It was the beating of the old man's heart. It increased my fury, as the beating of a drum stimulates the soldier into courage.

But even yet I refrained and kept still. I scarcely breathed. I held the lantern motionless. I tried how steadily I could maintain the ray upon the eye. Meantime the hellish tattoo of the heart increased. It grew quicker and quicker, and louder and louder every instant. The old man's terror *must* have been extreme! It grew louder, I say, louder every moment!—do you mark me well? I have told you that I am nervous: so I am. And now at the dead hour of the night, amid the dreadful silence of that old house, so strange a noise as this excited me to uncontrollable terror. Yet, for some minutes longer I refrained and stood still. But the beating grew louder, louder! I thought the heart must burst. And now a new anxiety seized me—the sound would be heard by a neighbor! The old man's hour had come! With a loud yell, I threw open the lantern and leaped into the room. He shrieked once—once only. In an instant I dragged him to the floor, and pulled the heavy bed over him. I then smiled gaily, to find the deed so far done. But, for many minutes, the heart beat on with a muffled sound. This, however, did not vex me: it would not be heard through the wall. At length it ceased. The old man was dead. I removed the bed and examined the corpse. Yes, he was stone, stone dead. I placed my hand upon the heart and held it there many minutes. There was no pulsation. He was stone dead. His eye would trouble me no more.

If still you think me mad, you will think so no longer when I describe the wise precautions I took for the concealment of the body. The night waned, and I worked hastily, but in silence. First of all I dismembered the corpse. I cut off the head and the arms and the legs.

I then took up three planks from the flooring of the chamber, and deposited all between the scantlings. I then replaced the boards so cleverly, so cunningly, that no human eye—not even *his*—could have detected any thing wrong. There was nothing to wash out—no stain of any kind—no blood spot whatever. I had been too wary for that. A tub had caught all—ha! ha!

When I had made an end of these labors, it was four o'clock—still dark as midnight. As the bell sounded the hour, there came a knocking at the street door. I went down to open it with a light heart,—for what had I *now* to fear? There entered three men, who introduced themselves, with perfect suavity, as officers of the police. A shriek had been heard by a neighbor during the night; suspicion of foul play had been aroused; information had been lodged at the police office, and they (the officers) had been deputed to search the premises.

I smiled,—for *what* had I to fear? I bade the gentlemen welcome. The shriek, I said, was my own in a dream. The old man, I mentioned, was absent in the country. I took my visitors all over the house. I bade them search—search *well*. I led them, at length, to *his* chamber. I showed them his treasures, secure, undisturbed. In the enthusiasm of my confidence, I brought chairs into the room, and desired them *here* to rest from their fatigues, while I myself, in the wild audacity of my perfect triumph, placed my own seat upon the very spot beneath which reposed the corpse of the victim.

The officers were satisfied. My *manner* had convinced them. I was singularly at ease. They sat, and while I answered cheerily, they chatted familiar things. But, ere long, I felt myself getting pale and wished them gone. My head ached, and I fancied a ringing in my ears: but still they sat and still chatted. The ringing became more distinct:—it continued and became more distinct: I talked more freely to get rid of the feeling: but it continued and gained definitiveness—until, at length, I found that the noise was *not* within my ears.

No doubt I now grew *very* pale;—but I talked more fluently, and with a heightened voice. Yet the sound increased—and what could I do? It was a *low, dull, quick sound—much such a sound as a watch makes when enveloped in cotton.* I gasped for breath—and yet the officers heard it not. I talked more quickly—more vehemently; but the noise steadily increased. I arose and argued about trifles, in a high key and with violent gesticulations, but the noise steadily increased. Why *would* they not be gone? I paced the floor to and fro with heavy strides, as if excited to fury by the observation of the men—but the noise steadily increased. Oh God! what *could* I do? I foamed—I raved—I swore! I swung the chair upon which I had been sitting, and grated it upon the boards, but the noise arose over all and continually increased. It grew louder—louder—*louder!* And still the men chatted pleasantly, and smiled. Was it possible they heard not? Almighty God!—no, no! They heard!—they suspected!—they *knew!*—they were making a mockery of my horror!—this I thought, and this I think. But any thing was better than this agony! Any thing was more tolerable than this derision! I could bear those hypocritical smiles no longer! I felt that I must scream or die!—and now—again!—hark! louder! louder! louder! *louder!*—

"Villains!" I shrieked, "dissemble no more! I admit the deed!—tear up the planks!—here, here!—it is the beating of his hideous heart!"

Reviewing "The Tell-Tale Heart"

Here is an analysis of "The Tell-Tale Heart," based on the questions listed previously.

Title.   The story is "The Tell-Tale Heart" by Edgar Allan Poe. The title shows how important the heart of the murdered man is to the story. The heart ends up betraying the murderer in a strange way.

Setting.   The house of the old man is the setting. Most of the action takes place in the old man's bedchamber. The setting is important because the narrator (and murderer) buries the dismembered body of the old man under the floorboards of the bedchamber. The time in which the story takes place is important because it takes place before the invention of electric lights. The lantern plays an important role in the story.

Characters.   The main character in the story is the murderer who tells the story and the old man. The three officers who investigate the shriek also are important to the plot. The narrator-murderer is a man who protests too much that he is not mad. His actions and his monologue gradually reveal that he is crazy. The old man is described as kind, but the narrator is first obsessed with the old man's "vulture eye" and then with the heartbeat of the "tell-tale heart." Though their names are not provided, they both stand out as vivid characters because of Poe's description.

They both change during the story. The old man is killed and dismembered, and the narrator convicts himself because he imagines the heartbeat after the old man dies.

They are believable people. Poe does make it easier for himself by having an insane murderer tell the story. A mad person can do almost anything in a story, and it could be possible. The old man is merely a prop that triggers the action, but he is also believable. He is described as kind; but I feel he also was not a very good judge of character, or he would have lasted longer.

The murderer is interesting because his speech reveals his character. Poe develops his character with great skill and care. After the murder, fantasy takes the place of reality, and the imagined beating of the "tell-tale heart" leads to the murderer's confession.

Plot.   The main character is insane. He is at first bothered by the kind old man's "vulture eye." Before he kills him, he is bothered by the sound of the man's muffled heartbeat. He dismembers the old man and hides his body beneath the floorboards. His sick imagination leads him to continue to hear the beat of the heart, which grows louder and louder, even though the old man is dead. When three officers come to investigate a shriek that has been heard, the heart becomes so loud to the narrator that he confesses his crime to relieve himself. The tell-tale heart has acted as a conscience—representing guilt—that betrays the murderer by forcing the murderer to reveal his crime.

The conflict in the story is that of a sick man at war with his guilty conscience. His crazed obsession with the old man's eye, and then with the heartbeat, leads to the old man's murder and the murderer's revelation of his guilt. He can be at peace only when he confesses. We never know why he had to kill the old man. The only explanation is the murderer's insanity.

Suspense is created by posing the question, "Why does he continue to hear the heartbeat, and what effect will the heartbeat have on the narrator?"

Poe describes the effect of the eye and the heartbeat extremely well. He also reveals the madman's character skillfully through the madman's own words.

Style and Theme.   Poe uses repetition and symbols in the story. He repeats that he is not mad several times. He also describes the heart as a muffled watch twice. The heart is a symbol for a guilty conscience. The theme of the story is that a guilty conscience can betray you and force admission of guilt.

Impact.   The monologue is very well written, and the use of description is very striking. I felt it was a powerful story, and I want to read more of Poe's work.

After reviewing the notes, read the review that was written about "The Tell-Tale Heart."

"The Tell-Tale Heart": A Review

"The Tell-Tale Heart" by Edgar Allan Poe is a gripping study of the effects of insanity upon the narrator. The first line contains the strong hint that the narrator is strange: "True—nervous—very, very nervous I had been and am; but why *will* you say that I am mad?" The narrator protests that he "loved the old man," but he is obsessed with the old man's eye. They have obviously been living in the same house, but the reader never knows what their relationship has been. The narrator cannot tolerate the eye, however. He describes it in this way: "One of his eyes resembled that of a vulture—a pale, blue eye with a film over it. Whenever it fell upon me, my blood ran cold; and so by degrees—very gradually—I made up my mind to take the life of the old man, and thus rid myself of the eye forever."

The story takes place in a very brief period of time. After eight days of thinking about it, the narrator strikes. He repeats that he is afflicted with "acuteness of the senses." When his lantern beam strikes the old man's eye, the narrator also hears the beating of the old man's heart, ". . . a low, dull, quick sound, such as a watch makes when enveloped with cotton." He kills the old man, dismembers his body, and buries him under the floorboards of the bedchamber. It is almost the perfect crime.

A neighbor, however, has heard a shriek. Three officers knock on the door early in the morning. They have come to investigate the shriek. The narrator says he has had a nightmare and has cried out. It seems a logical explanation.

While he talks with the officers, however, the narrator begins to suffer a ringing in his ears. The sound increases, and the narrator feels the sound is not in his ears. It is a "low, dull, quick sound—much such a sound as a watch makes when enveloped in cotton." The narrator becomes more and more upset, foaming, raging, swearing. The visitors do not seem to hear a thing. Finally, the narrator screams, "I could bear those hypocritical smiles no longer! I must scream or die!—and now—again!—hark! louder! louder! louder! *louder!* . . . tear up the planks!—here, here!—it is the beating of his hideous heart!"

The heart that has continued to beat for the narrator is obviously his guilty conscience. The monologue of the narrator gradually reveals his madness and finally his guilt. The suspense builds as the reader is drawn into the story, wanting to know why it is a tell-tale heart.

Poe uses description, repetition, and symbols very effectively in the story. The "vulture eye" of the old man, the heart compared to the "watch when enveloped with cotton," and the symbol of the heart as the betraying conscience of the narrator are good examples of Poe's techniques.

Poe has, of course, stacked the odds for himself as a writer by making the narrator insane. A madman can do anything in a story, and it can be believable. The characters have no names, which makes the atmosphere of the story more strange. The impressive quality of the story is the power it creates in so few words. The story has a chilling effect upon the reader, similar to the effect of the heartbeat upon the narrator.

"The Tell-Tale Heart" is one of those stories that lingers with the reader. It seems to say that a guilty conscience will trap even the most clever criminals in the end. It is a grotesque, vivid story by a master storyteller. Those who like horror movies will love this tale.

| Writing Activity 3 | **Writing a Review of a Short Story** |

Select a short story from an anthology or magazine, or use a story that your teacher recommends or assigns. Take notes on the story.

After you have reviewed your notes, write a review of the story, using the techniques you have learned.

Writing a Book Review

You can use many of the basic techniques for a book review that you use for the short story. A short story does differ from a book, however, in several respects:

1. The action is compressed. Novels usually are lengthier and are more complicated.
2. There is ordinarily one basic plot in a short story. Novels may include more than one plot.
3. There are fewer characters. Novels often involve many characters.

Writing Activity 4   **Writing a Review of a Novel**

Using the 5Ws and the H approach and the elements you have studied, review a novel that you have read. Include several body paragraphs, an introduction, and a conclusion in your written review.

Writing a Movie Review

When you review a movie, many of the elements you applied to the short story will apply to a movie. These are:

title	style
setting	theme
characters	impact
plot	

There are some additional elements to consider, however, when you review a film. A film is primarily a sight and sound experience, although it does result from the writing of a script. The director plays the major role in making a film. He or she works with the actors, the cinematographers (the people who photograph the film), and all other aspects of production. The director is primarily responsible for the success or the failure of the film. Although the scriptwriter certainly deserves recognition, the director should be mentioned instead of the author. You have to look at the credits at the beginning of the film to discover the director's name. The camera work and the pace of the film also are important. Pay particular attention to the photography, since it is the image—not the written word—that creates the scene. The actors are very important and usually are mentioned by name when you review the film.

Add these elements to your review of a film:

Direction and acting: How well are the roles acted by the actors? Do they portray the characters well? Does the director produce a powerful effect through the use of the elements of film?

Cinematography: Is the photography of high quality? Why? Why not? Is the pace of the film appropriate to the story? Does it ever drag or go too fast?

Script: Does the movie seem well written? Is the dialogue natural and well delivered? Is it ever false or stilted?

Impact: Making a film is a different enterprise from writing a book. It is much more of a combined effort among the director, actors, scriptwriter, camera crew, and everyone concerned with the production. A book is an individual effort by one writer, working with an editor in a publishing house. Most of the credit for a film usually goes to the director and the actors. Although this may not seem fair, the director does oversee and deliver the film, while the actors carry out the director's concept.

When you do review a film, remember that you cannot pick it up and quote from it, as you can with a book. Do try to avoid one trap that some critics fall into. Do not judge a film in terms of a book it is based on. A film is a film, and a book is a book. A good film can come from a bad book, and a bad film can result from basing it on a good book. Judge a film, or a book, on its own terms.

Writing Activity 5	**Writing a Review of a Film**

Review a film you have seen recently, using the techniques you have learned.

Chapter 13

BUSINESS COMMUNICATIONS

WARM-UP

Read the following letter:

Mr. Jones, President
Jones Nail Company
Naidir, Wisconsin
Tuesday morning, October 17

Dear Mr. Jones,

I saw your ad in the paper wanting a good assembly line checker for your nails. I am a super good mechanic, and I have sharp eyes. I have passed everything in school, and my mother thinks I'm a great person. I would try to do a good job for you. I don't get sick much. I like to look at nails. I think they are great. So why don't you hire me. I'll wait for your call. My phone number is in the book. If you don't hire me soon, I'll take a job somewhere else. You can bet on that. So, hurry up!

Mike Schmidt

Mike Schmidt

P.S. Don't waste any time. Call me now, while the getting is good.

Do you think Mike got the job? He didn't. List the reasons that Mr. Jones quickly wadded up his letter and threw it in the wastebasket.

What kind of a letter do you think Mike should have written? List some changes you would make in his letter. You will learn more in this section about the business letter.

The Importance of Business Communication

Often you will need to use writing to communicate with people in the business and professional world. Prominent business and professional people have criticized the writing of persons who have applied for jobs, sought information, or attempted to communicate with them for various reasons. Criticism has been directed at poor spelling, awkward sentence structure, badly organized paragraphs, and foggy thinking.

How well you present yourself through writing could determine whether you get a job, gain admission to a college or university, or achieve some other goal that is important to you.

When writing a business communication, you must always be careful to present yourself in the best possible way. Your communication should be neat, accurate, clear, and concise. People do not like to waste time with sloppy writing and thinking. Do not forget that your writing gives the reader an image of you as an individual. Whatever your purpose, you will want to make the best possible impression with the most effective words.

You probably have discovered that the world of school is different from the world outside the walls of the classroom. The years you spend with books, classmates, and teachers are rewarding in many ways, both socially and academically. The real world of commerce, industry, and professions, however, is a world in which you will be responsible for yourself and your livelihood.

This chapter focuses on writing skills that will help you to cope in the practical world. They are skills you will use for important reasons. All of these writing skills can be valuable to you now or at some time in the future.

The Business Letter

The format of a business letter is very precise. Most business letters are typed on white bond paper. The block format presently is most frequently used by businesses. Study the model of the block format on page 156. For more information on writing addresses, refer to pages 157–58.

Elements of a Business Letter

Heading. The heading contains your address and the date. It usually comprises three lines.

1. Your street address
2. Your city, state, and ZIP code
3. The date and the year of the letter

Inside Address. Beginning at the left margin, the inside address contains the name of the person to whom you are writing, the person's title, the department, the name of the business or organization, the street address, and the city, state, and ZIP code. If the name of a specific person is not known, the title is used. If there is no title, the name of the business comes first.

Salutation. Very often, you do not know the gender of the person to whom you are writing: It is perfectly acceptable now to address the person by the title, as in Dear Director. You may also address the business itself, as in Dear Acme Products.

Some other salutations you may use are:

• Dear Sir:

• Dear Madam:

• Gentlemen:

If you know the name of the person, you should write your salutation as follows:

Dear Miss Lee:	Dear Mrs. Lee:
Dear Mr. Lee:	Dear Dr. Lee:
Dear Ms. Lee:	Dear Peter Lee:
Dear Sonja Lee:	

Notice that a colon follows the salutation.

The Body. There are two different styles for writing the body of the letter. With one style, you indent the first paragraph five typewriter spaces. Using the other style, you do not indent at all. Instead, you indicate a new paragraph by adding an extra line of space.

Indented

Dear Mr. O'Rourke:

It has come to my attention that the economy needs stimulating. I am writing to offer you some suggestions that might help us all to live a better life.

Block Style

Dear Mr. O'Rourke:

It has come to my attention that the economy needs stimulating. I am writing to offer you some suggestions that might help us all to live a better life.

The body of the letter contains the message of the letter. You should take care that the letter is properly punctuated and that there are no spelling errors.

Either style (indented or block) is acceptable. The style you choose to use is a matter of personal preference. More and more businesses, however, are using the style that does not use indentation.

Closing.   There are various ways to close your letter. Here are some of them:

Sincerely,	Cordially,
Very truly yours,	Cordially yours,
Sincerely yours,	Respectfully,

The first word of the closing is capitalized. The others are not. Note that there is a comma after the closing.

Signature.   Type your full name four spaces below the closing. In the space between the closing and your typed name, sign your letter in ink.

Modified Block Style Business Letter

Heading
752 Green Lane Road
Evanston, IL 60210-4567
January 5, 1996

Inside Address
Director
Council on Wage and Price Stability
726 Jackson Place, N.W.
Washington, D.C. 20506-2066

Salutation
Dear Director:

_____

_____

_____ **Body of Letter** _____

_____

_____

Closing
Sincerely,

Signature
Derek Roberts
Derek Roberts

Writing Activity 1	**Writing Headings and Inside Addresses**

Write headings that include the following information:

1. A person who lives in the city of Harvey, in the state of Illinois. The letter is written on the fourth of June, 1997. The street address is 812 Elm Street. The ZIP code is 60426-1234.

2. A person who lives at 325 Holly Lane in Alden, Utah. The letter is written in the month of May on the twelfth day of 1997. The ZIP code is 84403-4321.

Write inside addresses for the following:

1. The person who is the Director of the Office of Public Inquiries of the Social Security Administration. The office is in Baltimore, Maryland, on 6401 Security Boulevard. The ZIP code is 21235-0123.

2. The Consumer Affairs Officer for the Federal Railroad Administration. The department is the Department of Transportation. The office is located in Washington, D.C. The ZIP code is 20590-3210. There is no street address.

Addressing Mail

The post office processes millions of letters per day. The probability of your letter arriving at the correct place will be greatly increased if the addresses are correct, legible, and complete. Accurate information will help to insure that your letter will get to your receiver. It is obvious that you should check the spelling and the address numbers very carefully to be sure that all information is correct. Also, the United States Postal Service prefers that all addresses on the outside of packages and letters be printed *without punctuation marks.*

All envelopes and parcels must have a destination address and a return address. A destination address is the place to which the letter is to be sent. A return address is the place to which the letter will be returned if it cannot be delivered. For this reason, the return address should never be omitted. Study the model envelopes.

Here is the accepted way to address an envelope:

Return Address

Destination Address

J R Moore
2530 Arroyo Dr #61
Santa Ana CA 94912-1357

Ms Sylvia De Marco
5951 Capitol Pkwy
Dallas TX 75228-2468

1. In addresses clearly print or type all items, especially numbers.
2. Keep a straight margin at the left.
3. Capitalize each word or abbreviation.
4. Write the city or town, state, and ZIP code directly below the street address.
5. Use the Postal Service's two-letter abbreviations for state names (refer to page 315).
6. Write the ZIP code after the state name.

Return Address

The return address contains the following information:

1. The full name of the sender. It is acceptable to write only the last name, but preferable to write the full name, if a specific person is writing the letter. If an organization is sending the letter, the full name of the organization should be written or typed.
2. The sender's street address, post office box number, or rural route number. If the letter is from an apartment house, office building, or multidwelling, the unit number should appear to the right of the street address.
3. The writer's city, state, and ZIP code.

The return address is typed or printed legibly in the upper left-hand corner of the envelope.

Destination Address

The destination address lists the person or organization to whom the letter is being sent. It contains the following information:

1. The receiver's name (person or organization).
2. The receiver's street address, post office box number, or rural route number. The unit number of an apartment, office, or multidwelling should appear to the right of the street address.
3. The receiver's city, state, and ZIP code number.

The destination address is typed or printed legibly in the center of the envelope.

Writing Activity 2   **Addressing Envelopes**

On a piece of paper (size 8½" by 11", if possible) draw the outlines of three envelopes. Write the return address and the destination address for each of the following three situations:

1. The Director of Consumer Affairs is writing a letter to Amy Carlson, who has a post office box number. The box number is

1681. She lives in Maple Plain, Minnesota. The ZIP code is 55359-2222.

The Director of Consumer Affairs works in the Office of Consumer Affairs. The office is part of the Department of Energy in Washington, D.C. The ZIP code is 20585-4444.

2. Colleen Hogan is writing to her best friend, Sara Mandel. Colleen lives in Apartment 2-A, 787 South Fourth Street, in Minneapolis, Minnesota. The ZIP code is 55415-1212. Sara lives on Rural Route #2 in Mobile, Alabama. The ZIP code is 36652-3434.

3. Jason Sadowski is writing to W. J. Tuser, Chief Inspector of the Bureau of Weights and Measures in Concord, New Hampshire. Mr. Tuser's office is at 85 Manchester Street. The ZIP code is 03301-6789.

Jason lives at 85 Caramba Street in El Paso, Texas. The ZIP code is 79975-9876.

Letters of Inquiry

When you write a letter that seeks information, you should make your letter brief, clear, and concise. You should explain why you wish to have the information you are requesting.

Read the following model letter:

752 West Flagler Street
Miami, FL 33130-0369
June 8, 1997

Director
National Library Service
  for the Blind and Physically
  Handicapped
1291 Taylor Street, N.W.
Washington, D.C. 20542-4255

Dear Director:

    My grandmother is blind. I would like information about the regional library nearest to my home where I can obtain talking books and magazines for her use. Thank you for your help.

Cordially yours,

William Evers

William Evers

Writing Activity 3   **Writing Letters of Inquiry**

Notice that the model letter told why the information was wanted. It was brief and polite. Write brief, polite letters to the following agencies, asking for the information described.

1. Write a letter to Amtrak at the Office of Consumer Relations. The post office box number is 2709. It is in Washington, D.C. The ZIP code is 20013-2709. Ask for information about the train service between Chicago and San Francisco. Use your own return address.

2. Write to the National Cartographic Information Center. It is part of the Geological Survey at 507 National Center, in Reston, Virginia. The ZIP code is 22092-8765. Ask for information about marine maps in the Westport, Connecticut, area. Use your own return address.

3. Write to the Inspection and Safety Division of the National Marine Fisheries Service, which is part of the Department of Commerce in Washington, D.C. The ZIP code is 20235-2345. Ask for information about the salmon that is caught in Lake Michigan near Waukegan, Illinois. You want to know whether these fish are safe to eat. Use your own return address.

Letters to Colleges

If you plan to attend a trade school, college, or university, it is a good idea to investigate schools that interest you well before you graduate from high school. When you write to a school, ask specifically for the information that you wish. To help the receiver answer your letter, supply the following information about yourself:

1. Your name, school, date of graduation, and grade level

2. The area or areas you are interested in studying

3. Availability of scholarships and/or other financial aid

Much of this information should be in their catalog, so include a request for one.

Read the model letter that follows.

810 Central Street
Portland, OR 97204-2165
October 18, 1997

Director of Admissions
Indiana University
Bloomington, IN 47405

Dear Director of Admissions:

I am presently a sophomore at Taft High School in Portland. I am interested in attending your school when I graduate in June, 2000.

I am very interested in your music program, which I understand is excellent. I would like to know about the cost of out-of-state tuition and the availability of scholarship aid and financial aid. I would also like to know how long I must live in Indiana before I can qualify as a resident.

Please send me your catalog and any other information that might help me learn more about your university.

Sincerely yours,

Juan Clemente
Juan Clemente

Writing Activity 4   **Writing Letters to Institutions of Higher Learning**

Write letters to the following institutions, using the information supplied:

1. You are a senior in high school in your town. Write a letter to the School of Cooking Arts, 815 Colfax Street, Lincoln, Nebraska 68509-9999. You are interested in becoming a chef. You want to know the course requirements and financial costs for attending the school. You would also like to know about opportunities for employment. What percentage of their graduates actually get jobs in restaurants after graduation?

2. Write to Nelson Junior College, 864 Barnette Street, Fairbanks, Alaska 99707-7878. You want to attend school in Alaska, and your interest is in biology. You wish a catalog and information on continuing your studies at another university after you complete a two-year course at Nelson. You also want to know about scholarships and financial aid.

3. Write a letter to the University of Washington, Seattle, Washington 98104-4567. You wish to attend the university. Your field of interest is English literature. You want to know out-of-state tuition costs, opportunities for part-time employment, and availability of scholarships and financial aid.

Letters of Complaint

There will be times when you wish to write a letter of complaint. When you do so, consider these points:

1. Include your name, address, and home and work phone numbers.

2. If possible, type your letter. If it is handwritten, make sure it is neat and legible.

3. Make it brief and concise. Include all important facts. If your complaint is about defective merchandise, include date of purchase, item and order number, place of purchase, and other important facts. Also include specific information stating what you think is a fair settlement for the problem. Attach *copies* of receipts, not originals.

4. Avoid sarcasm, threats, or anger when you write your letter. Simply state the facts and the reasons for your complaint.

5. Keep a copy for your records.

Read the following model letter:

8912 Lawrence Street
Santa Fe, NM 87501-9360
April 2, 1997

Ms. Maria Rajala
President
Googol Electronics Corporation
Little Rock, AR 72201-3221

Dear Ms. Rajala:

Last month, I purchased your Whiz-Bang Space Game #519 at the Elmo Super Market here in Santa Fe. I enclose a copy of the receipt, as well as a copy of the warranty.

I am writing to you because the game has never worked properly. I tried new batteries on the unit, but still it did not work.

I would appreciate your sending me either a game that does work or a check for $32.97, the total cost of the purchase.

I look forward to hearing from you within two weeks. Thank you for your attention to this problem.

Sincerely yours,

Kim Lee-Sing

Kim Lee-Sing

Phone numbers:
Home: (505) 643-8857
Work: (505) 643-6723

Writing Activity 5 **Writing Letters of Complaint**

1. Write a letter of complaint to Fiddle's, 5415 Deerhunt Road, Wheeling, Illinois 60090-8668. You had an expensive meal there, but the red snapper that you ordered tasted strange. It had been represented to you as fresh fish, but you suspect that it had been frozen. The meal cost you $21.84 cents. You did complain to the waiter (named Jean), but you received no satisfaction. The owner of the restaurant is Nick Fiddle.

2. Write a letter to the Cyclops Bicycle Company, 7621 Pontica Street, Austin, Texas 78711-3412. Your twelve-speed bicycle collapsed when you hit a rock on the street. The front wheel and the spokes were completely bent out of shape. According to specifications and advertising, the bike should have been able to withstand such stress with ease. It cost you $284.60.

3. Write a letter to the Environmental Protection Agency, 324 East 11th Street, Kansas City, Missouri 64106-6643. You wish to complain about industrial waste that is being dumped in a river near you by a chemical company. You specifically saw this dumping occur on two different occasions.

Letters of Application

You will find numerous occasions throughout your life for writing letters of application. Often, a dozen or more letters of application to various potential employers are required to secure a position. In addition to applying for jobs, you may also find other occasions for writing letters of application, nearly all of which will be competitive. For example, if you want to attend a conference or a workshop or to obtain a grant or a fellowship, you probably will have to write a letter of application.

It will help you to keep the following points in mind when writing a letter of application:

1. Restrict your letter to one page. Employers and institutions receive hundreds of letters of application when a position is advertised. Your letter stands a better chance of being read if it is brief.

2. State your business immediately. Say what you're applying for and why. Then sell yourself by describing briefly your outstanding qualifications and the reasons you believe you are well suited for this particular position.

3. Give pertinent information about when you will be available for an interview and how you can be reached by phone or mail.

4. Be certain that your letter looks professional. It should be typed in business letter form, free of errors, and include the date and the full addresses of both yourself and the person to whom you are writing.

5. Keep a copy for your files of each letter you write.

456 White Stag Lane
Cary, IL 60013-1415
June 3, 1997

Director
Personnel Department
Oak Furniture Company
562 Eames Street
Cary, IL 60013-5544

Dear Director of Personnel:

I would like to know if you have any part-time jobs available during the summer vacation. I would be particularly interested in working in the warehouse. Last summer I worked for Acme Products, Lansing, Michigan. I packaged and loaded products for them in the warehouse. They asked me to return this summer, but we moved to Cary in September.

I will be available for work from June 15 to August 28. I am in excellent health, and am going into the eleventh grade of high school. Since I play football, I enjoy the hard work in the warehouse because of the exercise and muscle-building activity.

I can be contacted by mail at the above address, or by phone at 562-2801. Thank you for your consideration. I would be happy to come in for an interview at your convenience.

Sincerely,

Alonzo Hill

Alonzo Hill

| Writing Activity 6 | **Writing Letters of Application** |

Write a letter inquiring about possible employment to each of the following potential employers, using the information given.

1. Write to the Zenith Baby-Sitting Service, which is located at 410 Greenbow Street, Columbia, South Carolina 29240-0722. You are writing to ask for baby-sitting employment. You have had experience in baby-sitting with your family, and you have also done some baby-sitting for neighbors' children. You will supply references on request, and you would be available for an interview at their convenience. You are interested in part-time work.

2. Write to Black Eagle Summer Camp, on Rural Route #5, Missoula, Montana 59801-2003. You are interested in a summer job as a counselor. You have had some experience at a day camp near your home.

3. Write to the Pegasus Hotel, 816 Palm Drive, Jackson, Mississippi 39205-1810. You are interested in working in the restaurant as a waiter. You have had experience in a restaurant in your hometown. You will be moving to Jackson after you graduate this year, and you would be interested in full-time employment, starting in September.

Writing Activity 7	**Job Hunting**

Choose an area of employment in which you'd like to work. Use the yellow pages of the local phone book to locate a specific business in your area of interest. Next, call or write this business and ask to visit the office or manufacturing plant. If you fail to obtain a visit to this employer, try another.

When you make your visit, take notes on everything you observe. Ask questions while you are there. What qualities does the management look for in its employees? Consider your own skills and imagine where you might fit in the organization.

After your visit, write down your observations and your goals regarding this particular business. What skills will you need to develop or strengthen in order to reach these goals?

Finally, write a letter of thanks to the person who hosted your visit and express your desire to work at that business at some future time.

Note: You can use this same technique for jobs that you see listed in the classified section of the newspaper. If you cannot arrange a visit, write a letter of application. Or, simply write a letter expressing your interest in future or perhaps part-time employment. Ask to be contacted when an opening is available. Part-time employment is an excellent opportunity to gain business experience and determine whether the nature of the work suits you.

Writing a Résumé

Résumé comes from a French word meaning *begin again*. In English, it is a summary of your work experience and important facts about your life. Frequently, résumés are requested by employers as a first step in considering a person for a job.

Learning to write a résumé is important. The employer can quickly get a picture of you and your experience from a résumé. If you can write a good one, it can help you to get the job you want.

In fact, a résumé can be helpful in several ways. It can quickly impress an employer if you fit the job qualifications. It can demonstrate how well organized you are and how clearly you perceive yourself. It can also save time, for if you do not fit the qualifications for the job, you will not have to waste time with an interview and/or a job application.

Parts of a Résumé

The style of a résumé is different from an ordinary writing style. A résumé is a quick image of you through words on paper. In a résumé, you list important facts about yourself and your experience briefly and concisely. You must say a lot with a few words. Résumés are written in phrases, not in complete sentences.

Study the model résumé. Notice that there are no complete sentences. The information is delivered in brief, but clear, "bullet" statements, as in a telegram. It gives the reader a picture of Nicholas's life very quickly. Like a letter of application, résumés should not be more than one page.

Writing Activity 8 **Writing a Résumé**

Study the model résumé shown on page 167, and then write your own. Follow the form and writing style of the model shown.

Application Forms

Throughout your life you will likely have many occasions to fill out applications. Probably one of the most important applications you will be asked to complete is a job application. What you learn about filling out a job application will apply to many other forms that you will be asked to complete in the future.

How well you fill out an application may affect the decision to hire you or to offer the job to someone else. Given its importance, you should prepare yourself to fill out an application for employment. Follow these steps:

1. Memorize your social security number accurately. If you have no social security number, apply for one.

2. Ask the permission of another person beforehand to list him or her as an emergency contact. Know the address and phone number of the emergency contact.

3. Know your employment experience and your skills. Be able to list them briefly and clearly.

4. Know your educational experience. Be able to list dates, places, and corresponding years you attended school.

5. Ask three reliable people if you may list them as references. (It is an important courtesy to ask a reference before you list the name.) Most people will agree to give you a recommendation if you are a good prospect for employment. List respected people as references. You may want to list a former teacher, a former employer, a member of the clergy, or another respected member of the community. Be careful about listing close friends, however, and *never* list relatives.

RÉSUMÉ

Nicholas T. Swoboda   566 Harms Woods Drive
                          Glenview, Illinois 60025-1020
                          Telephone: 801-485-5826

Job Goal: Bank Teller in Elmwood Bank and Trust Company,
                          Winnetka, Illinois

Experience:

Sept. 1995 to June 1996   Treasurer, Student Council, Glenview High School
                          President, Economics Club

June to Sept., 1996   Sales Clerk, Martin's Hardware Store, 506 Main
                             Street, Evanston, Illinois 60202-1725

Sept. 1994 to August 1995 Parking Attendant, Ace Garage, 601 Chestnut
                             Street, Winnetka, Illinois 60093-4747

Jan. to July, 1994   Newspaper Delivery, Shore Distributors, 62 Brown
                             Street, Winnetka, Illinois 60093-4229

Education: Glenview High School, Glenview, Illinois 60025-9747
                             Student Council
                             Mathematics and Economics Clubs
                             National Honor Society
                             Ranked third academically in Senior Class

Personal Data: Born in Columbus, Indiana, June 4, 1979
                          Excellent Health
                          Captain, Football Team, Glenview Young Adult League
                          Chess Champion, Young Adult Competition,
                             State of Illinois Chess Society, 1994
                          Hobbies: Stamp Collecting, Jogging, Swimming,
                             Football, Karate, Chess, Reading, Computers

References: Ms. Sheila Weinstein
                          President, League of Women Voters
                          66 Butternut Lane
                          Glenview, Illinois 60025-8257

                          The Reverend Robert Hughes
                          St. John's Episcopal Church
                          122 Third Street
                          Glenview, Illinois 60025-3210

                          Mr. Winston Hernandez
                          Department of Mathematics
                          Glenview High School
                          Glenview, Illinois 60025-9797

Filling Out the Application

When you fill out an application for employment, do the following:

1. Read the application very carefully. Be certain that you understand the entire form.

2. Complete the application with a pen. If you can possibly do so, type the application. If not, print unless specifically told to do otherwise. Business organizations place much emphasis on neatness and legibility. Print very neatly and legibly. Spell correctly.

3. If you make a mistake, erase it carefully or ask for a new form. Do not cross out an error.

4. Answer all the questions that apply to you on the form. Be completely honest. A false application can cost you your job. Where questions do not apply to you, write N/A, which means "not applicable," or D/A, which means "doesn't apply" in the appropriate blank.

5. When you finish the application, check it carefully for accuracy of spelling, punctuation, and information. Be sure to sign the application on the proper blank.

6. If you have written a résumé, submit it with the application. This professional gesture can impress an employer.

Study the model application on the next page.

Writing Activity 9   **Filling Out an Application Form**

On a piece of paper (8½" by 11"), copy the application form. Then fill it out accurately and neatly.

HERMES TOOL AND DIE COMPANY

Employment Application

Date _____ Soc. Sec. No. _____

Name _____
            Last   First   Middle

Home address _____
                    Number   Street

            _____
                    City   State   Zip

Tel. No. _____

Type of position wanted _____

When could you begin work? _____

Educational Experience

                        Name   City   Highest Year Completed

Elementary School _____

High School _____

College _____

Postcollege _____

List any job experience and skills that qualify you for this job.

1. _____

2. _____

3. _____

If necessary, use the back of the application to list further information.

References

                    Name   Address   Phone Number

1. _____

2. _____

3. _____

Person to contact in case
of accident or emergency _____
                                                    Name

                        _____
                            Address   Tel. No.

Part 4

LANGUAGE SKILLS REVIEW

A Brief Reference for Correct Usage

THE CHIEF VIRTUE THAT

LANGUAGE CAN HAVE

IS CLEARNESS.

HIPPOCRATES

A good writer is able to communicate in writing what he or she means. As we write, though, sometimes we are unsure of a word, a phrase, or a sentence and decide to toss it out rather than write something that might be wrong. This section is a quick reference that you can use to check specific areas of usage about which you are uncertain. You will not find lengthy lists of rules here, however. We believe that most people learn to speak and write naturally with practice, rather than by memorizing rules. Yet, in the midst of writing a paper, occasionally a quick review may be just what is needed to sharpen language skills in a particular area. This section will be a handy reference for those times. You'll find here not only answers to specific questions, but also activities and tests you can use to practice areas of usage that are troublesome for you.

WHAT YOU WILL LEARN

In this section you will find information on each of the following:

1. Correct sentences
2. Phrases and clauses
3. Verbs
4. Pronouns
5. Correct agreement
6. Words often misused and misspelled
7. Punctuation
8. Capitals and abbreviations

Chapter 14

SENTENCE SENSE

Try to read the following:

Eggs to How Well Boil

Enough cover to eggs fill water pan a with the. On turn stove the bring and water the boil to a. Eggs with spoon a, water place boiling in the the.

This group of words does not make much sense. Why? For words to have meaning in the English language, they must be arranged in the right order. Compare the first group of words with the following:

How to Boil Eggs Well

Fill a pan with enough water to cover the eggs. Turn on the stove and bring the water to a boil. With a spoon, place the eggs in the boiling water.

The second group of words has meaning because the words are arranged in ordered groups that we call sentences. Indeed, words are just words until they are put into a meaningful arrangement in a sentence. When we communicate with others, we expect sentences to be formed in familiar patterns that we can understand. Interestingly, even though the patterns of sentences may vary, two elements that we listen for immediately in each sentence are a *subject* and a *verb*.

| Skills Activity 1 | **Arranging Words for Sentence Sense** |

On a separate sheet of paper, rearrange the following words so they make sense as sentences. Underline the subject once and the verb twice.

1. took Ramona night Juan movies the to last
2. because the it meowed cat hungry was
3. the on stranger street barked the at dog the
4. eating George cream cone enjoyed ice the
5. tennis Sally with friend played her

Finding Subjects and Predicates

Definition: **The *subject* of a sentence is who or what the sentence is about.**

Example: <u>Comic strips</u> have been popular for nearly a century.

Definition: **The *predicate* of a sentence tells what the subject is or does. (*Predicate* means "to tell.") The verb is always part of the predicate.**

Example: Comic strips <u>have been popular for nearly a century</u>.

To find the subject and predicate, follow these steps:

1. Find the *verb*.
2. Ask *who* or *what* before the verb. The answer should be the subject.
3. The rest of the sentence, including the verb, is the predicate.

Example: Comic strips have been popular for nearly a century.

1. The verb is <u>have been</u>.
2. *Who* or *what* have been? <u>Comic strips</u>
3. The rest of the sentence: <u>have been popular for nearly a century</u>.

Example: Joseph Pulitzer published the first color comic.

1. The verb is <u>published</u>.
2. *Who* or *what* published? <u>Joseph Pulitzer</u>
3. The rest of the sentence: <u>published the first color comic</u>

Example: The Hearst papers began an entire comic section.

1. The verb is <u>began</u>.
2. *Who* or *what* began? <u>The Hearst papers</u>
3. The rest of the sentence: <u>began an entire comic section</u>

Skills Activity 2   **Finding Subjects and Predicates**

Read each sentence and find the verb. Find the subject by asking *who* or *what* before the verb. The find the predicate. Copy each sentence on the next page. Underline the subject once.

Example: The daily comics have changed over the years.
<u>The daily comics</u> have changed over the years.

1. "Garfield" has remained a favorite for many years.
2. Another popular comic is "Peanuts."
3. "Cathy" has stayed in top place, too.

4. Children have been comic fans since the beginning.
5. Many adults read one or more comics daily.
6. Daily readers include about forty percent adults.
7. Story-telling comic strips seem on the way out.
8. Humorous comics have become more and more popular.
9. The popular strips are becoming funnier each year.
10. Many people buy newspapers because of their comics.

| Skills Activity 3 | **Replacing Subjects** |

Read each sentence and find the subject. Think of another subject that makes sense in the sentence. Rewrite the sentence on your paper, replacing the subject with your subject.

Example: The house was built on a steep hill.
The building was built on a steep hill.
or
The garage was built on a steep hill.

1. The morning paper carried the election returns.
2. A heavy rain can cause lots of damage.
3. Texas has become a vacation destination.
4. Some motorbikes burn low-cost fuel.
5. The crosstown expressway can carry heavy traffic.
6. The shopping mall gets crowded by midday.
7. London is one of the world's great cities.
8. Metric measurements should be easy for most people.
9. Coins can increase in value over the years.
10. Soup and a sandwich can make a good lunch.

| Skills Activity 4 | **Replacing Predicates** |

Read each sentence and find the predicate. Think of another predicate that makes sense in the sentence. Rewrite the sentence on your paper, replacing the predicate with your predicate.

Example: Permanent-press fabrics have become very popular.
Permanent-press fabrics are easy to care for.
or
Permanent-press fabrics have made ironing unnecessary.

1. A sudden freeze can ruin a flower garden.
2. Jet airplanes have changed the way people travel.
3. Good, bright light makes reading easy on the eyes.
4. Weather forecasts can be very accurate.
5. The Atlantic Ocean can become extremely stormy.

6. A rainbow may show six distinct colors.
7. Franklin D. Roosevelt was elected president four times.
8. The forty-eight adjoining states are divided into four time zones.
9. Lightning does strike the same place twice.
10. Southern California enjoys a moderate climate.

Combining Sentence Parts

Sometimes you may be telling about two different subjects. You can write two sentences:

Examples: Good highways had encouraged suburban development.
Cheap gas had encouraged suburban development.

Or, you can write one sentence:

Example: Good highways <u>and</u> cheap gas had encouraged suburban development.

The same goes for actions. You can write two sentences:

Examples: People moved far out from the city.
People built homes far out from the city.

Or, write one sentence:

Example: People moved <u>and</u> built homes far out from the city.

Definition: **Build subject and predicate parts by *compounding*, or combining, them. (*Compound* means "put together.")**

Subject:

Connect subjects with *and* or *or* (conjunctions):

Example: Good highways <u>and</u> cheap gas had encouraged suburban development.

Predicate:

To tell about actions, connect verbs with *and* or *or:*

Example: People moved <u>and</u> built homes far out from the city.

Skills Activity 5   **Writing Sentences with Compound Subjects and Verbs**

Rewrite each of the following sentences, giving the first five sentences compound subjects and the last five sentences compound verbs.

Examples: Henrique found ten dollars in the parking lot.
Henrique and Louise (compound subject) found ten dollars in the parking lot.

The couple wandered aimlessly across the field.
The couple wandered aimlessly across the field and picked wildflowers (compound verb).

1. She fell knee-deep into the mud.
2. Boston has many skyscrapers.
3. A cellular phone is great for emergencies.
4. Flora wanted to go to the play that night.
5. You can have a free meal at any restaurant in town.
6. The delivery service lost the tickets for the show.
7. Horace waited impatiently for their arrival.
8. They missed the bus, as usual.
9. This city needs to repair all the sidewalks.
10. A well-run business keeps its customers happy.

Also, you can put two complete sentences together with *and, but, or,* or *nor.*

Examples: A suburban area should provide good schools, <u>and</u> it should also be visually attractive.

The suburbs usually are quiet, <u>but</u> sometimes they are boring on weekend evenings.

A house can be built on a concrete foundation, <u>or</u> it can be built on wooden stilts.

A flimsily built house will not survive a flood, <u>nor</u> is it likely to survive a hurricane.

| Skills Activity 6 | **Writing Compound Sentences** |

Rewrite each of the following sentences to make them compound. Use *and, but, or,* or *nor* to connect the sentences.

Example: Self-service stations are convenient.

Self-service stations are convenient, but they often are crowded on weekends.

1. A tiny calculator does problems instantly.
2. Antibiotics offer people good chances for healing.
3. That FM station plays the top ten hits every day.
4. She didn't want to buy a new car.
5. Subways and trains can be faster than a car in the city.

6. An unrepaired faucet leaks constantly.
7. You might find an apartment or a townhouse that you can afford.
8. A burglar alarm will provide protection for your house.
9. Not everyone has an answering machine.
10. Fuel costs probably will rise.

Sentence Patterns

Nearly all sentences in the English language will fall into the following six sentence patterns:

- Noun-Verb
- Noun-Verb-Noun
- Noun-Verb-Noun-Completer
- Noun-Verb-Adverb
- Noun-Linking Verb-Noun
- Noun-Linking Verb-Adjective

The Noun-Verb Pattern

The *noun-verb pattern* is one of the basic sentence patterns in English. A noun or pronoun is the subject; the verb follows the subject. The verb completes the sentence. The noun or pronoun is the subject that does the acting. In any of the patterns, wherever there is a noun, a pronoun can be substituted.

Examples: The dog barked.
Julia cooked.
He fell.

Noun	Verb
The grass	grew.
The flowers	bloomed.
The cats	fought.
He	laughed.
She	cried.
It	shook.
The car	started.
The play	ended.

Skills Activity 7 **Noun-Verb Patterns**

On a separate sheet of paper, complete the following as *noun-verb sentences.*

1. The audience _____.
2. _____ won.
3. The sparrows _____.
4. _____ lost.
5. She _____.
6. _____ yelled.
7. It _____.
8. They _____.
9. _____ roared.
10. _____ returned.

Skills Activity 8 **Writing Noun-Verb Sentences**

Write five sentences of your own using the *noun-verb pattern.*

The Noun-Verb-Noun Pattern

When you use action verbs preceded by a noun, the first noun is the subject. The verb follows the subject. After the verb, the other noun is the direct object.

Examples: Tiffany played the guitar.
Roberto made popovers.
They auctioned the painting.

Noun	Verb	Noun
The butcher	chopped	the meat.
The pilot	landed	the plane.
The cat	devoured	its food.
She	bought	the dress.
He	dated	her.
The snow	covered	the garden.
They	applauded	the show.

Skills Activity 9   **Noun-Verb-Noun Patterns**

On a separate sheet of paper, complete the following so that the *noun-verb-noun pattern* forms a sentence with meaning.

Noun	Verb	Noun
1. The boy	chewed	_____.
2. _____	hammered	the nail.
3. He	cooked	_____.
4. _____	sewed	the hem.
5. The woman	cut	_____.
6. _____	planted	the seeds.
7. They	ate	_____.
8. _____	returned	the slacks.
9. Barbara	broke	_____.
10. _____	threw	the football.

Skills Activity 10   **Writing Noun-Verb-Noun Sentences**

Write five sentences of your own that fit the *noun-verb-noun pattern*.

The Noun-Verb-Noun-Completer Pattern

Sometimes the final noun of a *noun-verb-noun pattern* is followed by another noun or an adverb, a word that describes the action. These words complete the sentences when they are used.

Examples: Shana asked Robert for a date.
The airplane hit the ocean immediately.
He gave his opponent a handshake.

Noun	Verb	Noun	Noun
Her mother	bought	EmmaLou	a dress.
He	baked	his friend	a cake.
She	offered	the dog	a bone.
Willy	told	the crowd	a joke.

Noun	Verb	Noun	Adverb
Sandy	burned	the letter	quickly.
The batter	smacked	the ball	hard.
A clown	amused	the audience	cleverly.
She	performed	her part	expertly.
My father	made	dinner	slowly.

Skills Activity 11	**Noun-Verb-Noun-Noun Patterns**

On a separate sheet of paper, complete the following *noun-verb-noun-noun patterns* to form sentences.

	Noun	Verb	Noun	Noun
1.	The teacher	gave	the class	_____.
2.	The clerk	sold	_____	_____.
3.	_____	told	Joyce	_____.
4.	She	offered	_____	_____.
5.	_____	sent	_____	_____.

Skills Activity 12	**Noun-Verb-Noun-Adverb Patterns**

On a separate sheet of paper, complete the following *noun-verb-noun-adverb patterns* to form sentences.

	Noun	Verb	Noun	Adverb
1.	Mark	made	the team	_____.
2.	Sarah	prepared	the roast	_____.
3.	The movie	impressed	_____	_____.
4.	The dog	bit	_____	_____.
5.	_____	ended	the game	_____.

Skills Activity 13	**Writing Noun-Verb-Noun-Completer Sentences**

Write five *noun-verb-noun-noun sentences* and five *noun-verb-noun-adverb sentences* of your own.

The Noun-Verb-Adverb Pattern

Sometimes the verb is followed by a word that describes the action. Such a word is called an *adverb*.

Examples:
I agreed instantly.
The sun set slowly.
Margarita ate hurriedly.

Noun	Verb	Adverb
The choir	sang	loudly.
The glider	soared	silently.
The grass	grew	quickly.
The team	lost	badly.
The horse	ran	swiftly.

Skills Activity 14   **Noun-Verb-Adverb Patterns**

On a separate sheet of paper, complete the following sentences in the *noun-verb-adverb pattern.*

Noun	Verb	Adverb
1. The soldiers	marched	_____.
2. The girls	worked	_____.
3. The pilot	landed	_____.
4. The driver	honked	_____.
5. She	cooked	_____.
6. _____	_____	fast.
7. _____	_____	gently.
8. _____	_____	slowly.
9. _____	_____	well.
10. _____	_____	sadly.

Skills Activity 15   **Writing Noun-Verb-Adverb Sentences**

Write five sentences of your own that fit the *noun-verb-adverb pattern.*

The Noun–Linking Verb–Noun Pattern

Some verbs are called linking verbs. They differ from action verbs. They connect a subject with a predicate noun or a predicate adjective. Remember that a predicate is the part of a sentence that says something about the subject. Linking verbs are like equal signs in mathematics.

Examples: Sarah became a great guitar player.
The puppy is a cocker spaniel.
Manuel has always been a good writer.

Sarah	became	guitar player
Sarah	=	guitar player
puppy	is	cocker spaniel
puppy	=	cocker spaniel
Manuel	has been	good writer
Manuel	=	good writer

The following verbs are linking verbs. You will find it helpful to learn them.

All Forms of *Be*

am	was	be
are	were	been
is		being

Sense Verbs

look	looks	looked	looking
smell	smells	smelled	smelling
taste	tastes	tasted	tasting
sound	sounds	sounded	sounding
feel	feels	felt	feeling

By memorizing the word *GRABS*, you can remember some linking verbs beginning with these letters.

GRABS

grow	grows	grew/grown	growing
remain	remains	remained	remaining
appear	appears	appeared	appearing
become	becomes	became	becoming
seem	seems	seemed	seeming

Study the following *noun-linking verb-noun sentences*.

Noun	**Linking Verb**	**Noun**
Harry	is	a teacher.
I	am	a writer.
Eisenhower	was	a general.
The girls	were	swimmers.
He	has been	an actor.
The car	remained	a junker.
The girl	became	a carpenter.
The animal	seemed	a monster.
They	appeared	fools.

In each case, the subject and the noun following the linking verb are equal, in that they describe or represent the same thing.

Skills Activity 16   **Noun-Linking Verb-Noun Patterns**

On a separate sheet of paper, complete the following *noun-linking verb-noun patterns.*

Noun	Linking Verb	Noun
1. Claire	is	_____.
2. The old man	became	_____.
3. _____	remains	a threat.
4. _____	became	a star.
5. Maria	was	_____.
6. I	am	_____.
7. You	are	_____.
8. Margaret	will be	_____.
9. The neighbors	have been	_____.
10. The kids	were being	_____.

Skills Activity 17   **Writing Noun-Linking Verb-Noun Sentences**

Write five sentences of your own using the *noun-linking verb-noun pattern.*

The Noun–Linking Verb–Adjective Pattern

In this pattern, an adjective follows the linking verb. It is called the *predicate adjective.* It always describes the subject.

Examples: The bread seems stale. (stale bread)
The spaghetti tastes wonderful. (wonderful spaghetti)
The music sounded romantic. (romantic music)

Noun	Linking Verb	Adjective
The elephant	looks	old.
The pizza	smells	tempting.
The milk	tastes	sour.
The thunder	sounds	frightening.
The skin	feels	rough.
The donkey	grew	restless.
The patient	remained	ill.
The snake	appeared	dangerous.
The movie	became	successful.

Skills Activity 18   **Noun-Linking Verb-Adjective Patterns**

On a separate sheet of paper, complete the following *noun-linking verb-adjective patterns.*

Noun	Linking Verb	Adjective
Be		
1. _____	are	good.
2. I	am	_____.
3. You	are	_____.
4. Steak	is	_____.
5. _____	was	funny.
6. The play	will be	_____.
7. _____	has been	upset.
8. _____	were being	silly.

Sense Verbs

1. The future	looks	_____.
2. _____	smells	strange.
3. Ice cream	tastes	_____.
4. The singer	sounds	_____.
5. _____	feels	sharp.

GRABS

1. _____	grew	old.
2. The acrobat	remained	_____.
3. _____	appears	afraid.
4. He	will become	_____.
5. _____	seems	odd.

Skills Activity 19   **Writing Noun-Linking Verb-Adjective Sentences**

Write ten *noun-linking verb-adjective sentences* of your own.

Two Common Sentence Errors

Run-on Sentences

The *run-on sentence* is a common error that occurs when the writer tries to make a comma function in the wrong way. Read these examples:

I like Aaron, he has a good sense of humor.

The store is full of delicious food, the fresh vegetables are the best.

Walking along a city street is fun, there is much activity there.

In each of the above examples, the writer tried to glue two sentences together with a comma. Commas were never intended to join two complete sentences, however. Read the following sentences aloud:

Baseball is a popular sport, it is more fun to watch at the ballpark than on television.

I eat a lot of vegetables, spinach is my favorite.

I like to go to the movies, many Western movies have too much violence.

Did you notice that when you read these run-on sentences aloud, there was a natural pause when you reached the comma? That pause was due to the fact that a period (which indicates a *stop*) should have been there instead of a comma.

Read these sentences. They are correct because the original run-on sentence has been split into two sentences.

Baseball is a popular sport. It is more fun to watch at the ballpark than on television.

I eat a lot of vegetables. Spinach is my favorite.

I like to go to the movies. Many Western movies have too much violence.

Another way to correct run-ons is to separate the sentences with a comma and one of the *coordinating conjunctions*. These are the coordinating conjunctions:

and   or   but   nor   for   yet

Baseball may be a popular sport, but I don't like it.

I eat a lot of vegetables, and spinach is my favorite.

Another set of words, called *conjunctive adverbs*, can be used to correct a run-on sentence. These are some of the most commonly used conjunctive adverbs:

accordingly	consequently	however	still
also	furthermore	moreover	therefore
besides	hence	nevertheless	thus

In sentences, a semicolon precedes the conjunctive adverb, and a comma follows it.

> Baseball is a popular sport; however, it is more fun to watch at the ballpark than on television.

Use conjunctions and punctuation to separate run-on sentences only when the sentences that have been run together are related in meaning. For example, "I like to go to the movies" and "Many Western movies have too much violence in them" are not related. Separate sentences such as these with a period and a capital letter.

| Skills Activity 20 | **Correcting Run-on Sentences** |

On a separate sheet of paper, correct these run-on sentences in one of the ways discussed in the previous section. If the two sentences are not related in meaning, be sure to separate them with a period and a capital letter.

1. I enjoy playing basketball, it is a fast game that develops your skill.
2. Mr. Tikada is an excellent teacher, he is fair and cares about his students.
3. Reading books is more fun than watching television, you imagine what happens in books instead of seeing what comes over the tube.
4. Andy plays soccer, he is quite skillful in the guard position.
5. Sarah heard the phone ring, it was probably Vanessa.
6. The truth is I didn't care how he acted, they didn't care either.
7. Nothing bothers a cat, cats just seem to take it easy every day.
8. Sometimes everything seems to go wrong, I just want to give up.
9. Going to the movies is Patrice's idea of a good time, she seems never to get tired of going to them.
10. Why would you argue with me, I'm just trying to keep us out of trouble.

Sentence Fragments

Another common problem in writing is the *sentence fragment*. A sentence fragment is a group of words that tries to function as a sentence but is incomplete in some way. A fragment leaves the reader hanging because an important part of the sentence is not there. Read the following:

> Here was Jenny. Grinning, skipping along, as if she had no care in the world.

The second group of words is not a sentence because it lacks a subject. The writer intended <u>Jenny</u> to be the subject, but Jenny is not part of the group of words. The problem can be solved by joining the two groups of words with a comma.

Here was Jenny, grinning, skipping along, as if she had no care in the world.

Read the following example:

A giant among a group of ordinary mortals.

When you read this group of words, you do not know who is the giant. The group needs another element, or elements, to correct it.

She was a giant among a group of ordinary mortals.

A giant lived among a group of ordinary mortals.

Either way, the sentences above are correct. The writer chooses how to write the sentence by examining its purpose. Read the following:

Eating popcorn until the show began.

This group of words simply hangs there without a subject. Who is eating? This addition would correct it:

We were eating popcorn until the show began.

Here is another example:

Risa and I played catch. Until the sun went down.

The first group of words is a sentence. The second is a fragment. The two should be joined:

Risa and I played catch until the sun went down.

Skills Activity 21   **Correcting Sentence Fragments**

Rewrite the following groups of words, creating either one or two complete sentences from each set. Use a separate sheet of paper.

1. Jack stood nervously at the line. Concentrating to make a basket.

2. The dogs sniffed at each other. Growling and baring their teeth.

3. A terrible lunch like the one we had last week.

4. Each box has a prize in it. A ring, or a whistle, or something else.

5. The Washington Monument, a miracle of design.

—6. Barnum, the greatest showman on earth.

7. Tyrone has liked water-skiing. Since he was a child.

— 8. Keesha bought a new dress. And some lovely shoes to wear with it.

9. The team behind two points, with fifty seconds to play.

— 10. The little boy, crying because he could not find his father.

Skill Test 1	**Finding Subjects and Verbs**

Copy each sentence below and underline the subject or subjects once and the verb or verbs twice. Watch for compound sentences.

1. Daylight Savings Time continues for more than half the year.

2. High-speed railroads connect major cities in Europe and make traveling to different countries very easy.

3. Car accidents and automobile deaths decrease with lower speed limits.

4. Charles Lindbergh flew across the Atlantic alone and he later wrote several books about his experience.

5. Many people have been eating and cooking Chinese foods lately.

6. Mexico City has a lot to offer tourists but it is also very polluted.

7. Rain can both nurture and destroy crops.

8. The number of smokers and drinkers has been decreasing.

9. Traffic has become lighter with higher fuel costs.

10. Matilda doesn't want to go with us nor does she want us to call.

Skill Test 2	**Identifying Sentence Patterns**

Copy each sentence below and indicate which of the six sentence patterns it follows most closely.

1. In the winter, fresh foods usually are shipped from California.

2. Nearly everyone watches a few hours of TV each week.

3. The hum of a refrigerator can be very loud.

4. Barbara sends me a postcard from every vacation spot.

5. The ice skater floated gracefully across the rink.

6. They returned only moments later.

7. Charlie Chaplin was a great comedian.

8. She looks quite tired today.

9. Edison gave the world electricity.

10. The plants grew strong and healthy under the bright lights.

| *Skill Test 3* | **Identifying and Correcting Run-ons and Fragments** |

Study each of the following sentences. Determine whether a sentence is a run-on or a fragment and then rewrite it correctly.

1. A digital watch is water-resistant it runs on a battery.

2. The store has a big sale. When their inventory gets too high.

3. I want to move to Dallas, this small town bores me.

4. Marvin guessed the number of beans in the jar, he won the prize.

5. A great idea that came into her mind all of a sudden.

6. The dog stood patiently. Hoping his master would appear again.

7. Some days nothing goes right you think you should've just stayed in bed.

8. The cabinets are crammed full, they can't hold another thing.

9. Juanita got very nervous and just stopped on the balance beam. Chewing her fingernails.

10. You never know what's around the corner. A success or a failure.

Chapter 15

BUILDING SENTENCES WITH PHRASES AND CLAUSES

Once you understand the structure of simple and compound sentences, you can easily begin to experiment with *complex* sentences. These are sentences that contain phrases or clauses. In speech, we naturally expand our sentences with clauses and phrases, as in the following:

> I wanted to go see a movie but Anita insisted on having her own way, as she usually does, so we ended up going to the boxing match, which is the way things always turn out when we go places with Anita.

In writing, you can add phrases and clauses to your sentences to give them grace and rhythm. Phrases and clauses are similar in that each is a cluster of related words. To determine which is which, however, check the group of words for a subject and a verb: A *phrase* is a group of words without a verb. A *clause* is a group of words that includes a subject and a verb.

You can add a single phrase to a sentence:

> People can be watchful <u>with litter</u>. (phrase)
> People can be watchful <u>in public places</u>. (phrase)

You can also add phrases one after another in a sentence:

> People can be watchful <u>with litter</u> <u>in public places</u>. (two phrases)

The same goes for clauses. You can use them one by one:

People can be watchful <u>if they are reminded</u>. (clause)
People can be watchful <u>wherever they see a litter basket</u>.
(clause)

Add them together:

People can be watchful <u>if they are reminded</u> <u>wherever they
see a litter basket</u>. (two clauses)

Finally, string both phrases and clauses together:

People can be watchful with litter in public places if they
are reminded wherever they see a litter basket.

In fact, we tend to follow such a pattern in our normal speech,
adding one phrase or clause after another to build up an idea.

Phrases

Remember that a *phrase* is a group of words that does not contain
a verb. The most commonly used phrases are *prepositional phrases;*
but there also are *infinitive phrases* and *participial phrases*. This
review will cover these three types of phrases.

You can build up a word anywhere in a sentence. Simply add one
or more describing words.

Examples: Forecast is bad.
                <u>The</u> forecast is bad.
                The <u>weather</u> forecast is bad.
                The <u>latest</u> weather forecast is bad.
                The <u>very</u> latest weather forecast is bad.

In the previous examples, all the single words are added in front
of the noun. Now find the added words in this sentence:

The very latest weather forecast on TV is bad.

You can add onto a noun with a word group *after* the noun. This
word group will tell *which* or *what kind*.

Examples: The weather forecast <u>on TV</u> is bad. (Which forecast?)
                The forecast <u>in the paper</u> looks better. (Which forecast?)
                The forecast <u>for the next five days</u> is encouraging. (What kind of
                forecast?)

Prepositional Phrases

Definition: **Begin the word group with a *preposition* and end it with a noun or pronoun. (*Pre-* means "before," so *pre-position* means "position before"—a noun or pronoun.) A preposition joins a noun or pronoun to another part of the sentence. The word group is a *prepositional phrase.***

Common Prepositions

about	before	from	over
above	behind	in, into	through, throughout
across	below	of	to
after	by	off	under
around	during	on	up, upon
at	for	out	with, without

A prepositional phrase is a handy structure to know about and use. It helps to clarify meaning. Use a prepositional phrase when you have already added single words in front of the noun:

Example: The latest weather forecast <u>on TV</u> is bad.

Use a prepositional phrase when single words won't do the job:

Example: Is weather a visitor <u>from outer space</u>?

Remember, a prepositional phrase can go after a noun *anywhere* in a sentence.

Skills Activity 1 | **Adding Prepositional Phrases to the Subject**

Read each sentence and find the subject. Decide where the prepositional phrase in parentheses belongs in the subject. Rewrite the sentence on your paper, adding the prepositional phrase where it belongs.

Example: Weather information usually is interesting. (on TV)
Weather information on TV usually is interesting.

1. Nearly everyone watches the weather. (in the U.S.)
2. Some people really understand computers. (with mathematical skills)
3. Other people experience physical discomforts on the job. (besides outdoor workers)
4. Baseball or football fans are very interested. (during the season)
5. Most residents watch the winter weather. (of northern areas)

6. A heavy snow can happen very quickly. (during winter months)

7. A temperature variation can mean the difference between rain and snow. (of just one degree)

8. One degree makes an even greater difference. (on the Celsius scale)

9. The hurricane season is closely watched. (in summer and fall)

10. The weather bureau picnic is a classic joke. (on a rainy day)

Skills Activity 2   Adding Prepositional Phrases to the Predicate

Read each sentence and find the predicate. Decide where the prepositional phrase in parentheses belongs in the predicate. Rewrite the sentence, putting in the prepositional phrase.

Example: The weather forecast is an important feature. (of a local newscast)
The weather forecast is an important feature of a local newscast.

1. A TV forecaster gives the statistics. (of temperature and precipitation)

2. The forecast also includes data. (about approaching conditions)

3. The anchorperson usually makes an opening remark. (about yesterday's weather)

4. The forecaster begins the presentation. (with a satellite photo)

5. The photo shows weather systems. (in much of the nation)

6. Next he or she gives a forecast. (for the next 24 hours)

7. The segment ends with a prediction. (for the next five days)

8. No one can trust a forecast. (beyond one full day)

9. Some conditions can make a forecaster only a good guesser. (of any weather)

10. Rain or sleet or snow is often the prediction. (throughout the mid-Atlantic region)

Skills Activity 3   Adding Prepositional Phrases to Sentences

Read each sentence and think of a prepositional phrase that would make sense after the underlined word. Rewrite the sentence, putting in your own prepositional phrase.

Example: Weather forecasters use all sorts of <u>information</u>.

Weather forecasters use all sorts of information in their work (*or* from sophisticated instruments, *or* for their forecasts).

1. The National Weather Service provides basic <u>data</u>.

2. Another service, Accu-Weather, supplies many TV <u>stations</u>.

3. A good weather <u>person</u> is like a doctor.

4. The "<u>doctor</u>" examines the "patient's" symptoms.
5. The same symptoms can yield many different <u>opinions</u>.
6. Some <u>people</u> can predict the weather.
7. An aching knee or elbow may give a <u>clue</u>.
8. The appearance of the sky tells other <u>observers</u>.
9. A red sky in the morning can mean a <u>storm</u>.
10. Heavy fur growth on animals can mean cold <u>weather</u>.

Adverb Prepositional Phrases

Compare these sentences:

The factory robot dropped the auto parts.

The factory robot dropped the auto parts <u>instantly</u>.

The factory robot dropped the auto parts <u>precisely</u>.

The factory robot dropped the auto parts <u>there</u>.

Definition: **The added words in the sentences are *adverbs*. Adverbs tell when, how (or how much), or where.**

Now compare these sentences:

The factory robot dropped the auto parts <u>in an instant</u>.

The factory robot dropped the auto parts <u>with precision</u>.

The factory robot dropped the auto parts <u>in the right slots</u>.

Do the added word groups tell when, how, or where? What kind of word do you think begins each underlined word group?

Definition: **A *prepositional phrase* can act as an adverb. It tells when, how, or where, just as a single-word adverb does.**

When
Word: dropped the auto parts <u>instantly</u>.
Phrase: dropped the auto parts <u>in an instant</u>.

How (or **how much**)
Word: dropped the auto parts <u>precisely</u>.
Phrase: dropped the auto parts <u>with precision</u>.

Where
Word: dropped the auto parts <u>there</u>.
Phrase: dropped the auto parts <u>in the right slots</u>.

Sometimes a prepositional phrase adverb tells *why*.

Why

Phrase: The robot works <u>for a living</u>.

Begin a prepositional phrase adverb with a preposition and end
it with a noun or pronoun. Add adjectives before the noun if needed.
A prepositional phrase can be an adjective or an adverb. It depends
on what the phrase does in the sentence.

Prepositional Phrase Adjective:

The phrase goes after the noun and describes that noun.

Examples: The robot <u>in the factory</u>
The robot <u>with steel pincers</u>

Prepositional Phrase Adverb:

Definition: **The phrase (like any adverb) can go almost anywhere in a
sentence. An adverb usually tells about a verb. (*Adverb* means
"about a verb.")**

Examples: The robot dropped the auto parts <u>in an instant</u>.
<u>In an instant</u> the robot dropped the auto parts.
The robot <u>in an instant</u> dropped the auto parts.

Sometimes a phrase adverb tells about an adjective and goes right
after it.

Example: A robot is alert <u>at all times</u>.

Skills Activity 4   **Placing Adverb Prepositional Phrases**

Decide where the prepositional phrase in parentheses makes sense
in each sentence. Rewrite the sentence, inserting the prepositional
phrase adverb.

Examples: A robot can do several tasks. (in a factory)
A robot can do several tasks in a factory.
or
In a factory a robot can do several tasks.

1. A robot is designed. (with flexible arms and hands)
2. Like a human hand, the mechanical hand can grasp. (with
   great precision)
3. Some 5,000 robots already are working. (in factories)
4. A robot may pick up and insert parts. (into complex machinery)
5. Or, it can unload items. (from packing cases)

6. Some robots can actually see. (with TV camera "eyes")
7. A seeing robot matches images and objects. (with its eyes)
8. It then selects the objects from an assembly line. (without any mistakes)
9. Another robot can grind and polish surfaces. (with efficiency and care)
10. Specially designed robots can reach. (into difficult places)

| Skills Activity 5 | **Adding Adverb Prepositional Phrases** |

Think of a prepositional phrase adverb that would make sense in each sentence. Your phrase should answer the question word in parentheses. Rewrite the sentence, inserting your prepositional phrase adverb.

Examples: One robot can weld several points. (When?)
One robot can weld several points at the same time.
or
One robot can weld several points in a few seconds.

1. Another robot can weld and paint. (When?)
2. A small factory robot does cost. (How much?)
3. But it pays for itself. (When?)
4. A robot doesn't actually replace a worker. (Where?)
5. Instead, it assists a worker. (How?)
6. Also, someone should be near or work with a robot. (When or why?)
7. A robot can do only its programmed tasks. (When?)
8. If something goes wrong, a robot doesn't change its behavior. (How?)
9. A person has to make any changes. (How or when?)
10. Actually a robot does the many boring, unpleasant tasks. (Where?)

Infinitive Phrases (*to* Phrases)

Definition: **Begin the phrase with *to* and add a verb form to finish the idea. The entire phrase (including *to*) is called an *infinitive phrase*. (*In* means "not" and *finite* means "limit"; so *infinitive* means "not limited"—to any particular subject or time.)**

Examples: Paper money <u>to be destroyed</u> . . .
Paper money <u>to spend</u> . . .

The meaning is not limited to any subject or time. <u>Anyone</u> may do the destroying or spending at <u>any</u> time.

Like the other kinds of phrases (prepositional or participial), an infinitive phrase can work when nothing else does. Use it when you want to tell about actions *to do* or *to be done* with something or someone.

Examples: **To Do:**   The money <u>to spend</u> is in circulation.
          To Be Done: The money <u>to be destroyed</u> is set aside.

An infinitive phrase (like a prepositional phrase) can be an adjective or an adverb. It depends on what the phrase does in the sentence.

Infinitive Phrase Adjective

The phrase goes after a noun and describes that noun.

Examples: The money <u>to spend</u> is in circulation.
          The money <u>to be destroyed</u> is set aside.

Infinitive Phrase Adverb

The phrase usually tells about a verb and usually goes after the verb.

Examples: The people telephoned <u>to make an appointment</u>.
          They were going <u>to take a vacation</u>.
          The reservations were written <u>to give details</u>.

Sometimes the adverb phrase tells about an adjective and goes right after it.

Example: Everyone was eager <u>to get started</u>.

Like any adverb, an infinitive phrase adverb doesn't have to follow any word.

Examples: <u>To make the appointment</u>, we telephoned a week ahead.
          We telephoned <u>to make the appointment</u> a week ahead.
          We telephoned a week ahead <u>to make the appointment</u>.

Put an adverb phrase where it sounds most natural to you.

Skills Activity 6   **Placing Adverb Infinitive Phrases**

Decide where the infinitive phrase in parentheses makes sense in each sentence. Rewrite each sentence on your paper.

Example: Any family can plan. (to have a low-cost vacation)
          Any family can plan to have a low-cost vacation.

  1. Months ahead of time a family began. (to plan their trip)
  2. Their early start was needed. (to get a reservation)

3. The reservation was made. (to exchange houses)
4. Another family in Europe had also planned. (to do the same thing)
5. The two families wrote letters. (to arrange the exchange)
6. At vacation time the American family traveled. (to stay in the house in Europe)
7. The European family made the trip. (to use the house in the U.S.)
8. Both families were ready. (to take good care of the houses)
9. In fact, they were eager. (to please one another)
10. Everyone was happy. (to save on hotel bills)

Skills Activity 7 **Adding Adverb Infinitive Phrases**

Think of an infinitive phrase adverb that would make sense in each sentence. Your phrase should answer the question word in parentheses. Rewrite the sentence, inserting your infinitive phrase adverb where it makes best sense.

Examples: The families made the house exchange. (Why?)
The families made the house exchange to save money.
or
The families made the house exchange to make their vacations more interesting.

1. Each family started early. (Why?)
2. A house exchange group provided the names. (Why?)
3. Home-owning families joined the exchange group. (Why?)
4. Their names and addresses are listed. (Why?)
5. Sometimes cars and food supplies are included. (How or why?)
6. Then the families sent each other letters. (Why?)
7. Both families had been anxious. (How?)
8. At last the two families were traveling. (Where?)
9. Everyone had certainly promised. (Why?)
10. Even the neighbors were ready. (How?)

Skills Activity 8 **Placing Adjective Infinitive Phrases**

Read each sentence and find the subject. Decide where the infinitive phrase in parentheses belongs in the subject. Rewrite the sentence, including the infinitive phrase.

Example: Dollar bills shouldn't last more than two years. (to spend)
Dollar bills to spend shouldn't last more than two years.

1. Bills stay in circulation until worn out. (to be spent)
2. Money is brought into the banks. (to be deposited)
3. However, the money is now in larger bills than one dollar. (to be saved)
4. The everyday money is more and more in dollar bills than in coins. (to be used as change)
5. Bills are set aside in the bank. (to be inspected)
6. Special new machines are being used. (to inspect paper money)
7. Worn-out bills are put into a shredding machine. (to be destroyed)
8. The better bills are paid out by the tellers. (to be recirculated)
9. The one-dollar coin never caught on. (to spend every day)
10. Perhaps the two-dollar bill will grow more popular. (to use for many purchases)

| Skills Activity 9 | **Adding Adjective Infinitive Phrases** |

Read each sentence and find the predicate. Decide where the infinitive phrase in parentheses belongs in the predicate. Rewrite the sentence, inserting the infinitive phrase.

Example: Sometimes the public quickly accepts a new coin. (to use every day)
Sometimes the public quickly accepts a new coin to use every day.

1. Late in 1963 the president issued an order. (to make a new coin)
2. The Kennedy half-dollar became an instantly popular coin. (to collect)
3. Many people collected the 1964 all-silver coin. (to keep as a souvenir)
4. Other people collected these silver coins. (to melt down into metal)
5. Artisans used the handsome coins in jewelry. (to be worn)
6. A number of the coins were made into charms. (to be worn on bracelets)
7. Many of these half-dollars did not stay in circulation. (to be spent)
8. The latest issues of the coin contain no silver. (to be melted down)
9. These later coins have the same value. (to be used as money)
10. Yet they are still very handsome coins. (to keep and admire)

Participial Phrases (-*ing* and -*ed* Phrases)

Definition: **These word groups are called *participial phrases*. They function partly as verbs and partly as adjectives. Participial phrases begin with the -*ing* or -*ed* form (a participle) of a verb. (Remember that a participle is a verb form that is used as an adjective.) Like a prepositional phrase, a participial phrase can come in handy in describing. However, you have to decide when to use it.**

Use it when your description is too complicated for single words.

Example: The suitcase <u>spilling its contents</u>

Often you can choose between a prepositional phrase and a participial phrase. Choose the one that sounds better to you or that says exactly what you want to say.

Examples: **Prepositional:** The suitcase <u>with too many provisions</u>
Participial: The suitcase <u>overfilled with provisions</u>

Prepositional: The suitcase <u>with spilling contents</u>
Participial: The suitcase <u>spilling its contents</u>

Remember, a participial phrase (like a prepositional phrase) can go after a noun *anywhere* in a sentence.

Examples: The amused passengers saw the suitcase <u>spilling its contents</u>.
The suitcase <u>spilling its contents</u> was a surprise.

Some verbs have an irregular -*ed* form. You already know these forms because you use them all the time.

Examples: **Regular:** The suitcase <u>filled</u> with things . . .
Irregular: The program <u>seen</u> on public TV . . .
The items <u>lost</u> in the flood . . .

Skills Activity 10 | **Adding Participial Phrases to the Subject**

Read each sentence and find the subject. Decide where the participial phrase in parentheses belongs. Then rewrite the sentence, inserting the participial phrase in the subject.

Example: Some travelers are quite a sight. (carrying too much luggage)
Some travelers carrying too much luggage are quite a sight.

1. People can bring too many things. (lacking travel know-how)
2. Other travelers carry needed supplies. (knowing of emergencies)
3. Travelers do need detailed maps. (visiting large cities)
4. Some people carry extra candles. (accustomed to power blackouts)

5. One woman always brings air freshener. (disliking stuffy rooms)

6. A particular person takes his own packaged foods. (avoiding fast-food places)

7. Some people must carry all their food supplies. (following strict diets)

8. Pet owners may bring them along. (attached to their animals)

9. Special carriers are available for pets. (designed for their safety)

10. Many pets are poor travelers. (accustomed to their secure homes)

Skills Activity 11   **Adding Participial Phrases to the Predicate**

Read each sentence and find the predicate. Decide where the participial phrase in parentheses belongs. Then rewrite the sentence, inserting the participial phrase in the predicate.

Example: One couple always carries a kit. (filled with repair tools)
One couple always carries a kit filled with repair tools.

1. Most people can pack extra coat hangers. (taking little space)

2. Frequent travelers carry schedule books. (giving flight information)

3. Smart travelers bring a first-aid kit. (filled with medical supplies)

4. Every traveler's friend is drip-dry clothing. (needing no ironing)

5. Instant coffee is handy for small hotels. (lacking room service)

6. Another handy item is an immersion heater. (providing hot water)

7. One gourmet always carries a picnic basket. (packed with favorite foods)

8. A helpful travel item is some spray cleaner. (designed for spot cleaning)

9. Early risers use a small alarm clock. (intended for travel)

10. Some even carry a sewing kit. (filled with pins and buttons)

Skills Activity 12   **Adding Participial Phrases to Sentences**

Read each sentence and think of a participial phrase that would make sense after the underlined word. Rewrite the sentence, putting in your own participial phrase.

Examples: Supermarket <u>customers</u> can get annoyed.
Supermarket customers waiting in a checkout line can get annoyed.
or
Supermarket customers tired of price increases can get annoyed.

1. New <u>products</u> always are available.
2. Many <u>people</u> think they must drive everywhere.
3. A team's <u>fans</u> become furious over a lost game.
4. Out-of-the-way places attract certain <u>travelers</u>.
5. Certain <u>people</u> always buy the latest fashions.
6. Sun-block lotions can help most beach <u>visitors</u>.
7. Election results often surprise the so-called <u>experts</u>.
8. Some <u>movies</u> may be quite violent.
9. Someone left an unusually shaped <u>package</u>.
10. Several <u>drivers</u> will get tired of waiting.

Clauses

A *clause* is a group of words that contains a subject and a verb. This section will explain how to incorporate *adjective clauses* and *adverb clauses* into sentences.

Study the difference between the first group of sentences and the second group. The first three sentences have been expanded with *phrases;* the sentences in the second group have been expanded with *clauses.*

Examples: **Phrases:**   The telephone book <u>in the library</u>
                           The telephone book <u>lying on the shelf</u>
                           The telephone book <u>to be used</u>

             Clauses: The telephone book <u>that was lost</u>
                           The person <u>who took it</u>
                           The book, <u>which was falling apart</u>

Adjective Clauses

Definition: ***Adjective* means "add to"; *clause* means "closed" or "complete." Therefore, *adjective clause* means "a complete idea added to" a noun or pronoun. An adjective clause is a little sentence within a sentence. The clause has its own subject and predicate, just as a sentence does; however, an adjective clause alone is not always a complete sentence.**

Here is how to write one kind of adjective clause:
Begin with one of the following words:

which   that   who   whose   whom

The phone book <u>that</u>
The person <u>who</u>
The book, <u>which</u>

Note: An adjective clause can begin with *when* or *where,* although most do not. For your purposes now, stay with *which, that, who, whose,* or *whom.* The beginning word can act as the subject of the clause. Then add a verb form:

Examples: The phone book that <u>was lost</u>
The person who <u>took</u>
The book, which <u>was falling</u>

Add any more predicate words (if needed) to finish the idea, as you would in any sentence.

Examples: The phone book that <u>was lost</u> (no more words needed)
The person who took <u>it</u> (pronoun)
The book, which was falling <u>apart</u> (adverb)

Examples: The phone book <u>that was lost</u> could be valuable.
Could you offer the person <u>who took it</u> a reward?
No one wanted the book, <u>which was falling apart</u>.

Sometimes a noun or pronoun acts as the subject of the clause.

Examples: The trains <u>that Europeans use</u> go almost everywhere.
The trains <u>that they take</u> are convenient.
Good train service is a convenience <u>that everyone enjoys</u>.

Like a phrase, an adjective clause can describe or point out. A clause usually is more exact, because it tells just who is doing what.

Examples: **Phrases:**   The trains <u>in Europe</u>
The trains <u>to take</u>
The trains <u>going everywhere</u>

Clauses: The trains <u>that Europeans use</u>
The trains <u>that they take</u>
The trains <u>that everyone enjoys</u>

Skills Activity 13   **Adding Adjective Clauses to the Subject**

Decide where the adjective clause in parentheses belongs in the subject. Rewrite the sentence, inserting the adjective clause in the subject.

Example: A phone book was falling to pieces. (that was forty years old)
A phone book that was forty years old was falling to pieces.

1. An ancient ledger is in fairly good shape. (that is 3,000 years old)

2. The paper makes all the difference. (that is used in a book)

3. Modern paper destroys itself over the years. (that has lots of acid)

4. Most publications cannot last very long. (that were printed since 1850)

5. Many items have already disintegrated. (that were printed since 1900)

6. A book has a life expectancy of about fifty years. (that is published today)

7. People could do something about this. (who care about books)

8. Publishers could use nonacid paper. (who want to preserve their work)

9. Specialists could preserve valuable books on film. (who are experts)

10. The amount of money is a problem. (that would be needed)

| Skills Activity 14 | **Adding Adjective Clauses to the Predicate** |

Decide where the adjective clause in parentheses belongs in the predicate. Rewrite the sentence, inserting the adjective clause in the predicate.

Example: Much knowledge of history comes from fossils. (that have been unearthed)

Much knowledge of history comes from fossils that have been unearthed.

1. Fossils are the remains of animals and vegetables. (that have been preserved)

2. Over 100 years ago scientists began digging up fossils. (that are studied today)

3. Museums store these fossils. (which are irreplaceable)

4. Museum storage vaults are watched over by scientists. (who classified the fossils)

5. These fossils have often been inaccessible even to students. (who would like to study them)

6. However, the fossils are available to something. (that cannot be locked out)

7. The fossils have gradually been eaten into by the air. (which is acid-filled)

8. The air destroys dinosaur bones. (that had been buried for 100 million years)

9. Yet, you cannot blame the museum people. (who are trying to preserve their treasures)

10. Throughout the land, more fossils are destroyed by bulldozers and plows. (that chew into the earth)

Skills Activity 15   **Adding Adjective Clauses to Sentences**

Think of an adjective clause that would make sense after the underlined word. Rewrite the sentence, putting in your own adjective clause.

Example: The best-dressed teacher is <u>Mr. Morris</u>.

The best-dressed teacher is Mr. Morris, who always wears the newest fashions.

1. A new kind of <u>shampoo</u> is called Dandy Ruff.
2. The ancient <u>car</u> can hardly make it around the block.
3. The classified directory contains business <u>numbers</u>.
4. Many so-called <u>illnesses</u> come from eating the wrong foods.
5. The interstate highway system has opened up many <u>areas</u>.
6. <u>Wood</u> is an excellent source of energy.
7. Many states require the use of infant seats and <u>seatbelts</u>.
8. Sometimes a piece of <u>junk</u> may turn out to be valuable.
9. <u>Motorbikes</u> are becoming more popular.
10. Most department stores have sets of <u>escalators</u>.

Adverb Clauses

An adverb can be a single word:

Examples: People leave trash <u>everywhere</u>.
People leave trash <u>thoughtlessly</u>.
Trash is left <u>there</u>.

An adverb can be a phrase:

Examples: People leave trash <u>on city streets</u>.
People leave trash <u>every day</u>.
Trash is left <u>to be collected</u>.

Look at the underlined word groups in these sentences:

Examples: People leave trash <u>where they drop it</u>.
People leave trash <u>when no one is watching</u>.
Trash is left <u>wherever someone else will collect it</u>.

Another kind of word group that can act as an adverb is a clause. An *adverb clause* often tells *where* or *when*.

Examples: **Where:**   People leave trash <u>where they drop it</u>.
Trash builds up <u>wherever people are careless</u>.

When: People leave trash <u>when no one is watching</u>.
An area looks bad <u>after people leave trash</u>.

Definition: An adverb clause (like an adjective clause) is a little sentence within a sentence. The clause has its own subject and predicate, just as a sentence does.

Here is how to write an adverb clause that tells *where* or *when*. Begin with one of the following words:

where	when	after	once	until
wherever	whenever	before	since	while

People leave trash <u>where</u>

Trash builds up <u>wherever</u>

People leave trash <u>when</u>

An area looks bad <u>after</u>

Put in a noun or pronoun. (This will be the subject of the clause.)

People leave trash where <u>they</u>

Trash builds up wherever <u>people</u>

People leave trash when <u>no one</u>

An area looks bad after <u>people</u>

Add a verb form. (This will be the main word in the predicate of the clause.)

People leave trash where they <u>drop</u>

Trash builds up wherever people <u>are</u>

People leave trash when no one <u>is watching</u>

An area looks bad after people <u>leave</u>

Add any more predicate words (if needed) to finish the idea, as you would in any sentence.

People leave trash where they drop <u>it</u>. (pronoun)

Trash builds up wherever people are <u>careless</u>. (adjective)

People leave trash when no one is watching. (No more words needed.)

An area looks bad after people leave <u>trash</u>. (noun)

An adverb clause (like an adverb or adverb phrase) can go almost anywhere in a sentence. Usually an adverb clause goes at the beginning or the end.

Examples: <u>After people leave trash</u>, an area looks bad.
                An area looks bad <u>after people leave trash</u>.

   Rule: **When you put an adverb clause at a sentence beginning, put a comma after the clause.**

Skills Activity 16   **Adding Adverb Clauses to Sentences**

Think of an adverb clause that would make sense in each sentence. Your clause should answer the question word in parentheses. Rewrite the sentence, inserting your adverb clause where it makes best sense.

Example: Communities can be made more attractive. (when?)
                Communities can be made more attractive when people want them to be.

1. Littering is not the only problem. (when?)
2. Bare patches of ground can be seeded. (when?)
3. Community gardens are attractive. (where?)
4. Trash collection areas can be fenced. (where?)
5. Some neighborhoods plant new trees. (where?)
6. Regular pickups of discarded items should be set up. (when?)
7. Street sweeping should also be done. (when?)
8. A coat of paint can help. (where?)
9. A rake and a broom are the basic tools. (where?)
10. Of course, someone has to use the rake or broom. (when?)

Skills Activity 17   **Inserting Adverb Clauses in Sentences**

Think of, or choose from the list, an adverb clause that would make sense in each sentence. Rewrite the sentence, putting in the adverb clause where it makes best sense.

Examples: Littering habits will not die.
                Littering habits will not die before fines are imposed.
                or
                Until people change their attitudes, littering habits will not die.

Adverb Clauses:

until people change their minds

whenever people disobey them

before fines are imposed

where violations are found

before it is too late

when loose trash falls off

where littering habits are learned

where trash piles up quickly

where people can do something right away

wherever littering is the worst

where people can see a difference

while people are aware of the problem

when they are needed

before the cleanup begins

when people expect them

1. Your area can clean up litter.
2. Begin at home.
3. Work on garages, yards, and trash collection areas.
4. See that trash pickups are scheduled.
5. Educate the public about littering.
6. Set up littering laws.
7. Watch for problem areas.
8. Construction sites can be bad areas.
9. Uncovered trucks can be problems.
10. Enforce the laws.

Skills Activity 18   **Combining Phrases and Clauses to Expand Sentences**

Use the add-on method to write your own sentence about drivers in rush hour traffic. Begin with the sentence *People drive.* Add at least two adverb phrases, one by one. Rewrite the whole sentence with each added phrase, as in the examples.

Go on to clauses. Write at least two sentences using a clause in each sentence. The result will be a list of sentences, each one more detailed than the one before.

When you have finished, select the sentence you think sounds best.

Phrases and Clauses (Use as needed)

at great speeds	because they are tired
with (or without) care	because they are in a hurry
during rush hour	where high speeds are permitted
on the expressways	whenever they change lanes
in carpools	as if they were crazy
in special lanes	unless they want a ticket
	so that they can stop fast

| *Skill Test 1* | **Phrases** |

Copy the following sentences and underline all the phrases, identifying whether each phrase is *prepositional, infinitive,* or *participial.*

1. A good pitcher may not be good at hitting.
2. The expressway has a special lane for fast traffic.
3. Everyone was too tired to stay up for the late show.
4. A course teaching first aid is a must for campers.
5. The best shows to watch often are reruns of old movies.
6. Many stores sell gourmet foods displayed in a special department.
7. A fresh coat of paint may be all that is needed to make a table look like new.
8. The exit ramp is the last one before the tollgate.
9. Energy-saving measures should be taken in every household.
10. Many people will shop a long time for a good bargain to take home.

| *Skill Test 2* | **Clauses** |

Copy the following sentences and underline each clause. Tell whether the clause is adjective or adverb.

1. Your skin needs protection while you are in the sun.
2. Before the speech ended, people began leaving.
3. Radio was once the major entertainment medium that drew millions of listeners every day.
4. Hang gliding is dangerous whenever wind conditions are uncertain.
5. A men's jacket style that is always in fashion is called the blazer.
6. There are cosmetic products that are made for teenage skin problems.
7. The TV personalities who get high audience ratings stay on the air.
8. Plain old blue jeans were popular before designer labels came into fashion.
9. You pay for "free" TV through advertisements that persuade you to buy.
10. When the political conventions end, the election campaign begins.

Skill Test 3   **Identifying Phrases and Clauses**

Copy the following sentences. Put parentheses around each *phrase* and underline each *clause.* Identify the type of phrase or clause each one is.

1. Preventive maintenance means solving repair problems before they become serious.
2. A banner headline across the front page announced who had won the election.
3. The American hotdog which is a favorite at ball games was created in Germany before becoming a fast-food dish.
4. Solar energy collectors work only where there is plenty of sunshine to activate them.
5. Jet planes which can go faster than the speed of sound have changed the way we travel.
6. Chicago was the nation's rail transportation center before truck and air freight were important.
7. Products that were unknown ten years ago are now everyday items.
8. A weekend when the weather's stormy is a great time to catch up on reading.
9. Everyone was interested in the championship game seen on cable TV.
10. During the winter months, ads for Caribbean cruises attract the eye of travelers who can afford to pay the airfare for a week in the sun.

Chapter 16

VERB POWER

Verbs give sentences their power—their direction. Changing only the verb in the following sentences brings a complete change in meaning.

1. The doctor petted a dog. (active verb)
2. The doctor was given a dog. (passive verb)
3. The doctor smelled a dog. (linking verb)
4. The doctor fell over a dog. (complete verb)

These four sentences illustrate the four types of verb patterns: *active, passive, linking,* and *complete.*

Active Verbs

Definition: An *active verb* tells what someone or something does or did. An active verb can be used alone or with auxiliary verbs in an *action verb phrase.*

Examples: **Active Verb**
The team <u>won</u> every game.
The team <u>beat</u> the champions.

Active Verb Phrase: (Action verb + auxiliary verb[s])
The team <u>has won</u> every game.
The team <u>has beaten</u> the champions.

Active verbs have a direct object. To find an active verb or active verb phrase, ask yourself the following: "What does (or did) someone or something do?"

Examples: The team practiced their formations.
What did something do? (practiced)

The fans expected the team to win.
What did someone do? (expected)

The coach knew the team's record.
What did someone do? (knew)

The fans shouted encouragement to the team members.
What did someone do? (shouted)

The action may be *physical* or *mental:*

Physical	**Mental**
(What you can see, hear, etc.)	(What you cannot see, hear, etc.)
play	know
shout	expect
practice	want
run	think
win	plan

Skills Activity 1   **Active Verbs**

Read each sentence and find the active verb or active verb phrase. Then write the verb or verb phrase on your paper.

Examples: The TV schedule gives a week's programming.
gives

Last week's schedule had listed the movies incorrectly.
had listed

1. Oranges need some cold weather for full flavor.
2. New autos should save fuel.
3. Astronauts constantly risk their lives.
4. Many cities have improved the quality of their air.
5. A digital watch can show the time in numerals only.
6. Few animals attack humans without warning.
7. The president approved the new budget.
8. People have been learning the benefits of exercise.
9. Both hot sunny weather and cold windy weather can harm the skin.
10. Elvis Presley earned twenty-eight golden records during his career.

Passive Verbs

A *passive* sentence has a subject that is acted upon by a verb. The verb always contains a form of *be* plus another verb form.

The dinner was eaten by George. (passive)

In this sentence, dinner (the subject) *receives* the action. It also receives the attention in the sentence and seems more important than George, who is placed at the end of the sentence. The feeling of action also is weakened by was (a form of *be*).

In order to understand active and passive sentences, the writer must know the forms of *be*. Memorize them:

am	was	be
are	were	been
is		being

In the passive voice, there are two or more words in the verb. The first verb form always is a form of *be*, and the word that follows it is the past participle of a second verb. Here are examples:

(form of be)	*(past participle)*
were	followed
was	given
are	delivered
is	played
be	awarded
will have been	finished
shall be	saved

Here are the above verbs used in passive sentences:

The clowns <u>were followed</u> by the elephants.

The retiring teacher <u>was given</u> a reception by the staff.

See that the sausages <u>are delivered</u> by two o'clock.

Rugby <u>is played</u> by many people in Great Britain.

The jury directed that the film <u>be awarded</u> a prize.

The cake <u>will have been finished</u> when you get home.

Many dollars <u>shall be saved</u> by cautious motorists.

Notice that sentences in the passive voice frequently have verbs that are followed by a group of words beginning with *by:* The fish was caught <u>by the little girl</u>. Remember also that the subject receives the action in a passive sentence.

Skills Activity 2   Passive Versus Active Verbs

Read the following paragraph and, on a separate sheet of paper, list all the verbs you notice. Indicate an *A* next to those verbs that seem to have someone or something actually performing an activity.

At 1:00 P.M. the group met in the grand ballroom. Introductory remarks, which included a review of last week's meeting, were given by the chairperson. When the speaker from the zoning commission was introduced, some people in the back of the room began to yell interruptions. Apparently, the speaker had not been told that several nearby residents of the proposed nuclear plant site would attend the meeting. The speaker, obviously angry, slammed his fist on the podium and walked off the stage, shaking his head in disgust.

There are a total of ten words used as *verbs* in the above paragraph. Did you find all ten? Seven of the verbs are *active* words, where a person or thing actually performs the activity of the verb. Did you find them? The other three verbs are *passive;* the person or thing receives the action. Whenever possible, write with active rather than passive verbs.

Why should a writer prefer active verbs to passive verbs? Think about the meaning of the word *active*. It means "working" or "operating effectively." Some synonyms (words with similar meanings) for *active* are *alive, dynamic,* and *functioning.* Effective writers use active sentences that show vitality and energy. They usually avoid making their thoughts appear passive.

In contrast, *passive* has the opposite meaning of *active.* Passive means "inactive." Some synonyms of passive are *idle, quiet, inert,* and *docile.* The word passive suggests a feeling of dullness and laziness. It is no wonder that the effective writer avoids the passive voice most of the time. Unless there is a good reason for using the passive voice (and sometimes it is appropriate), a writer should concentrate on writing active sentences.

Note: A sentence can be active when the present participle (the form ending in -*ing*) of a verb is used with a form of *be*. Here are examples:

> The champion is <u>defeating</u> George.
>
> I <u>am defeating</u> George.
>
> You <u>are defeating</u> George.
>
> I <u>have been defeating</u> George.

Skills Activity 3   **Changing Passive Verbs to Active**

The ten sentences that follow are written with passive verbs. Copy each sentence and then rewrite it, making the verb active.

Passive: The audience was thrilled by the acrobat.
Active: The acrobat thrilled the audience.

1. The herd was stampeded by the cowhands.
2. The test was passed by Abraham.
3. The snow was shoveled by Nancy.

4. The game is being won by me.
5. You were fooled by the trick.
6. The dog was bitten by the flea.
7. The guests were served dinner by the host.
8. The fire was lit by the campers.
9. A fierce bull was ridden by a tough cowhand.
10. His aunt was delighted by the surprise party.

Writing Passive Sentences

There are three situations when the passive voice is appropriate for you to use:

1. When you want to focus upon a subject that receives the action.

   Emily was astounded by her huge raise in salary.
   The evil monster finally was destroyed by the knight.

2. When you do not know or do not want to reveal the person or thing that is doing the action.

   The diamond ring was stolen.
   The ice cream that was in the refrigerator had been eaten.

3. When you want to add variety to the rhythm of the sentences.

   Sometimes a string of active sentences, one after the other, can become monotonous. You might choose to include a passive sentence to vary the sentence rhythms, as in the following paragraph:

   The Baltimore orioles flew into the garden in May. They ate from the birdhouse and fluttered around the garden. They warbled sweetly at twilight, delighting the birdwatchers. Flashes of their black and orange bodies were noticed by the people throughout the day. They enjoyed observing and hearing these lovely feathered guests, who seemed to be announcing springtime.

Linking Verbs

Compare the underlined words in the sentences:

The team <u>was</u> the best.

The team <u>looked</u> the best.

The team <u>became</u> the best.

The team <u>seemed</u> the best.

The team <u>appeared</u> the best.

Each sentence has the same, or nearly the same, meaning. Each underlined word is a *linking verb*.

A *linking verb* connects, or links, a sentence beginning and a sentence ending. Often you can exchange one linking verb for another without changing the meaning. A linking verb sentence describes or gives information about someone or something.

Examples: The team <u>was</u> excellent. (describes)
The team <u>became</u> the league champions. (gives information)

A linking verb acts like the equal sign in a math problem. The equal sign connects, or links, the problem and its answer.

Examples: $25 - 14 = 11$ $25 - 14$ <u>is</u> 11
The team = the best.   The team <u>is</u> the best.

Common linking verbs are forms of *be* and verbs whose first letters are included in the acronym *GRABS* as shown below.

Be

am	was	be
are	were	been
is		being

GRABS

grow	grows	grew/grown	growing
remain	remains	remained	remaining
appear	appears	appeared	appearing
become	becomes	became	becoming
seem	seems	seemed	seeming

Other linking verbs are those for the five senses. (Your senses give you firsthand information; so do the senses verbs.)

Sense Verbs

look	looks	looked	looking
smell	smells	smelled	smelling
taste	tastes	tasted	tasting
sound	sounds	sounded	sounding
feel	feels	felt	feeling

Note: Many of the verbs discussed in this section are not *always* linking verbs. To be a linking verb, the verb must link a noun or pronoun in the first part of the sentence with a word that describes or names it in the second part. When the verb is followed by an object, or when an adverb or adverb phrase follows the verb, the verb is not called a linking verb.

Examples: She smelled the milk to check if it was sour.
(<u>Milk</u> is the object that received the action of the verb.)

The ghost appears in the evening.
(<u>In the evening</u> is an adverb phrase telling when the ghost appears.)

Note: If the verb is the last part of speech in the sentence, it is not a linking verb because there is nothing to link.

Examples: I <u>am</u>.
The ghost <u>appeared</u>.

Skills Activity 4   **Finding Linking Verbs**

Find the linking verb in each sentence below. Write it on your paper.

Example: The team became overconfident.
The team <u>became</u> overconfident.

1. Fresh fruits and vegetables are nutritious.
2. A hurricane appears calm in its center or eye.
3. Country and western music remains popular even in eastern cities.
4. Some silk flowers look real.
5. Saving fuel became more vital in auto design.
6. The common cold remains a mystery to medical science.
7. Most foods taste better with proper seasoning.
8. Do you feel well today?
9. Compact discs played on the new equipment sound clear and true.
10. Gradually the U.S. became less dependent on foreign oil.

Skills Activity 5   **Exchanging One Linking Verb for Another**

Read each sentence and find the linking verb. Then think of another linking verb that can replace the one in the sentence. Rewrite the sentence.

Example: The weather often is a mystery.
                The weather often <u>becomes</u> a mystery.

1. Predicting weather seems scientific.
2. Actually, it remains more an art than a science.
3. Scientific information appears important to a weather forecaster.
4. Yet, exact weather information often remains doubtful.
5. In many areas, rain, snow, and fog become impossible to predict.
6. Sometimes the atmosphere almost feels snowy.
7. Also, the sky looks a certain way during tornado conditions.
8. Some storms actually smell musty.
9. Before a snow, the air sounds deadened.
10. Weather prediction often becomes good guesswork.

Complete Verbs

A *complete* verb is one that sometimes stands alone or that is followed by an adverb, as in the following examples:

1. The bells <u>chimed</u>.
   The bells <u>chimed</u> loudly.

2. The crowd <u>vanished</u>.
   The crowd <u>vanished</u> quickly.

3. Raindrops <u>fell</u>.
   Raindrops <u>fell</u> outside the window.

   The added words are adverbs—*loudly, quickly, outside the window.*
   An *adverb* tells when, how or how much, or where about a verb or verb phrase.

When

Examples: The *Titanic* <u>immediately</u> became the finest ship afloat.
                Passengers <u>quickly</u> signed up for the maiden voyage.

When Adverbs

always	never	rarely	soon
eventually	now	recently	still
ever	occasionally	seldom	usually
frequently	often	sometimes	yet
immediately	quickly		

How or How Much

Had the ship been <u>carefully</u> designed for safety?

The builders were <u>absolutely</u> confident of the ship's seaworthiness.

How Adverbs

accurately	certainly	only	rather
actually	definitely	partially	really
almost	gradually	possibly	surely
also	lengthwise	probably	truly
carefully	not		

Where

Icebergs were drifting <u>ahead</u> in the ship's path.

Other ships were sailing <u>nearby</u>.

Where Adverbs

above	behind	forward	outside
ahead	below	here	there
away	beside	inside	underneath
backward	elsewhere	nearby	

Above, below, beside, inside, outside, and *underneath* also can be used as prepositions in adverbial phrases, where the phrases act as adverbs.

Examples: She hid <u>behind the post</u>.
He hid <u>underneath the bed</u>.
The plane flew <u>above the clouds</u>.

Adverbs can move around. An adverb telling about a verb can go almost anywhere, as long as it makes sense.
Next to a single-word verb:

Examples: Navigators <u>carefully</u> planned for the maiden voyage.
Navigators planned <u>carefully</u> for the maiden voyage.
Did navigators plan <u>carefully</u> for the maiden voyage?

Between verbs in a verb phrase:

Examples: Icebergs had <u>often</u> drifted into the shipping lanes.
Had icebergs <u>often</u> drifted into the shipping lanes?

Note: Remember, when an adverb is within a verb phrase, it still is an adverb. It is not part of the verb phrase.

Sometimes at the beginning or end of the sentence:

Examples: <u>Immediately</u> the ship was considered the world's finest.
The ship was considered the world's finest <u>immediately</u>.

For a *where* adverb, usually after the verb or verb phrase:

Examples: Investigators looked <u>everywhere</u> for survivors.
The ship was speeding <u>forward</u> in spite of the icebergs.

Skills Activity 6   **Finding Complete Verbs**

Read each sentence and find the verb or verb phrase. Decide where the adverb in parentheses makes sense in the sentence. (If it makes sense in more than one place, choose one.) On your own paper rewrite the sentence, putting in the adverb.

Example: The luxurious *Titanic* had begun her voyage. (triumphantly)
The luxurious *Titanic* had triumphantly begun her voyage.
or
The luxurious *Titanic* triumphantly had begun her voyage.
or
The luxurious *Titanic* had begun her voyage triumphantly.

1. World-famous people were making the voyage. (definitely)
2. People had questioned the safety of the ship. (never)
3. The vessel had been designed as "unsinkable." (faultlessly)
4. The ship was traveling through iceberg-filled waters. (actually)
5. A huge iceberg scraped the ship. (beside)
6. The iceberg was cutting into the ship like a can opener. (lengthwise)
7. Passengers ran for the lifeboats. (desperately)
8. Many of the boats had become stuck. (unfortunately)
9. The situation worsened for the next two hours. (steadily)
10. Then the unsinkable *Titanic* did sink. (quickly)

Skills Activity 7   **Adding Adverbs to Complete Verbs**

Read each sentence and find the verb or verb phrase. Think of an adverb to answer the question in parentheses. Then decide where the adverb makes sense in the sentence. Rewrite the sentence on your own paper, inserting the adverb.

Example: Crossing the Atlantic has been an adventure. (When?)
Crossing the Atlantic always has been an adventure.
or
Crossing the Atlantic often has been an adventure.

1. The early trans-Atlantic travelers drifted. (How?)
2. The trip could take several weeks. (When?)
3. Later the steamship took passengers to Europe. (How?)
4. The steamship trip would take several days. (When?)
5. Steamships could be elegant and luxurious. (How?)
6. Some of them seemed more like floating palaces. (How?)
7. However, they had become expensive. (How?)
8. Today only a few of them cross the sea. (When?)
9. A regular jet makes the crossing in seven hours. (When or how?)
10. A supersonic jet can make the trip in three hours. (When or how?)

Skill Test 1   **Distinguishing between the Four Verb Types**

Study each of the following sentences. Underline the main subject and the main verb of each sentence and tell whether it is *active, passive, linking,* or *complete.*

1. Usually governments add sales taxes onto goods.
2. Fog can move quickly across the water.
3. Properly frozen meats and vegetables taste perfectly fresh.
4. Each year the sky becomes more crowded with aircraft.
5. Lady Ashton was given a yacht for her birthday.
6. Sometimes they don't show up for appointments.
7. At that exact moment, the photographer snapped a picture of the eclipse.
8. Thin, melting ice on a lake appears discolored.
9. The price of coffee has risen dramatically during the winter.
10. The television set was stolen from right under our noses by a masked thief.

Skill Test 2   **Converting Passive Verbs into Active**

Study the following passive verb constructions in each sentence. Rewrite each sentence, turning the passive verb into an active one.

1. The goods normally are shipped by the company every Monday morning.
2. We were treated to a steak by our friends.
3. The game has been won by the green and white team.
4. The leader was considered outstanding by most of the people.

5. In a five-star restaurant, superb food always will be served by attentive and competent waiters.

6. Was Phillip injured by the falling tree?

7. I haven't been sent a letter by Stefanie in over a month.

8. You obviously were supported strongly by your admirers.

9. The name of the winner was revealed accidentally by the newspaper.

10. Your bid must be given before the end of the day.

Chapter 17

TROUBLESOME VERBS

Sometimes verbs can be very confusing, especially those verbs that change their form. This chapter gives a brief review of the most commonly used *irregular* verbs, as well as a group of verbs that often cause confusion.

Irregular Verbs

There are four principal parts most commonly used for a verb:

Present Tense

Today, I <u>bring</u> water.
Today, he/she/it <u>brings</u> water.

Past Tense

Yesterday, I <u>brought</u> water.

Present Participle

I am <u>bringing</u> water now.

Past Participle

I have <u>brought</u> water before.

Many students have trouble with the *past* form and the *past participle* form of irregular verbs. It is a good idea to study and learn them.

The best formula for testing the principal parts of a verb is to place the verb forms in the following pattern:

Present:

Today, I _____.
Today, he/she/it _____.

Past:

Yesterday, I _____.

Present Participle:

I am _____ now.

Past Participle:

I have _____ before.

225

Examples: Today, I <u>break</u> a glass. (present)
Today, he/she/it <u>breaks</u> a glass.

Yesterday, I <u>broke</u> a glass. (past)

I <u>am breaking</u> a glass now. (present participle)
I <u>have broken</u> a glass before. (past participle)

Study the following groups of irregular verbs:

Group A: *begin, blow, bring, burst, buy*

begin: begin, began, beginning, begun
Today, I begin a task.
Today, he/she/it begins a task.
Yesterday, I began a task.
I am beginning a task now.
I have begun a task before.

blow: blow, blew, blowing, blown
Today, I blow my trumpet.
Today he/she/it blows my trumpet.
Yesterday, I blew my trumpet.
I am blowing my trumpet now.
I have blown my trumpet before.

bring: bring, brought, bringing, brought
Today, I bring news.
Today, he/she/it brings news.
Yesterday, I brought news.
I am bringing news now.
I have brought news before.

burst: burst, burst, bursting, burst
Today, I burst a balloon.
Today, he/she/it bursts a balloon.
Yesterday, I burst a balloon.
I am bursting a balloon now.
I have burst a balloon before.

buy: buy, bought, buying, bought
Today, I buy stocks.
Today, he/she/it buys stocks.
Yesterday, I bought stocks.
I am buying stocks now.
I have bought stocks before.

Skills Activity 1 **Group A: *begin, blow, bring, burst, buy***

On a separate sheet of paper, write the correct form of the verb for each of the following sentences:

1. Yesterday, I (begun, began) school.
2. The wind has (blew, blown) for four days.
3. Has he (brung, brought) our newspaper?
4. I have (busted, burst) the bubbles in the bath.
5. I should have (buyed, bought) comic books a long time ago.
6. The show has just (began, begun).
7. Wait until the heat of the argument has (blowed, blown) over.
8. I (brang, brought) you a rose.
9. Many homes were flooded when the Morristown dam (bust, burst).
10. She (buy, buys) a lot of clothes.

Group B: *catch, choose, come, cost, do, drink*

catch: catch, caught, catching, caught
Today, I catch fish.
Today, he/she/it catches fish.
Yesterday, I caught fish.
I am catching fish now.
I have caught fish before.

choose: choose, chose, choosing, chosen
Today, I choose a book.
Today, he/she/it chooses a book.
Yesterday, I chose a book.
I am choosing a book now.
I have chosen a book before.

come: come, came, coming, come
Today, I come to your house.
Today, he/she/it comes to your house.
Yesterday, I came to your house.
I am coming to your house now.
I have come to your house before.

cost: cost, cost, costing, cost
Today, I cost a lot to feed.
Today, he/she/it costs a lot to feed.

Yesterday, I cost a lot to feed.

I am costing a lot now to feed.

I have cost a lot before to feed.

do: do, did, doing, done

Today, I do a good deed.

Today, he/she/it does a good deed.

Yesterday, I did a good deed.

I am doing a good deed now.

I have done a good deed before.

drink: drink, drank, drinking, drunk

Today, I drink water.

Today, he/she/it drinks water.

Yesterday, I drank water.

I am drinking water now.

I have drunk water before.

Skills Activity 2	**Group B: *catch, choose, come, cost, do, drink***

On your own paper, write the correct form of the verb for each of the following sentences:

1. I (catched, caught) a lot of mosquitoes last night.
2. Haven't you (chose, chosen) a seat yet?
3. Why haven't you (come, came) to deliver the pizza?
4. Have things always (cost, costed) so much?
5. Have you (did, done) all you can to improve?
6. I (drank, drunk) a lot of cider yesterday.
7. I (caught, catched) the ball when he threw it to me.
8. Ralph (choosed, chose) a new car today.
9. The mail carrier has not (came, come) to leave the mail.
10. Rosita has (did, done) a great deal for charity.

Group C: *drive, eat, fall, feel, fly*

drive: drive, drove, driving, driven

Today, I drive a car.

Today, he/she/it drives a car.

Yesterday, I drove a car.

I am driving a car now.

I have driven a car before.

eat: eat, ate, eating, eaten

Today, I eat my food.

Today, he/she/it eats my food.

Yesterday, I ate my food.

I am eating my food now.

I have eaten my food before.

fall: fall, fell, falling, fallen

Today, I fall in love.

Today, he/she/it falls in love.

Yesterday, I fell in love.

I am falling in love now.

I have fallen in love before.

feel: feel, felt, feeling, felt

Today, I feel good.

Today, he/she/it feels good.

Yesterday, I felt good.

I am feeling good now.

I have felt good before.

fly: fly, flew, flying, flown

Today, I fly my plane.

Today, he/she/it flies my plane.

Yesterday, I flew my plane.

I am flying my plane now.

I have flown my plane before.

Skills Activity 3   **Group C: *drive, eat, fall, feel, fly***

On a separate sheet of paper, write the correct form of the verb for each of the following sentences:

1. I (drived, drove) a tractor yesterday.
2. Have the three of you (ate, eaten) yet?
3. Max has (falled, fallen) on hard times.
4. I haven't (feeled, felt) so good in years.
5. People have (flied, flown) airplanes for more than seventy years.
6. I have (driven, drove) cattle in Wyoming.
7. I already (eat, ate) my dinner before I came.
8. Sherri has (fell, fallen) and broken her arm.
9. Bill has (feeled, felt) that the plan is not a good one.
10. We have (flied, flown) as high as the moon.

Group D: *freeze, give, go, grow, know*

freeze: freeze, froze, freezing, frozen
Today, I freeze the vegetables.
Today, he/she/it freezes the vegetables.
Yesterday, I froze the vegetables.
I am freezing the vegetables now.
I have frozen the vegetables before.

give: give, gave, giving, given
Today, I give a gift.
Today, he/she/it gives a gift.
Yesterday, I gave a gift.
I am giving a gift now.
I have given a gift before.

go: go, went, going, gone
Today, I go to the movies.
Today, he/she/it goes to the movies.
Yesterday, I went to the movies.
I am going to the movies now.
I have gone to the movies before.

grow: grow, grew, growing, grown
Today, I grow more patient.
Today, he/she/it grows more patient.
Yesterday, I grew more patient.
I am growing more patient now.
I have grown more patient before.

know: know, knew, knowing, known
Today, I know better.
Today, he/she/it knows better.
Yesterday, I knew better.
I am knowing better now.
I have known better before.

Skills Activity 4   **Group D: *freeze, give, go, grow, know***

On a separate sheet of paper, write the correct form of the verb for each of the following sentences:

1. I think the lake has (froze, frozen) over.
2. Had you (gave, given) any thought to a vacation?
3. I believe Marlon has (went, gone) home.

4. I (growed, grew) corn in the garden last year.
5. If I had (knowed, known) the danger, I would not have gone there.
6. We almost (freezed, froze) in the cold apartment.
7. Last Tuesday, I (give, gave) a speech.
8. The snow has melted and (went, gone) away.
9. It seems that you have (growed, grown) two inches this summer.
10. Jason (knowed, knew) Alex when he was a little boy.

Group E: *lead, lend, lie, lose, make, put*

lead: lead, led, leading, led
Today, I lead the class.
Today, he/she/it leads the class.
Yesterday, I led the class.
I am leading the class now.
I have led the class before.

lend: lend, lent, lending, lent
Today, I lend a hand.
Today, he/she/it lends a hand.
Yesterday, I lent a hand.
I am lending a hand now.
I have lent a hand before.

lie: lie, lay, lying, lain
Today, I lie in bed.
Today, he/she/it lies in bed.
Yesterday, I lay in bed.
I am lying in bed now.
I have lain in bed before.

lose: lose, lost, losing, lost
Today, I lose the game.
Today, he/she/it loses the game.
Yesterday, I lost the game.
I am losing the game now.
I have lost the game before.

make: make, made, making, made
Today, I make an impression.
Today, he/she/it makes an impression.

Yesterday, I made an impression.

I am making an impression now.

I have made an impression before.

put: put, put, putting, put

Today, I put a nickel in the slot.

Today, he/she/it puts a nickel in the slot.

Yesterday, I put a nickel in the slot.

I am putting a nickel in the slot now.

I have put a nickel in the slot before.

Skills Activity 5   **Group E: *lead, lend, lie, lose, make, put***

On your own paper, write the correct form of the verb for each of the following sentences:

1. Joe (lead, led) the class in spelling last week.
2. I (lended, lent) my sister five dollars.
3. Here (lays, lies) Whiskers, resting in peace.
4. I (lost, losed) my watch at the movies.
5. Has Antonio (maked, made) the salad?
6. Last year I (put, putted) a lot of money in stocks.
7. She is (leading, leads) the team in base hits.
8. Maria (lent, lended) her support to the candidate.
9. Jessica has (laid, lain) on the beach for four hours.
10. Alonzo has not (maked, made) any progress with his algebra.

Group F: *ride, ring, rise, run, say*

ride: ride, rode, riding, ridden

Today, I ride a horse.

Today, he/she/it rides a horse.

Yesterday, I rode a horse.

I am riding a horse now.

I have ridden a horse before.

ring: ring, rang, ringing, rung

Today, I ring the bell.

Today, he/she/it rings the bell.

Yesterday, I rang the bell.

I am ringing the bell now.

I have rung the bell before.

rise: rise, rose, rising, risen
Today, I rise early.
Today, he/she/it rises early.
Yesterday, I rose early.
I am rising early now.
I have risen early before.

run: run, ran, running, run
Today, I run the race.
Today, he/she/it runs the race.
Yesterday, I ran the race.
I am running the race now.
I have run the race before.

say: say, said, saying, said
Today, I say my poem.
Today, he/she/it says my poem.
Yesterday, I said my poem.
I am saying my poem now.
I have said my poem before.

Skills Activity 6	**Group F:** *ride, ring, rise, run, say*

On a separate sheet of paper, write the correct form of the verb for each of the following sentences:

1. Have you (rode, ridden) a wild mustang?
2. Has the bell (rung, rang) yet?
3. Have you (rose, risen) early often?
4. Has Mark (ran, run) for office before?
5. I (says, said) what I thought to the referee.
6. I (rode, rid) the range for five years.
7. The salesperson has (rang, rung) the doorbell.
8. The sun (rose, rised) before 6 A.M.
9. Have you often (ran, run) from an argument?
10. What did you (say, said) to him?

Group G: *see, set, shrink, sing, sit*

see: see, saw, seeing, seen
Today, I see the sun.
Today, he/she/it sees the sun.

Yesterday, I saw the sun.

I am seeing the sun now.

I have seen the sun before.

set: set, set, setting, set

Today, I set my goals.

Today, he/she/it sets my goals.

Yesterday, I set my goals.

I am setting my goals now.

I have set my goals before.

shrink: shrink, shrank, shrinking, shrunk

Today, I shrink my jeans.

Today, he/she/it shrinks my jeans.

Yesterday, I shrank my jeans.

I am shrinking my jeans now.

I have shrunk my jeans before.

sing: sing, sang, singing, sung

Today, I sing a ballad.

Today, he/she/it sings a ballad.

Yesterday, I sang a ballad.

I am singing a ballad now.

I have sung a ballad before.

sit: sit, sat, sitting, sat

Today, I sit at my desk.

Today, he/she/it sits at my desk.

Yesterday, I sat at my desk.

I am sitting at my desk now.

I have sat at my desk before.

Skills Activity 7   **Group G: *see, set, shrink, sing, sit***

On your own paper, write the correct form of the verb for each of
the following sentences:

1. I (saw, seen) you going to the store.
2. I have (sat, set) twenty tomato plants in the garden.
3. Have you ever (shrank, shrunk) a dress in the wash?
4. At the party, Corrine (sang, sung) "Jambalaya."
5. Please (set, sit) the book on that table.
6. Mary has (saw, seen) eight movies this month.

7. Jim never (shrinked, shrank) from a challenge.
8. I have (sang, sung) all the verses.
9. I (set, sat) and waited for you for an hour.
10. Charlie just (sat, set) quietly and said nothing.

Group H: *speak, steal, swim, take, teach*

speak: speak, spoke, speaking, spoken
Today, I speak to the group.
Today, he/she/it speaks to the group.
Yesterday, I spoke to the group.
I am speaking to the group now.
I have spoken to the group before.

steal: steal, stole, stealing, stolen
Today, I steal a nap.
Today, he/she/it steals a nap.
Yesterday, I stole a nap.
I am stealing a nap now.
I have stolen a nap before.

swim: swim, swam, swimming, swum
Today, I swim in the pond.
Today, he/she/it swims in the pond.
Yesterday, I swam in the pond.
I am swimming in the pond now.
I have swum in the pond before.

take: take, took, taking, taken
Today, I take a bath.
Today, he/she/it takes a bath.
Yesterday, I took a bath.
I am taking a bath now.
I have taken a bath before.

teach: teach, taught, teaching, taught
Today, I teach school.
Today, he/she/it teaches school.
Yesterday, I taught school.
I am teaching school today.
I have taught school before.

Skills Activity 8   **Group H: *speak, steal, swim, take, teach***

On your own paper, write the correct form of the verb for each of the following sentences:

1. Leon has not (spoke, spoken) to me for two days.
2. Has somebody (stealed, stolen) my watch?
3. Larry (swum, swam) in the pool yesterday.
4. Saul has (tooken, taken) an interest in golf.
5. Mr. Giovanni (teached, taught) us well.
6. She (speaked, spoke) sharply to me.
7. The cat (stealed, stole) the piece of meat from the table.
8. The instructor has (swam, swum) twenty lengths.
9. The plane (took, taked) off two hours ago.
10. The coach (taught, teached) the players basic skills.

Group I: *tear, think, throw, wear, write*

tear: tear, tore, tearing, torn
Today, I tear my fort down.
Today, he/she/it tears my fort down.
Yesterday, I tore my fort down.
I am tearing my fort down now.
I have torn my fort down before.

think: think, thought, thinking, thought
Today, I think clearly.
Today, he/she/it thinks clearly.
Yesterday, I thought clearly.
I am thinking clearly today.
I have thought clearly before.

throw: throw, threw, throwing, thrown
Today, I throw my football.
Today, he/she/it throws my football.
Yesterday, I threw my football.
I am throwing my football now.
I have thrown my football before.

wear: wear, wore, wearing, worn
Today, I wear my ring.
Today, he/she/it wears my ring.

Yesterday, I wore my ring.

I am wearing my ring now.

I have worn my ring before.

write: write, wrote, writing, written

Today, I write a paper.

Today, he/she/it writes a paper.

Yesterday, I wrote a paper.

I am writing a paper now.

I have written a paper before.

Skills Activity 9   **Group I: *tear, think, throw, wear, write***

On a separate sheet of paper, write the correct form of the verb for each of the following sentences:

1. The dog has (teared, torn) up my paper.
2. Carmen (thinked, thought) you were coming to dinner.
3. Joan has not (throwed, thrown) a football for a long time.
4. Haven't you (wore, worn) that jacket before?
5. You have (wrote, written) a good story.
6. He (tore, teared) into the parking lot on his motorcycle.
7. I (thought, thunk) you were coming with us.
8. The batter was (throwed, thrown) out at third base.
9. I have (worn, wore) myself out by running too far.
10. Dominic is (writing, written) an essay on John Smith.

Confusing Verbs

may/can

Definition: ***May* is a verb that expresses permission to do something or "suggests possibility."**

Examples: You <u>may</u> go to the movies. (permission)
The sun <u>may</u> shine today. (possibility)
Bill <u>may</u> attend the game if he wishes. (permission)

Might is another form of *may.*

Example: You <u>might</u> win the race, if you have luck with you. (possibility)

Definition: ***Can* indicates the "ability to do something."**

Examples: I <u>can</u> climb Mount Everest.
                 I am sure you <u>can</u> win the race.

                 Could is another form of *can.*

Example: I <u>could</u> win the race if I tried.

                 May (might) and *can (could)* frequently are confused by students.

                 Wrong: <u>Can</u> I have this dance? (It should be <u>may</u>.)

                 Right: <u>May</u> I have this dance? (permission)

                 May, might, can, and *could* usually are helping verbs.

Skills Activity 10   ***may/can***

Write the correct verb form for the following sentences on your paper:

1. Steve is happy that he (can, may) play the trumpet well.
2. You (may, can) want to see the movie at the Esquire.
3. You (can, may) start eating now.
4. It is uncertain, but I (might, could) join you later.
5. I knew you (could, might) do it if you tried hard enough.
6. (Can, May) I please be excused?
7. You (can, may) not go to bed later than ten o'clock.
8. Will I win? I (might, could) and I (might, could) not.
9. I (might, could) not bear to see the horses abused.
10. I (can, may) cook well enough to prepare a meal. (May, Can) you?

---

let/leave

Definitions: ***Let*** **means to allow permission to do something.** ***Leave*** **means "to depart or go away from" or "to let something remain in place."**

Examples: <u>Let</u> Olga go with us to the park. (permission)
                 Please <u>let</u> me go! (permission)
                 <u>Leave</u> the dog alone. (remain in place)
                 Shall we <u>leave</u> the party now? (depart)

                 let: let, let, letting, let
                 Today, I let my bird go free.

Today, he/she/it lets my bird go free.

Yesterday, I let my bird go free.

I am letting my bird go free now.

I have let my bird go free before.

leave: leave, left, leaving, left

Today, I leave for Brazil.

Today, he/she/it leaves for Brazil.

Yesterday, I left for Brazil.

I am leaving for Brazil now.

I have left for Brazil before.

Skills Activity 11   ***let/leave***

Write the correct verb form for the following sentences on your paper:

1. I wish the principal would (leave, let) the students go early.
2. I will (leave, let) my cat stay at your house for the weekend.
3. Has Barbara (let, left) the restaurant yet?
4. Mrs. Marcus is going to (leave, let) Sam have another chance.
5. "(Let, Leave) me alone," said Tommy.

lie/lay

Definitions: **Lie is a verb that can mean "at rest" or "in a prone position." Lay can mean "to put or to set down." Students frequently confuse these forms.**

Here are the correct forms of *lie:*

You <u>lie</u> down and get some sleep right now!

Yesterday, Sarah <u>lay</u> down and slept for four hours.

The dogs <u>are lying</u> outside by the fence.

The travelers <u>have lain</u> in bed all morning.

Here are the correct forms of *lay:*

I want Billy to <u>lay</u> the plates on the table immediately.

Mary <u>laid</u> the cards on the table last night for the players.

The teacher <u>is laying</u> the dictionaries on the desks for the students.

Henry <u>has laid</u> the tennis balls on the court to dry out.

Here are the present and past forms of each verb:

lie:

Present

Today, I lie down.   Today, we lie down.

Today, you lie down.   Today, you lie down.

Today, he/she/it lies down.   Today, they lie down.

Past

Yesterday, I lay down.   Yesterday, we lay down.

Yesterday, you lay down.   Yesterday, you lay down.

Yesterday, he/she/it lay down.   Yesterday, they lay down.

lay:

Present

Today, I lay the rocks in the garden.   Today, we lay the rocks in the garden.

Today, you lay the rocks in the garden.   Today, you lay the rocks in the garden.

Today, he/she/it lays the rocks in the garden.   Today, they lay the rocks in the garden.

Past

Yesterday, I laid the rocks in the garden.   Yesterday, we laid the rocks in the garden.

Yesterday, you laid the rocks in the garden. Yesterday, you laid the rocks in the garden.

Yesterday, he/she/it laid the rocks in the garden.   Yesterday, they laid the rocks in the garden.

Skills Activity 12   *lie/lay*

On a separate sheet of paper, write the proper form of *lie* or *lay* in the following sentences:

1. _____ down and take a nap before you go to the show.
2. _____ the silverware on the dining room table.
3. I _____ down last evening and slept for an hour before dinner.
4. I have _____ on the beach for three hours without getting sunburned.
5. Have you _____ the stones for your patio yet?
6. You _____ the nets on the dock to dry out.
7. We _____ on the deck of the boat yesterday morning, listening to the waves.
8. Why don't we _____ on the lawn and watch the eclipse of the moon?
9. The dogs are _____ in the backyard asleep.
10. The workers are _____ concrete for the new sidewalk.

rise/raise

Definition: ***Rise* means to "assume a standing position" or "to go from a lower to a higher level."**

Examples: Let us <u>rise</u> early tomorrow. (stand)
He watched the sun <u>rise</u> over the hills. (higher level)

Definition: ***Raise* means "to cause something to move upward."**

Examples: He <u>raised</u> his hand in class.
She <u>raised</u> the blind and let in the sunshine.

rise: rise, rose, rising, risen	**raise:** raise, raised, raising, raised
Today, I rise early.	Today, I raise the flag.
Today, he/she/it rises early.	Today, he/she/it raises the flag.
Yesterday, I rose early.	Yesterday, I raised the flag.
I am rising early now.	I am raising the flag now.
I have risen early before.	I have raised the flag before.

Skills Activity 13   ***rise/raise***

Write the correct verb form for the following sentences on your paper:

1. He (rose, raised) his head when he woke up.
2. Melinda (raised, rose) from her chair and walked out.
3. The moon (raised, rose) at seven o'clock last night.
4. I hope my boss will (rise, raise) my salary next week.
5. Has the sun (raised, risen) yet?
6. Henry (rose, raised) his voice to call his dog.
7. When will the curtain (raise, rise) for the play to begin?
8. John, will you (raise, rise) the curtain at eight o'clock?
9. The audience has (raised, risen) and is leaving the theater.
10. A mist is (raising, rising) over the lake.

set/sit

Definition: ***Sit* means "to be seated, resting on your hindquarters with your torso upright."**

Example: I think I'll <u>sit</u> in that chair.

Definition: *Set* **means "to place or put something somewhere."**

Example: I will <u>set</u> the plates on the table.

sit: sit, sat, sitting, sat
Today, I sit on the bench.
Today, he/she/it sits on the bench.
Yesterday, I sat on the bench.
I am sitting on the bench now.
I have sat on the bench before.

set: set, set, setting, set
Today, I set the trap.
Today, he/she/it sets the trap.
Yesterday, I set the trap.
I am setting the trap now.
I have set the trap before.

Skills Activity 14   *set/sit*

Write the correct verb form for each of the following sentences on your paper:

1. Will you (set, sit) with me at the movies?
2. Rosa, (set, sit) the plant on the table.
3. You must (set, sit) still at the award ceremony.
4. We must (set, sit) the tomato plants in neat rows.
5. I have (set, sat) in the moonlight for two hours, waiting for you.
6. Angela has (set, sat) up all night in the dark.
7. Desmond has (set, sat) up all the chairs for the game.
8. Has Emily been (setting, sitting) in her room all day?
9. Will Mikhail (set, sit) the milk bottles on the kitchen table?
10. Many great Americans have (set, sat) on the Supreme Court Bench.

---

teach/learn

Definition: *Learn* **means to "receive knowledge from teaching or experience."**

Example: I <u>learned</u> a new word in school yesterday.

Definition: *Teach* **means "to give instruction to someone or something."**

Examples: I <u>taught</u> a new word to the class yesterday.
Susan is <u>learning</u> poetry from José.
Lenny <u>teaches</u> English composition to freshmen at Indiana University.

You usually "learn from experience or instruction" and you "teach something to a person or a group."

teach: teach, taught, teaching, taught

I teach Spanish today.

Today, he/she/it teaches Spanish.

Yesterday, I taught Spanish.

I am teaching Spanish now.

I have taught Spanish before.

learn: learn, learned, learning, learned

I learn to sew today.

Today, he/she/it learns to sew.

Yesterday, I learned to sew.

I am learning to sew now.

I have learned to sew before.

Skills Activity 15   *teach/learn*

On a separate sheet of paper, write the correct verb for each of the following sentences:

1. Will you (learn, teach) me how to skate?
2. I want to (learn, teach) how to skate from you.
3. He has (taught, learned) the scales of the piano from Mr. Lopez.
4. Sally (taught, learned) Japanese by living in Yokohama for a year.
5. Lupe (learned, taught) how to draw through practicing a lot.
6. Will you never (learn, teach) to say "please" when you want something?
7. You can't (learn, teach) an old dog new tricks easily.
8. I want to (learn, teach) a new song from that musical.
9. (Teaching, Learning) to play tennis well demands a good teacher.
10. Many have (taught, learned) a great deal of information from doing homework.

Forms of *be*

Be is a special verb. It is used frequently in English in a variety of ways. In the present tense (where *the action* or *the state of being* is in the present), *be* has three forms, *am, is,* and *are.*

Examples: I <u>am</u> going to the movies.
You <u>are</u> going to the movies.
He/she/it <u>is</u> going to the movies.
We <u>are</u> going to the movies.
You <u>are</u> going to the movies.
They <u>are</u> going to the movies.

In each of these examples, the form of *be* is a *helping verb.*

Examples: I <u>am</u> here to see Henry.
You <u>are</u> here to see Henry.
He (she or it) <u>is</u> here to see Henry.
We <u>are</u> here to see Henry.
You <u>are</u> here to see Henry.
They <u>are</u> here to see Henry.

In each of these examples, *be* is a verb by itself—a *state of being* verb.

In the past tense (where the *action* or *state of being* has happened in the past), *be* has two forms, *was* and *were.*

Examples: I <u>was</u> here to see Henry.   We <u>were</u> here to see Henry.
You <u>were</u> here to see Henry.   You <u>were</u> here to see Henry.
He/she/it <u>was</u> here to see Henry. They <u>were</u> here to see Henry.

In the future tense (where the *action* or *state of being* is in a future time), the forms of *be* are *shall be* and *will be.*

Examples: I <u>shall be</u> here to see Henry.   We <u>shall be</u> here to see Henry.
You <u>will be</u> here to see Henry.   You <u>will be</u> here to see Henry.
He/she/it <u>will be</u> here to see Henry. They <u>will be</u> here to see Henry.

Singular and Plural Forms of *be*

Definition: **In writing, *singular* indicates one thing or one person.**

Examples: I am a carpenter. The house is a wreck. (singular)

Definition: ***Plural* indicates more than one thing or person.**

Examples: We both are carpenters. The houses are wrecks. (plural)

Rule: **A singular subject uses a singular verb form. A plural subject uses a plural verb form.**

be

Present Singular	Past Singular	Future Singular
I am	I was	I shall be
You are	You were	You will be
He/she/it is	He/she/it was	He/she/it will be

Present Plural	Past Plural	Future Plural
We are	We were	We shall be
You are	You were	You will be
They are	They were	They will be

Skills Activity 16   **Forms of *be***

On a separate sheet of paper, write the correct form of *be* for each of the following sentences:

1. _____ you people going to the movies tonight?
   (present)

2. I _____ hurrying to lunch when you called.
   (past)

3. We _____ happy that Leonardo got a promotion.
   (present)

4. _____ you really pleased with the movie?
   (past)

5. Where ___ Rosa and Pepe going to eat dinner after the show?
   (present)

6. You _____ _____ getting a card from me.
   (future)

7. I _____ _____ happy to come to your birthday party.
   (future)

8. _____ Henry and Amy supposed to be here for the ceremony?
   (past)

9. You _____ out when I called.
   (past)

10. Mario, Carla, and Eric _____ there when the accident happened.   (past)

Skill Test 1   **Irregular Verbs**

Write the correct form of the verb for these sentences:

1. Did you (brang, bring) the sandwiches?
2. The water balloon (burst, busted) on his head.
3. I (caught, catched) a firefly last night.
4. I (come, came) home early yesterday.
5. Have you (done, did) your chores?
6. The horses have (drunk, drinked) all the water in the trough.
7. I'm afraid they (drived, drove) too fast.
8. Have you (ate, eaten) all of the pizza?
9. The air (feel, feels) hot and sticky today.
10. Have you (given, gave) the tennis balls to my sister?
11. I believe Kelly has (gone, went) to the movies.
12. My mother (grew, growed) tomatoes in the garden this year.
13. The water in the pond (freezed, froze) quickly.
14. He (lost, losed) the key to his bicycle lock.
15. This year I (putted, put) a lot of effort into my school work.
16. She (made, maked) the team.
17. They (buyed, bought) a lot of hot dogs for the picnic.
18. They (chose, choosed) a team leader.
19. The band (led, lead) the parade.
20. Nancy has (laid, lain) in the sun for two hours.
21. Have you (rode, ridden) in their new car?
22. Has the warning bell (rang, rung) yet?
23. Did the fog (rose, rise) from the meadow?
24. The race horse has (runned, run) his last race.
25. What did Mark (said, say) to the teacher?
26. He (set, setted) out the plants in the garden.
27. The shirt (shrank, shrinked) in the wash.
28. They (sang, singed) songs around the camp fire.
29. I have been (sitting, setting) by the telephone all evening.
30. The dog (spoke, speaked) on the command of its owner.
31. The monkey (stole, stealed) a banana from the table.
32. That child has (swam, swum) the length of the pool.
33. The students (took, taked) their books back to the library.
34. The older children (teached, taught) the younger children how to catch the ball.
35. The wind has (torn, teared) some branches from the trees.
36. The players (thought, thinked) the umpire was wrong.

37. The catcher (throwed, threw) the ball to first base.

38. I am (wore, worn) out from too much work.

39. Have you (written, wrote) to your grandmother lately?

40. I (seen, saw) you at the movies.

Skill Test 2   **Confusing Verbs**

Choose the correct form of the verb in these sentences:

1. (Can, May) I go to the beach?
2. I am happy that I (can, may) play the piano well.
3. The coach is going to (let, leave) Steve have another chance.
4. Will you (leave, let) me alone!
5. You should (lay, lie) down and take a nap before the game.
6. Did you (lie, lay) the book on the table?
7. The teacher (rised, raised) the window shade.
8. The sun (rose, rised) before 6 A.M.
9. Will you (sit, set) beside me on the bus?
10. Ramon, please (set, sit) the dishes on the table.
11. Will you (learn, teach) me how to play the piano?
12. He (taught, teached) his brother how to play ball.
13. He (is, be) my best friend.
14. (Are, Be) you going to the beach today?
15. You (were, was) gone when I came to your house.
16. We (was, were) happy to hear your good news.
17. You (were, will be) getting a letter from me.
18. I (was, were) in a hurry when you called.
19. Lisa and Mikhail (were, was) late.
20. (Was, Were) you pleased with the gift?

Chapter 18

USING CORRECT PRONOUNS

Nominative and Objective Pronouns

Definition: A *pronoun* is a word that takes the place of a noun. The case form of the pronoun shows the function of the pronoun in the sentence. The following pronouns are in one of two cases—nominative or objective. We will call nominative pronouns "subject-type" pronouns. We will call objective pronouns "object-type" pronouns.

Nominative (subject-type) pronouns:

I   you   he   she   it   we   they

Objective (object-type) pronouns:

me   you   him   her   it   us   them

Study the following sentences:

1. Queen Victoria was a great monarch.
2. <u>She</u> ruled longer than any other queen of England.
3. Several plays have been written about <u>her</u>.

<u>She</u>—the personal pronoun in the second sentence—is the subject of the sentence. It replaces <u>Queen Victoria</u> and refers to her.

Definition: A personal pronoun takes the place of a noun. The noun it replaces is called the *antecedent.*

The pronoun in sentence 2 is <u>she</u>. The pronoun in sentence 3 is <u>her</u>. <u>Queen Victoria</u> is the *antecedent* for both pronouns, because they both refer to <u>Queen Victoria</u>.

Examples:

(antecedent)   *(pronoun)*
1. <u>Harley Johnson</u> is my name.   <u>I</u> am a stone mason.

(antecedent)   *(pronoun)*
2. <u>Harley Johnson</u> is your name?   <u>You</u> knew my father.

(antecedent)   *(pronoun)*

3. <u>Your father</u> worked with stone.   <u>He</u> was a fine cutter.

(antecedent)   *(pronoun)*

4. <u>My mother</u> was an artist.   <u>She</u> painted watercolors.

(antecedent)   *(pronoun)*

5. <u>Our house</u> was in Bedford.   <u>It</u> overlooked a lake.

(antecedent)   *(pronoun)*

6. <u>My brother and I</u> loved the lake.   <u>We</u> would often swim there.

Whenever you see a pronoun, ask *who* or *what* it refers to. The answer will be the noun that is the antecedent.

If a person or a group of people, including yourself, is speaking, the antecedent is the speaker and *I* or *we* is used. If *me* or *us* is used in a command or request, the speaker is the antecedent.

Examples: <u>I</u> am going to the movie. (speaker is the antecedent)
<u>We</u> are going to a play. (speaker is the antecedent)
Give <u>me</u> a dime. (speaker is the antecedent)
Lend <u>us</u> a dollar. (speaker is the antecedent)

Rule: **The number (singular or plural) of the antecedent should agree with the number of the personal pronoun.**

                  antecedent   *pronoun*
Examples: <u>My brother and I</u> were born on June 12.   My parents gave <u>us</u> a party.

                  antecedent   *pronoun*
            <u>Graduation day</u> was great.   <u>It</u> was sunny and pleasant.

Note: Subject-type pronouns usually are in the subject position or the predicate noun position. Object-type pronouns usually are objects of the verb or a preposition.

Skills Activity 1   **Using Correct Pronouns**

Select the correct pronoun in each of the following sentence pairs. Write it on your paper.

1. *Amadeus* is a wonderful play about Mozart. I saw (it, them) on Broadway.
2. Charlie and I are friends. (Me and Charlie, Charlie and I) see a play each week.
3. The two of us go to the movies a lot. (We, Us) liked the computer animation used in *Toy Story*.
4. My sister Sally goes with us sometimes. (Her, She) is fun to be with.

5. Sally sometimes brings Benita along. (Her and Benita, Benita and she) are a good pair.

6. Dominic won the tennis match fairly. Give the prize money to (he, him).

7. I know we disagree frequently. (Between you and I, Between you and me) I am right most of the time.

8. All of the kids in the next block like to play soccer. Let's challenge (they, them).

9. The Wright brothers invented the airplane. (They, Them) will be remembered for a long time.

10. Tiffany and I have never been to Wrigley Field. We probably will visit (it, them) someday.

Possessive Pronouns

Definition: *Possessive pronouns* **indicate ownership by one or more than one person. The following possessive pronouns can be used before nouns:**

my   your   his   her   its   our   their

Examples:

I have <u>my</u> food.	The dog has <u>its</u> food.
Do you have <u>your</u> food?	We have <u>our</u> food.
He has <u>his</u> food.	They have <u>their</u> food.
She has <u>her</u> food.	

These possessive pronouns can be used alone in sentences: *mine, yours, his, her, its, ours, theirs.*

Examples:

The food is <u>mine</u>.	The food is <u>its</u>. (this form is rare)
The food is <u>yours</u>.	The food is <u>ours</u>.
The food is <u>his</u>.	The food is <u>theirs</u>.
The food is <u>hers</u>.	

Skills Activity 2   Using Possessive Pronouns

On a separate sheet of paper, write the possessive pronoun in each of the following sentences:

1. Every dog has its day.

2. My daughter likes her teacher very much.

3. We should receive our tax return soon.

4. That seat in the back is mine.

5. I have my theater ticket.

6. Do you have yours?

7. All the students passed their exams today.
8. Did you borrow his pencil yesterday?
9. Pass the carrots, and you eat hers if she does not want any.
10. All the land beyond the street is ours.

Indefinite Pronouns

Definition: *Indefinite pronouns* do not refer to definite antecedents. They do not indicate definite people, animals, or things.

Singular Indefinite Pronouns

another	each	neither	somebody
any	either	nobody	someone
anybody	everybody	none	something
anyone	everyone	nothing	one
anything	everything		

Rule: Use the possessive pronouns *its, his,* and *her* with singular indefinite pronouns, since they refer to one person, animal, or thing.

Examples: Would <u>everyone</u> please take <u>his</u> or <u>her</u> seat?
<u>Each</u> of the girls has <u>her</u> backpack.
Give either <u>Rosa</u> or <u>Maria</u> the book.
Neither <u>Darnell</u> nor <u>John</u> has <u>his</u> pencil.
<u>Nobody</u> has a right to mistreat <u>his</u> or <u>her</u> pet.

The combination *his or her* avoids a bias toward either gender. When referring to a group including males and females, use it. Years ago, *his* was used to include both males and females in a group, but times have changed and the suggestion of sexism is unacceptable.

Plural Indefinite Pronouns

all	most	others	none
both	few	some	many
several	such		

Rule: Plural indefinite pronouns refer to more than one person, animal, or thing. Use the possessive pronoun *their* with these pronouns.

Examples: Many of the students forgot their pencils.
All of the tennis players had their rackets.
Most of the cooks brought their own recipes.
Both forgot their lines.

Several of the cyclists polished their bikes.
Many students kept their mouths shut.
Others voiced their objections to the assignment.
Some like their classes in the morning.
Others like their classes in the afternoon.
Many left their notebooks in the lockers.
Few would want to insult their best friends.

Rule: *Some, all,* and *none* **can be either plural or singular.**

Examples: Some of the cake is left. (singular)
Some of the students are unhappy. (plural)
None of the players cried when they lost. (plural)
None of the demolished building is standing. (singular)
All of the policemen were on duty. (plural)
All of the garden is planted. (singular)

Skills Activity 3   **Using Indefinite Pronouns**

On a separate sheet of paper, write the correct indefinite pronoun in these sentences:

1. Everyone has a right to say what (they, he or she) thinks.
2. Each summer, each bird builds (its, their) nest.
3. Some hide (its, their) nests in the branches.
4. Somebody left (his or her, their) dirty tray in the cafeteria.
5. Something has left (its, their) stain on your dress.
6. Few could do (his or her, their) best on the rainy track.
7. Many of the runners lost (his, their) tempers because of the heat.
8. Neither of the boys ran (his, their) best time in the race.
9. Anything worth doing has (its, their) reward.
10. Did everybody bring (his or her, their) swimming gear?
11. Everything has (its, their) place in the universe.
12. Nobody had a chance to say (his or her, their) lines.
13. None of the politicians at the rally satisfied (his or her, their) listeners.
14. No one with brains puts (his or her, their) safety in the hands of a drunk driver.
15. All were pleased with (their, his or her) prizes at the party.
16. Most find (his or her, their) work rewarding if it is interesting.
17. All the class went skating, and I was glad to see such a crowd enjoying (his or her, their) outing.
18. Nothing has (its, their) reward if no one cares about it.
19. One likes to spend (his or her, their) time wisely in this school.
20. Any can enter (his or her, their) project in the science fair.

Reflexive Pronouns

The following words are *reflexive pronouns:*

myself	yourselves	herself	ourselves
yourself	himself	itself	themselves

Definition: **A reflexive pronoun usually refers to a noun or another pronoun in the same sentence.**

Examples: He likes to carve the turkey <u>himself</u>.
Generally, we like to entertain <u>ourselves</u>.

Skills Activity 4   **Using Reflexive Pronouns**

On your own paper, write the reflexive pronouns in the following sentences:

1. I would rather do my homework myself.
2. Are you ever afraid to stay by yourself at night?
3. He always has to satisfy himself that he is right.
4. If she had graded the paper, she would have given herself an *A*.
5. The spider caught itself in its own web.
6. Give yourselves a break and see a movie tonight.
7. We make a lot of trouble for ourselves by not planning our time.
8. The politicians voted themselves a raise.
9. Help yourself when no one else will.
10. The dog hid itself under the table.

Interrogative Pronouns

The following words can be *interrogative pronouns:*

what	which	who	whom	whose

Definition: **The word *interrogative* indicates a question. Interrogative pronouns usually appear at the beginning of a question.**

Examples: <u>Who</u> is knocking at the door?
<u>What</u> is the matter with you?

Skills Activity 5   **Using Interrogative Pronouns**

On a separate sheet of paper, write the interrogative pronoun in each of the following sentences:

1. Who won the tennis match?
2. Whom did you want to see?
3. Which dress did you choose for the party?
4. Whose glass is this on the table?
5. What will you want for dinner?

Who and *Whom*

Rule: ***Who* and *whom* can cause confusion. *Who* always is the subject of the verb.**

Examples: <u>Who</u> is your teacher this year?
<u>Who</u> is staring at us?

Rule: ***Whom* always is an object of a verb or a preposition.**

Examples: <u>Whom</u> did you vote for in the election?
(Turned around, it equals, "You did vote for whom?")

To <u>whom</u> was the prize awarded?
(Turned around, it equals, "The prize was awarded to whom?") In both cases, *whom* is the object of a preposition.

Skills Activity 6   **Choosing *Who* or *Whom***

Select the correct interrogative pronoun in the following sentences:

1. (Who, Whom) was that on the phone?
2. (Who, Whom) were you talking to in the library?
3. (Who, Whom) was the 18th president of the United States?
4. To what or to (who, whom) would you assign the blame for the accident?
5. (Who, Whom) will care if you don't wear a hat?

Demonstrative Pronouns

The following words are *demonstrative pronouns:*

that   these   this   those

Definition: **Demonstrative pronouns indicate or point out people or things.**

Examples: This is my favorite car.
That is a beautiful chicken.

Skills Activity 7   **Using Demonstrative Pronouns**

Write on a separate sheet of paper the demonstrative pronoun in each of the following sentences:

1. This was certainly a lovely day.
2. These are the flowers for your wedding.
3. Those are the tomatoes for dinner tomorrow.
4. That is a harsh remark.
5. These are the antiques I bought.

Relative Pronouns

The following words can be *relative pronouns.*

that   which   who   whom   whose

Definition: **Relative pronouns are used to introduce *adjective clauses.* Adjective clauses are subordinate groups of words, each containing a subject and a predicate, that modify nouns or pronouns.**

Example: This recipe was from my grandmother, who was a great cook.

The adjective clause usually is introduced by a relative pronoun, which also is the subject of the clause.

Example: which is a famous play by Shakespeare

This clause, by itself, is incomplete. Used in a sentence as an adjective clause, it modifies a noun in the following example:

Hamlet, which is a famous play by Shakespeare, has been performed thousands of times.

Skills Activity 8   **Using Relative Pronouns**

On a separate sheet of paper, write the relative pronoun in each of the following sentences:

1. I like a tennis match that is close and exciting.
2. People who hate animals can't be considered for the job.

3. The person whom you have been waiting for has arrived.

4. I appreciate a person whose regard for others is obvious.

5. The class that meets at nine is my favorite class.

6. My Spanish class, which meets at nine, is my favorite class.

7. He was the kind of person who saw a glass as half empty, rather than half full.

8. The garbage collectors, whose hours are long, earn their money.

9. I like a play that has many characters.

10. This was the straw that broke the camel's back.

Skill Test	**Using Correct Pronouns**

Choose the correct pronoun in each of these sentences:

1. Each of the boys removed (his, their) jacket.

2. (Her and me) (She and I) like to write stories.

3. The director (himself, hisself) answered the phone.

4. Everyone in the group likes (his or her, their) steaks well done.

5. She was the kind of person (who, whom) saw good everywhere.

6. Neither Sue nor Valerie has (her, their) pen.

7. Who told Elaine about her and (I, me)?

8. (Him and me) (He and I) want to join the band.

9. I like soccer games (that, who) are close and exciting.

10. Somebody has left (their, his or her) ring on the table.

11. (Who, Whom) is your neighbor?

12. (This, These) are the gifts for the party.

13. Mr. Brown reported that (us, we) girls were late.

14. Most people find (his or her, their) vacations too short.

15. On what or (who, whom) would you blame this fire?

16. My sister and (me, I) can't stop laughing when we're together.

17. None of the boys wanted to give up (his, their) place in line.

18. Most everyone except Serina and (me, I) wanted a new teacher.

19. Latimore is the type of person (which, who) wants to win at everything.

Chapter 19

SUBJECT-VERB AGREEMENT

Subject-Verb Agreement

Rule: When using the present tense verb, the noun or pronoun acting as the subject agrees in number (singular or plural) with the verb. A singular verb is used with a singular noun or pronoun subject. A plural verb is used with a plural noun or pronoun subject.

Examples: <u>Juan</u> paints excellent pictures. (singular)
<u>Emily</u> loves to look at them. (singular)
<u>The ranchers watch</u> their sheep carefully. (plural)
<u>The dancers practice</u> five hours a day. (plural)

Skills Activity 1   **Simple Subjects and Verbs**

Write the correct verb for each of the following sentences on your paper:

1. The custodian (work, works) hard to keep the school clean.
2. Alice's assistant (finishes, finish) a project every week.
3. Lola's problem (is, are) that there is not enough material to do the job.
4. Terry's club (want, wants) to have a party.
5. The lawnmowers (break, breaks) down too often.
6. Your father (play, plays) a wonderful piano.
7. The bus schedule (puzzle, puzzles) many people.
8. Petunias (need, needs) regular watering to survive.
9. My dogs (bark, barks) loudly at strangers.
10. Enrico (love, loves) to knit sweaters.

Subject and Predicate Nominative

Rule: **The subject and the predicate nominative can differ in number. When they differ, the verb form agrees with the subject.**

Examples: <u>Your hobby</u> <u>is</u> old movies. (singular)
<u>My pet peeve on television</u> <u>is</u> corny comedians. (singular)
<u>Excellent athletes</u> <u>are</u> a team's greatest asset. (plural)
<u>Screaming students</u> <u>were</u> the greatest problem at the concert. (plural)

Skills Activity 2   **Subjects with Predicate Nominatives**

On a separate sheet of paper, write the correct verb in each of the following sentences:

1. The most popular act at the carnival (was, were) the clowns.
2. Pesticides (is, are) a controversial subject today.
3. A wink and a smile (seem, seems) to be his trademark.
4. Hard work and a strong will (is, are) his remedy for boredom.
5. Pinto beans (was, were) a staple food for farmers and their families in the pioneer days.
6. Interesting names for characters (was, were) one of Dickens's strong points as a writer.
7. The best part of the movie (was, were) the credits.
8. Jennifer, Pablo, and Christine (was, were) the group that won the prize.
9. Warming up and wearing proper shoes (is, are) important guidelines for good jogging.
10. Green peppers (seem, seems) a necessary ingredient for the salad.

Subject Modified by a Prepositional Phrase

Rule: **If a prepositional phrase modifies the noun or pronoun subject, the number of the verb stays the same as the number of the subject.**

Examples: The <u>actor</u> in the plays <u>is</u> wonderful. (singular)
The <u>girl</u> with the bicycles <u>is</u> a fine athlete. (singular)
The <u>grapes</u> on the table <u>are</u> delicious. (plural)
The <u>zebras</u> at the zoo <u>are</u> striking. (plural)

Skills Activity 3 **Subjects with Prepositional Phrases**

Write the correct verb for each of the following sentences on your paper:

1. One in a thousand (know, knows) the answer.
2. The larger of the monkeys (is, are) more energetic.
3. The toys in the attic (make, makes) noise.
4. The captains of industry (know, knows) arithmetic.
5. Your uncle from the suburbs (is, are) here.
6. Children in school (learn, learns) to use computers.
7. Anyone in the United States (know, knows) who George Washington was.
8. The lions from Africa (like, likes) heat.
9. The better of the two clarinet players (has, have) practiced a great deal.
10. The singer in the musical comedy series (enjoy, enjoys) her work.

Compound Subjects

Rule: **A compound subject joins two or more nouns, two or more pronouns, a noun and a pronoun, or nouns and pronouns. Compound subjects use a plural verb form.**

Examples: <u>Al and Dorothy</u> <u>jog</u> in the park. (plural)
<u>He and Henry</u> <u>are going</u> to the festival. (plural)
<u>She and he</u> <u>play</u> tennis every day. (plural)
<u>The cats and the dogs</u> <u>made</u> much noise. (plural)

Rule: **Two plural subjects joined by *or* or *nor* take the plural form of the verb.**

Examples: <u>The planes or the boats</u> <u>will transport</u> the people. (plural)
Neither <u>the children nor the adults</u> <u>enjoy</u> arguments. (plural)

Rule: **Two singular subjects joined by *or* or *nor* use a singular form of the verb.**

Examples: Either <u>Jason or Vincent</u> <u>took</u> notes in class today. (singular)
Neither <u>Kim nor Carlos</u> <u>wants</u> more potatoes. (singular)

Skills Activity 4   **Compound Subjects**

Write the correct verb for each of the following sentences on your paper:

1. The cousins, nephews, and other relatives (was, were) at the reunion.
2. Either Joseph or Danielle (sing, sings) well.
3. You and Betsy (help, helps) mother clear the table.
4. Gabriela and I (want, wants) to see the class play.
5. Roberto, Nick, and I (play, plays) guitars with the group.
6. Kanji and Mariko (is, are) related.
7. Either Nicole or Pak (act, acts) well enough to play the role.
8. Neither the students nor the teachers (support, supports) the candidate.
9. Either history or mathematics (is, are) Henry's favorite subject.
10. The monkeys, lions, and polar bears (was, were) the favorite animals at the zoo.

Indefinite Pronoun Subject Agreement

Singular Indefinite Pronouns

another	each	neither	one
any	either	nobody	other
anybody	everybody	none	somebody
anyone	everyone	no one	someone
anything	everything	nothing	something

Rule: **Singular indefinite pronouns agree in number with singular verb forms.**

Examples: Anybody will like this movie. (singular)
Each receives a prize. (singular)
No one knows what will happen. (singular)
None should benefit from the tragedy. (singular)

The following indefinite pronouns are plural. They agree with a plural verb form.

both   few   many   several   others

Examples: Few can stand the intense heat. (plural)
Many were selected to play in the band. (plural)
Others decided to drop out. (plural)

The following words are indefinite pronouns that can be either singular or plural.

all	some	most	any	none	such

Examples: <u>All</u> of the lemons <u>were</u> sour. (plural)
<u>All</u> of the beach <u>is</u> dry. (singular)
<u>Such</u> <u>are</u> the things that make dreams. (plural)
<u>Such</u> <u>is</u> life. (singular)
<u>Most</u> <u>will</u> not <u>like</u> the dessert. (plural)
<u>Most</u> of the cake <u>is</u> gone. (singular)

Skills Activity 5   **Indefinite Pronouns**

On a separate sheet of paper, write the correct verb for each of the following sentences:

1. Each (has, have) an hour to finish the test.
2. None of the apples (was, were) left.
3. Nothing (seem, seems) to satisfy them.
4. Both (jog, jogs) around the block daily.
5. Few (try, tries) to climb the mountain.
6. Either choice (is, are) a good one.
7. Nothing in the charts (show, shows) a problem.
8. One of the plates (is, are) missing.
9. Several (say, says) that the weather will be cold this winter.
10. Everyone (seem, seems) content with summer.

Here/There

Rule: **When a noun subject or a pronoun subject is singular and *here* or *there* begins the sentence, use the singular form of the verb.**

Examples: Here is the <u>car</u> you <u>ordered</u>.
There <u>goes</u> the <u>sailboat</u> into the wind.
Here <u>comes</u> the <u>bride</u>.

Rule: **When the noun subject or pronoun subject is plural and *here* or *there* begins the sentence, use the plural form of the verb.**

Examples: Here <u>are</u> the <u>eggs</u> for your breakfast.
There <u>were</u> many <u>students</u> at the concert.
Here <u>come</u> the <u>bride and groom</u>.

Skills Activity 6   *Here/There*

On a separate sheet of paper, write the correct verb for each of the following sentences:

1. Here (is, are) my father and mother.
2. There (was, were) apples, oranges, and mangos in the refrigerator.
3. There (is, are) light at the end of the lane.
4. Here (is, are) several shirts I want you to have.
5. There (is, are) free passes for Mary and Juan at the counter.
6. Here (is, are) my reasons for wanting to go to San Antonio.
7. There (is, are) rewards for doing good work.
8. Here (lie, lies) many victims of my fly swatter.
9. There (is, are) the tomatoes I grew in my garden.
10. There (goes, go) our last chances to win.

Amount

Rule: **When the amount is considered a single unit of measure, a singular form of the verb is used.**

Examples: Five days <u>is</u> a long time to wait. (singular)
Fifty dollars <u>is</u> a good discount for the suit. (singular)
Eighty bushels per acre <u>was</u> a good average yield for the corn. (singular)

Rule: **If the amount is considered as separate units, the plural form of the verb is used.**

Examples: Fifty percent of the players <u>want</u> to change the rules. (plural)
Ten gold pieces <u>are</u> worth a lot of money today. (plural)

Skills Activity 7   **Amount**

On your own paper, write the correct verb for each of the following sentences:

1. Five thousand miles (is, are) a long way to fly.
2. One-third of the voters (dislike, dislikes) the choices.
3. Twenty pesos (was, were) my change from the purchase.
4. Fifteen damaged silver dollars (was, were) in the collection.
5. One-half of the stamps in the book (is, are) worthless.
6. Thirty English pence (is, are) the price of admission.
7. Two tablespoons of chicken stock (goes, go) into the soup.

8. One-fourth of the sophomores (jog, jogs).

9. Twelve ounces of cat food (is, are) in the box.

10. Five hundred francs (is, are) the price of an ounce of French perfume.

---

do/does; don't/doesn't

Rule: **When the subject is singular, use *does* or *doesn't*.**

Examples: <u>Henry</u> <u>does</u> enjoy trigonometry. (singular)
<u>Millie</u> <u>does</u> as she pleases. (singular)
<u>She</u> <u>doesn't</u> like eggplant. (singular)

Rule: ***Do* and *don't* can be singular or plural, and they can agree with singular or plural subjects.**

Examples: <u>I</u> <u>do want</u> to go to the movies. (singular)
<u>I</u> <u>do</u> well in school. (singular)
<u>They</u> <u>do</u> well in school. (plural)
<u>They</u> <u>do</u> want to go to the movies. (plural)

> **do:** does, did, doing, done
> Today, I do nicely.
> Today, he/she/it does nicely.
> Yesterday, I did nicely.
> I am doing nicely now.
> I have done nicely before.
>
> **don't:** doesn't, didn't, am not doing, have not done
> Today, I don't do well.
> Today, he/she/it doesn't do well.
> Yesterday, I didn't do well.
> I am not doing well now.
> I have not done well before.

Examples: <u>The birds</u> <u>don't bother</u> me in the morning. (singular)
<u>They</u> <u>don't swim</u> in the lake at all. (plural)

Skills Activity 8   ***do/does; don't/doesn't***

On a separate sheet of paper, write the correct verb for each of the following sentences:

1. Celia and she (don't, doesn't) appreciate rowdy behavior.

2. I (do, does) want to argue.

3. Han and Daniel (do, does) qualify for the finals.

4. (Doesn't, don't) anybody want to play golf?

5. Carlotta and Joaquin (does, don't) wish to study together.

6. You (doesn't, don't) become a star overnight.

7. Aunt Juanita (does, do) make the best enchiladas when we visit her.

8. Anthony and Lisa (does, do) make a lovely couple.

9. Merely running (doesn't, don't) make you a good athlete.

10. The children (do, does) want to eat early.

Negative Words

These are negative words:

no	not	none	never
nobody	no one	nothing	hardly

Rule: **Negative words frequently are used to change the meanings of sentences. Only one negative word should be used to change the meaning of a sentence.**

Examples: **Wrong:** Janice didn't do nothing.
Right: Janice didn't do anything.
or
Janice did nothing.

Wrong: Robert didn't do no homework.
Right: Robert didn't do any homework.
or
Robert did no homework.

Wrong: She doesn't hardly smile at nobody.
Right: She hardly smiles at anybody.

Skills Activity 9   **Negative Words**

On a separate sheet of paper, rewrite the following sentences correctly, using only one negative word.

1. I don't hardly go to the movies these days.

2. I didn't have no luck on my fishing trip.

3. I won't give you no money to throw away.

4. She doesn't want none of those fish.

5. He doesn't think nothing is wrong with it.

6. Lupe don't let no one get near her new bicycle.

7. Chung didn't tell none of us about his high grades.
8. There isn't none of the players that don't want to win.
9. She don't see none of the people.
10. The new rules aren't doing nobody no good.

Skill Test   **Subject/Verb Agreement**

Choose the correct form of the verb for each of the following sentences:

1. During the summer, flowers (need, needs) frequent watering.
2. The families frequently (takes, take) picnics to the beach.
3. Dana (love, loves) to dance.
4. Neither (is, are) a skilled player.
5. There (were, was) no one to go to the store.
6. Both (run, runs) two miles every day.
7. Several (seems, seem) happy with the results of the test.
8. The boxes in the garage (is, are) empty.
9. A car that gets good mileage (are, is) a good investment.
10. The frogs and toads (hop, hops) across the road.
11. There (was, were) books and magazines on the table.
12. Here (are, is) the shirt you ordered.
13. There (come, comes) the race cars.
14. Thirty cents (was, were) my change.
15. Four hundred miles (are, is) a long drive.
16. The most exciting part of the game (was, were) all the home runs.
17. The will of the people (is, are) expressed on election day.
18. Vanessa (don't, doesn't) like to walk to work.
19. (Doesn't, Don't) anyone want to play tennis?
20. I won't give you (no, any) money.

Chapter 20

WORDS OFTEN MISUSED OR MISSPELLED

This chapter reviews several groups of words that often are misused or misspelled. These words frequently crop up as errors in compositions, so take the time necessary to learn their correct spelling and usage.

Words Often Misused

good/well

Definition: **Good** is an adjective that is used to modify a noun or a pronoun.

Examples: She cooked a <u>good</u> dinner.
Joseph is a <u>good</u> singer.

Well can be either an adjective or an adverb.

Definition: Used as an adverb, *well* means "an action completed properly or with skill."

Examples: David plays checkers <u>well</u>.
Michaela did <u>well</u> on the examination.

Definition: Used as an adjective, *well* means "healthy" or "in satisfactory condition."

Examples: José's fever is gone, and he seems <u>well</u> today.
Are you sure you feel <u>well</u>?
On such a beautiful morning, all is <u>well</u> with the world.

Skills Activity 1   ***good/well***

Write the correct word for each of the following sentences on your paper:

1. The band played (good, well) at the football game.
2. Johnny can cause a lot of trouble, but he was a (good, well) boy today.
3. The champion played tennis as (good, well) as ever yesterday.
4. It is really (good, well) to see you again.
5. You have been ill, but stay (good, well) so you can visit us soon.
6. Jessica is a (good, well) friend of mine. I have known her (good, well) for a long time.
7. It was (good, well) of you to come to my party.
8. If students do not pay attention, they may not learn (good, well).
9. Maria is a (good, well) judge of a person's character.
10. Lee and Kim get along together (good, well).

Comparisons with Adjectives

Rule: **When you compare two people or things, you can use the *comparative* form of an adjective.**

Examples: <u>old</u>   <u>older</u> (add *-er* ending)
Sally is <u>older</u> than Bill.

<u>large</u>   <u>larger</u>
This rock is <u>larger</u> than that one.

Rule: **Generally, you use *more* before adjectives of two syllables or more when you are comparing two people or things.**

Examples: <u>conscientious</u>   <u>more conscientious</u>
Alex was <u>conscientious</u>.   Alex was <u>more conscientious</u> than Johann.

<u>enthusiastic</u>   <u>more enthusiastic</u>
Anita was <u>enthusiastic</u>.   Anita seemed <u>more enthusiastic</u> about the play than Carla did.

Rule: **When more than two people or two things are compared, you use the *superlative* form. With adjectives of one syllable (and some of two syllables), add *-est*.**

Examples:	lovely She is <u>lovely</u>.	<u>loveliest</u> (superlative) She is the <u>loveliest</u> of the four girls.
	strong Mark is <u>strong</u>.	<u>strongest</u> (superlative) Mark is the <u>strongest</u> member of the wrestling team.
	<u>fine</u> Henri is a <u>fine</u> cook.	<u>finest</u> (superlative) Henri is the <u>finest</u> cook I know.
	<u>silly</u> He gave a <u>silly</u> answer.	<u>silliest</u> (superlative) He gave the <u>silliest</u> answer of all the students today.

Rule: **With adjectives of two syllables or more, use *most* before the adjective when you are comparing more than two people or things.**

Examples:	interesting That was an <u>interesting</u> play.	<u>most interesting</u> (superlative) That was the <u>most interesting</u> play I have ever seen.
	gorgeous He painted <u>gorgeous</u> watercolors.	<u>most gorgeous</u> (superlative) He painted the <u>most gorgeous</u> watercolors in the gallery.

Rule: **Sometimes you can use the *-est* ending with adjectives of two syllables.**

Examples:	tasty This is <u>tasty</u>.	<u>tastiest</u> (superlative) This is the <u>tastiest</u> meal I have ever eaten. *or* This is the <u>most tasty</u> meal I have ever eaten.
	muggy Today was <u>muggy</u>.	<u>muggiest</u> (superlative) Today was the <u>muggiest</u> day we've had this summer. *or* Today was the <u>most muggy</u> day we've had this summer.

Skills Activity 2	**Comparisons**

On your own paper, write the correct form of the adjective for each of the following sentences:

1. Sheila wore the (fancier, fanciest) dress in the whole crowd.

2. The (more intelligent, most intelligent) answer of the two was Ted's.

3. The (more intelligent, most intelligent) answer of the three was Ted's.

4. Juan's speech was (more humorous, humorouser) than Rico's.

5. Esa is (quicker, quickest) at chess than Christopher.

6. Which of the six trunks is the (smaller, smallest)?

7. This was the (cooler, coolest) evening we have had this week.

8. Anthony has a (more serious, seriouser) attitude than I do.

9. The carpenter is the (more meticulous, most meticulous) craftsman I have ever seen.

10. Which student is the (most energetic, more energetic) swimmer on the team?

good/bad

Rule: **The comparative form of *good* is *better*. It is used to compare two people or two things.**

Example: I like oranges <u>better</u> than apples.

Rule: **The superlative form of *good* is *best*. It is used to compare more than two people or things.**

Examples: Oranges are the <u>best</u> fruit in the whole world.
Of the five girls, Margarita is the <u>best</u> basketball player.

Rule: **The comparative form of *bad* is *worse*. It is used to compare two people or things.**

Examples: Oranges taste <u>worse</u> than grapefruit.
Meechi plays the violin <u>worse</u> than Colleen does.

Rule: **The superlative form of *bad* is *worst*. It is used to compare more than two people or two things.**

Examples: I saw five movies this summer, and that was the <u>worst</u> one.
Jack cooks the <u>worst</u> omelets in the world.

Skills Activity 3   *good/bad*

On a separate sheet of paper, write the correct form of the adjective for each of the following sentences:

1. I thought all of the speeches were bad, but Sam's was the (worse, worst).

2. All of their soaps are good, but this kind is the (better, best).

3. This kind of soap is (better, best) than that one.

4. Maria looks (better, best) than she did at the beginning of the year.

5. Which is the (better, best) of the three choices?

6. Which is the (better, best) of the two choices?

7. What do you like (better, best) to eat, bananas, apples, or kumquats?

8. The clarinet player is the (worse, worst) musician in the orchestra.

9. Mamoru sketches (better, best) pictures than John sketches.

10. Rosalie is the (best, better) dancer in the chorus.

less/fewer

Rule: **When a noun is singular, use *less* before it. When a noun is plural, use *fewer* before it.**

Examples: There seems to be <u>less</u> water in the fish tank. (singular)
There seem to be <u>fewer</u> mosquitoes this summer. (plural)

Skills Activity 4 **less/fewer**

Write the correct form of the adjective for each of the following sentences on your paper:

1. Emily has (less, fewer) fever than she had last night.

2. There are (less, fewer) boys in our algebra class than there are girls.

3. Use a little (fewer, less) paprika in the stew the next time.

4. Use (fewer, less) cubes of bouillon in the soup.

5. If you asked the students to help you keep the room clean, you would have (fewer, less) work to do.

6. Did you purchase (less, fewer) rolls for the banquet than you bought last year?

7. This room has (less, fewer) heat than it used to have.

8. Alice missed (fewer, less) questions than Jason did.

9. I wish we had (less, fewer) homework in our history course.

10. My muscular pains are (less, fewer) since I began a weight-lifting program.

this/that; these/those

Rule: **When using *kind, type,* and *sort,* use the singular form of *this* and *that.* Do not use *these* or *those,* unless the plural forms *kinds, types,* and *sorts* are modified.**

Examples: I like <u>this kind</u> of cereal. (singular)
                I think <u>that kind</u> of car is attractive. (singular)
                <u>Those types</u> of poisons are very dangerous. (plural)
                <u>These sorts of mistakes</u> should be avoided. (plural)

Skills Activity 5   ***this/that; these/those***

On your own paper, write the correct form of adjective for each of the following sentences:

1. I truly enjoy (these, that) kind of salsa.
2. Do you want to associate with (that, those) type of person?
3. (This, These) sort of humor makes me laugh.
4. (That, Those) kind of courage is not seen often.
5. I won't put up with (this, these) sorts of tricks.
6. (This, These) types of poisonous spiders are dangerous.
7. (That, Those) kinds of nasty remarks are in bad taste.
8. I love (this, these) types of organic vegetables.
9. Do you like (this, these) kind of cheese?
10. (These, This) sorts of meals should be served all the time.

them/those/these

Rule: ***Them* is always a pronoun and always an object of a verb or preposition. *Those* may be either an adjective or a pronoun. If *those* is followed by a noun, it is an adjective. If used by itself, it is a pronoun. *These* may be either an adjective or a pronoun. If *these* is followed by a noun, it is an adjective. If used by itself, it is a pronoun.**

Wrong: I like them things.
Right: I like them.

Examples: I like <u>those</u>. (pronoun)
                I like <u>those</u> jeans. (adjective)
                I hate <u>these</u>. (pronoun)
                I hate <u>these</u> hot days. (adjective)

I ate some of <u>those</u> plums and I did not like <u>them</u>.
All of <u>them</u> are going to the race.
<u>Those</u> people can be very critical.
Pass me some of <u>those</u> nuts, please.
I'll eat a few of <u>these</u> sunflower seeds.

Rule: ***Them* always is used by itself. It never is an adjective.**

Skills Activity 6   *them/those/these*

On a separate sheet of paper, write the correct word for each of the following sentences:

1. (Them, Those) are the kinds of fruits I want to serve after dinner.
2. Did you order (them, those) tamales with dinner?
3. Pass me some of (those, them) potatoes, please.
4. After (them, those) guests left, we cleaned up the kitchen.
5. (These, Them) are the times that give us trouble.
6. Aren't (those, them) hats beautiful?
7. Please do what you can to help (those, them) young people.
8. You can keep (those, them) beans.
9. I don't like (those, them) types of vegetables.
10. If you'll give me (those, them) boots, I'll try to fix them.

bad/badly

Rule: **After linking verbs, use the form *bad*.**

Examples: The weather turned <u>bad</u> today.
Alice's mood was <u>bad</u> yesterday.

Rule: ***Badly* is used as an adverb to modify a verb.**

Example: The team played <u>badly</u> in the finals.

Skills Activity 7   ***bad/badly***

On your own paper, write the correct word for each of the following sentences:

1. The weather report is (bad, badly) for tomorrow.
2. Is your eyesight (bad, badly) in the evening?
3. Mary Jane looked (bad, badly) when she went home from school.
4. I feel (bad, badly) when I hurt someone's feelings.
5. The orchestra really sounded (bad, badly) in that hall.
6. Ms. Lopez drove (bad, badly) on the highway.
7. He treated his friend (bad, badly) at the reception.
8. All his luck appeared (bad, badly) this year.
9. The audience behaved (bad, badly) during the play.
10. The outlook for the economy looks (bad, badly) from my point of view.

between/among

Rule: **The preposition *between* is used with *two* people or *two* things.**

Examples: The secret was kept <u>between</u> Donald and Julia.
The nest was built <u>between</u> two branches of the tree.

Rule: **The preposition *among* is used with *more than two* people or things.**

Examples: There was a dandelion growing <u>among</u> the roses.
A disagreement arose <u>among</u> the members of the club.

Skills Activity 8 ***between/among***

Write the correct word for each of the following sentences on your paper.

1. How can you make a choice (between, among) those stunning dresses?
2. How can you choose (among, between) those two nondescript suits?
3. (Among, Between) you and me, I think he is wrong.
4. Sarah is in a predicament caught (among, between) a rock and a brick wall.
5. How can they find a winner (between, among) all those contestants?
6. The antelope bounded (between, among) the trees in the forest.
7. Jacques threw flowers (between, among) the people in the audience.
8. The coin fell (among, between) the two rocks.
9. There is a real difference (between, among) winning and placing second.
10. Is there anyone (between, among) us who knows the answer?

---

in/into

Rule: **If you describe someone or something *inside* or *within* a place or a thing, use *in*.**

Examples: There are seeds <u>in</u> the orange.
I saw Janice sitting <u>in</u> the room.

Rule: **If you describe "moving toward the inside of an area or a building," use *into*.**

Examples: Ricardo walked <u>into</u> the office.
The tire sunk <u>into</u> the pothole.

Skills Activity 9   ***in/into***

On your own paper, write the correct word for each of the following sentences:

1. Debbie dashed (in, into) the restaurant.
2. I would like to be (in, into) her class.
3. The bear lumbered (in, into) the cave.
4. Ms. Santos tried to get (in, into) the theater, but the tickets were sold out.
5. He received his degree (in, into) business administration.
6. The criminal walked (in, into) the trap the police had set.
7. Julio has never lived (in, into) Puerto Rico.
8. It is difficult to enter (in, into) conversation with Ilana.
9. Michael swaggered (in, into) the room where the party was beginning.
10. The dog chased the cat (in, into) the barn.

of/at

Rule: **Never use *of* after *off*.**

Wrong: Bill scraped the paint <u>off of</u> the wall.
Right: Bill scraped the paint <u>off</u> the wall.

Rule: **Never use *at* after *where*.**

Wrong: <u>Where</u> is the bathroom at?
Right: <u>Where</u> is the bathroom?

Skills Activity 10   ***of/at***

On a separate sheet of paper, write the correct choice for each of the following sentences:

1. Sometimes I don't know (where I'm at, where I am).
2. Will you please get (off of, off) the sofa?
3. Do you know where my books (are, are at)?
4. He knows where the party is being (held, held at).

5. We watched as he dived (off, off of) the cliff.

6. He doesn't know where (it's at, it is).

7. Sally took the pitcher (off, off of) the table.

8. Lynette doesn't know where her glasses (are, are at).

9. Octavio took the chairs (off, off of) the speakers' stand.

10. Mr. Carlos knows where they hid the (treasure, treasure at).

beside/besides

Definition: **The preposition *beside* means "next to."**

Examples: The boy sat <u>beside</u> his father.
Park the car <u>beside</u> the house.

Definition: **The preposition *besides* means "added to" or "in addition to."**

Examples: <u>Besides</u> the driver, there were eight other people in the car.
<u>Besides</u> being very funny, the play had a good theme.

Skills Activity 11   ***beside/besides***

Write the correct word for each of the following sentences on your paper:

1. Rosa placed the chair (beside, besides) the table.

2. John played the clarinet (beside, besides) the pond.

3. Could Mother sit (beside, besides) Calvin at the table?

4. (Beside, Besides) the awful heat, it is raining outside.

5. (Beside, Besides) learning to cook chicken, Dolores learned to cook roast beef and potatoes.

6. The dog lay (beside, besides) the stove.

7. (Beside, Besides) spending the day with us, we asked Lisa and Chico to go to the movies this evening.

8. (Beside, Besides) folk songs, Pepe can play classical songs on his guitar.

9. Come and sit (beside, besides) me.

10. (Beside, Besides) green vegetables, you should include protein foods in your diet.

Words Often Misspelled

Words that Sound Alike

Words that sound alike often are confused with each other. These words have different meanings and different spellings. To make your writing clear, it is especially important to spell these words correctly.

all ready: everyone ready, all prepared.
When you are all ready, we will go.

already: by that time, previously.
We had already seen the show.

altar: the place that serves as the center of worship.
They stood at the altar.

alter: to change.
Will you alter my suit?

all together: everyone together in the same place.
We were all together at the celebration.

altogether: completely, entirely.
You are altogether right.

brake: a device for stopping.
The brake on my bicycle needs repair.

break: to come apart, to shatter.
Don't break the glass.

capital: a chief city; money; an upper-case letter.
Washington, D.C. is the capital of the United States of America.
Put your capital in the bank.
Use a capital letter.

capitol: a building in which a legislative body meets.
We visited the capitol building in Washington.

clothes: wearing apparel.
I like new clothes.

cloths: pieces of cloth.
Use these cloths to clean the car.

coarse: rough, crude.
They used coarse language.

course: path; a subject studied; part of a meal.
This is a difficult math course.

council: a group that makes decisions.
She is a member of the city council.

councillor: a member of a council.
The councillor voted for the new anti-loitering law.

counsel: advise; to give advice.
I need someone to counsel me.

counselor: one who gives advice.
I made an appointment with my counselor.

desert: dry, desolate land; to leave or abandon.
Do not desert me.

dessert: final course of a meal.
I enjoyed the rich dessert.

formally: in a proper or conventional manner.
He was dressed formally.

formerly: previously, in the past.
She was formerly in my class.

its: possessive pronoun.
The dog wagged its tail.

it's: contraction: it is.
It's mine!

later: afterward.
We will come later.

latter: the second of two.
You gave 8 and 10 as the answers; the latter is correct.

lead: present tense, to go in front.
You should lead us.

led: past tense.
He led the parade.

lead: (pronounced lĕd) a heavy metal.
It is made of lead.

loose: free; not tight.
The jacket is loose.

lose: misplace.
Did you lose your ball?

peace: absence of war.
We all want peace in the world.

piece: part of something.
I'd like a piece of cake.

plain: not fancy; clear; large area of flat land.
The dress is plain.
The answer is plain.
We crossed the Great Plains.

plane: a flat surface; a tool; an aircraft.
We studied plane geometry.
The carpenter used a plane to smooth it.
The plane was sleek and fast.

passed: verb.
The runner passed me in the race.

past: time gone by.
I like to think about past events.

principal: head of school; most important.
She is our principal.
The principal cause of errors is carelessness.

principle: rule, belief.
The principles of solar energy are clear.

quiet: still, silent.
We must be quiet in class.

quite: very, completely.
He is quite tall.

stationary: standing in one position.
The train remained stationary at the crossing.

stationery: writing paper.
Buy some stationery at the store.

there: in that place.
Put the book over there.

their: belonging to them.
It is their car.

they're: contraction: they are.
They're going to the movies.

to: preposition.
Give the books to me.

too: also.
You may go, too.

two: number.
She has two sisters.

weather: atmospheric conditions.
Did you listen to the weather report?

whether: if.
He did not say whether he could go.

who's: contraction: who is.
Who's your friend?

whose: possessive.
Whose jacket is this?

your: possessive.
Is this your hat?

you're: contraction: you are.
You're right about the test.

Skills Activity 12   **Words That Sound Alike**

Choose the correct word in each sentence. Write it on your paper.

1. The race horse (passed, past) the other horses at the beginning of the race.
2. I like chocolate cake for (desert, dessert).
3. There were (quiet, quite) a lot of children at the library today.
4. Lauren was (altogether, all together) shocked at the mess we made.
5. The (principal, principle) guitarist of our band has left.
6. (There, Their, They're) too busy to do (there, their, they're) homework.
7. If you throw the ball carelessly, you might (brake, break) the window.
8. The old (capital, capitol) building had interesting architectural details.
9. He was (formally, formerly) a neighbor.
10. The eagle suddenly spread (its, it's) wings and flew away.

Basic Spelling List

The following words are commonly misspelled. Study them carefully.

a lot	could've	heroine	October
(not *alot*)	countries	hoarse	often
accept	criticism	hoping	omitted
ache	dear	hour	once
across	December	humorous	passed
affect	define	interfere	past
again	definite	its	piece
all ready	definitely	it's	playwright
all right	definition	January	pleasant
(not *alright*)	dependent	July	please
alone	describe	June	precede
along	description	justify	prefer
already	development	knew	preferred
always	disappoint	know	prejudice
answer	doctor	knowledge	prejudiced
anyway	doesn't	laboratory	preparation
appearance	easy	laid	prepare
April	effect	lead	principal
article	enough	led	principle
August	every	library	privilege
author	except	license	probably
because	existence	literature	procedure
beginning	experience	loose	proceed
believe	extremely	lose	quiet
blew	familiar	losing	quite
blue	February	making	raise
brake	finally	March	read
break	foreign	May	really
built	forty	meant	receive
business	Friday	minute	receiving
busy	friend	Monday	recommend
buy	friendliness	much	refer
by	government	narrative	referred
can't	grammar	necessary	repetition
careful	guess	neighbor	rise
character	guest	ninth	rhythm
choose	half	no	said
chose	having	none	Saturday
chosen	hear	November	school
college	heard	now	science
color	height	occasion	seem
coming	here	occur	sentence
convenience	hero	occurred	separate
cough	heroes	occurrence	separation
could	heroic	occurring	September

(Continued)

shoes	then	tries	which
should've	their	trouble	whole
similar	there	truly	whose
since	they	Tuesday	who's
some	they're	two	witch
sophomore	thorough	until	woman
speech	though	used	women
stopping	threw	very	won't
stories	through	villain	would
straight	Thursday	weak	would've
studying	tired	wear	writer
sugar	to	weather	written
Sunday	tonight	were	wrote
sure	too	we're	your
tear	tragedy	where	you're
than	tried	whether	

Skills Activity 13   **Spelling Words**

Write the following words as they are dictated. Use each word in a sentence of your own.

1. a lot
2. all right
3. appearance
4. business
5. character
6. definitely
7. dependent
8. existence
9. extremely
10. humorous
11. knowledge
12. license
13. occurred
14. omitted
15. privilege
16. recommend
17. rhythm
18. separate
19. sophomore
20. thorough

Skill Test 1   **Correct Words**

Choose the correct word for each of the following sentences:

1. James feels (good, well) today.
2. The actor performed his part very (good, well).
3. He was the (more capable, most capable) player on the team.
4. She was (more friendlier, friendlier) than the others.
5. The weather today is (worse, worst) than yesterday.
6. This kind of ice cream is (best, better) than that one.
7. There are (less, fewer) students at the game this week.
8. I have (less, fewer) money than you do.
9. I like (this, these) kinds of games.
10. Please send me some of (those, them) stamps.
11. I'll send a few of (those, them).
12. I feel (bad, badly) about my angry words.
13. The traffic news is (bad, badly) today.
14. There was strong friendship (between, among) the five children.
15. (Between, Among) the two of us, we can raise the money.
16. We walked (in, into) my friend's house.
17. He swept the leaves (off of, off) the porch.
18. I don't know where my comb (is, is at).
19. (Besides, Beside) the trumpet, David also plays the piano.
20. The cat was asleep (besides, beside) the radiator.

Skill Test 2   **Spelling**

Choose the correctly spelled word for each of the following sentences.

1. The study of (grammar, grammer) is not all that difficult.
2. He needs to do something about his (appearance, appearence).
3. Which (auther, author) do you like better?
4. It's hard to (seperate, separate) fact from fantasy.
5. A sad (occurence, occurrence) happened last week.
6. I'm not sure (whether, weather) they will be there.
7. The (goverment, government) workers are retiring early.
8. Nice (stationary, stationery) makes a very good impression.
9. Sometimes citizens of this country lose their (priviledges, privileges).

10. By law, a (women, woman) can become president of the United States.

11. That drummer really has (rhythem, rhythm).

12. You'll get a fine if you drive without a (license, liscense) plate.

13. Be careful not to (lose, loose) the check she gave you.

14. The big (ocassion, occasion) has arrived at last.

15. Cloudy skies can (affect, effect) us in many different ways.

16. Dictionaries give several (defenitions, definitions) of each word.

17. A good manager should always have good (principals, principles).

18. Everyone (accept, except) Julia wore green and white.

19. Of (course, coarse) you can come with us if you like.

20. They have asked the leader to give them (council, counsel).

Chapter 21

PUNCTUATION

Try to read the following paragraph:

When and why did the *Titanic* sink the disaster happened on April 15 1912 during the ship's maiden voyage it ran into an iceberg in the North Atlantic and sank in just over two hours more than 1500 people drowned many of them were among the world's most famous or wealthy how shocked the world was

Now read the same paragraph below, written in the standard way.

When and why did the *Titanic* sink? The disaster happened on April 15, 1912, during the ship's maiden voyage. It ran into an iceberg in the North Atlantic and sank in just over two hours. More than 1,500 people drowned. Many of them were among the world's most famous or wealthy. How shocked the world was!

Clearly, punctuation and capitalization play important roles in a reader's ability to understand what is written.

Beginning and Ending Sentences

To write sentences in the standard way, do the following:

Rule: **Begin a sentence with a *capital letter.***

Examples: Homemade bread is inexpensive and delicious.
Why don't more people bake their own bread?
Take the time to bake at home.
How wonderful it tastes!

Rule: **End a sentence with a *mark of punctuation.* A sentence that tells something (statement) ends with a *period.***

Example: Homemade bread is inexpensive and delicious.

Rule: **A sentence that asks something (question) ends with a** *question mark.*

Example: Why don't more people bake their own bread?

Rule: **A sentence that gives a direction (command) usually ends with a** *period.*

Example: Take the time to bake at home.

Rule: **If a direction is urgent, it can end with an** *exclamation mark.*

Examples: Don't touch the hot pan!
                Watch out for the open flame!

Rule: **A sentence that exclaims something (exclamation) ends with an** *exclamation mark.*

Example: How wonderful it tastes!

Skills Activity 1   **Punctuating the Beginnings and Endings of Sentences**

Each paragraph below is missing capitals and punctuation marks for sentence beginnings and endings. Read each paragraph. Decide where each sentence should begin and end. Then decide on the end punctuation mark. (If it could be either a period or an exclamation mark, choose one.) On a separate sheet of paper write each paragraph, putting in the capitals and punctuation marks.

1. why does a jet aircraft leave a "smoke" trail it isn't smoke at all the exhaust from a jet engine includes fuel gases and water vapor these gases and steam hit the very cold upper air there they form cloudlike condensation and streams of water crystals

2. what can you do to make roller skating safe be sure the skate boots fit snugly and give ankle support wear cotton socks to help absorb perspiration do leg-stretching exercises for ten minutes before skating

3. what can you do to live longer get lots of exercise active people tend to be happier and healthier than inactive people for one thing they stay at a sensible weight they also recover faster from illnesses or accidents

4. what causes volcanoes these eruptions occur when pressures build up in underground reservoirs of molten rock and gas the materials force their way through cracks in the earth's crust some volcanoes also spew ash from their surface craters the eruption continues as long as there is great pressure underground

Using Commas

Commas probably are the most commonly used punctuation mark. They function like voice pauses in a conversation and can be used to add expression as well as clarity to your writing.

Commas in a Series

Rule: **A series is a group of related words separated by commas. Do not place a comma after the last word in a series.**

Example: Sarah, Carly, and Juanita are going to San Antonio for a vacation.

Rule: **A series may be groups of phrases.**

Example: Waking early, eating well, and sleeping enough hours are the rules for good health.

Rule: **A series may be groups of clauses.**

Example: How to select seed corn, when to plant it, and when to harvest it are important facts that good farmers need to know.

Skills Activity 2 | **Using Commas in a Series**

On a separate sheet of paper, write the following sentences and punctuate them correctly with commas.

1. Running walking and swimming are excellent exercise activities.
2. Macrame needlepoint and knitting have become popular crafts.
3. To work to learn and to achieve are guideposts for many who wish to be happy.
4. Learning to read write and add are basic skills for success in our society.
5. To fish well you have to learn to bait a hook you must know how to cast a line and you must have a lot of patience.
6. Jack stuck in this thumb he pulled out a plum and he said he was a good boy.
7. *Cats Les Miserables* and *Phantom of the Opera* were successful Broadway musicals.
8. Dracula Frankenstein and Superman are fantastic literary characters with unusual powers.
9. Baking the chicken mashing the potatoes and cooking the peas need to be done before we can eat.
10. I opened the letter I read it carefully and I tore it up in disgust.

Commas in Compound Sentences

These are common *coordinating conjunctions:*

      and   or   but   nor

Rule: **When coordinating conjunctions join two independent clauses in a compound sentence, place a comma before the conjunction.**

Examples: Tom likes swimming, <u>and</u> he likes to ski.
              Jessica enjoys movies, <u>but</u> she likes plays better.

Skills Activity 3   **Using Commas in Compound Sentences**

On a separate sheet of paper, write the following sentences and insert commas in the correct places.

1. We must try to save the whales or they will become extinct.
2. I do not like loud noise nor do I like messy rooms.
3. Andy and Han went to lunch and they enjoyed the food.
4. Kendra does not like to eat meat nor does she care for junk food.
5. I would love to play the mandolin but I have no musical talent.
6. Katrina said she would be here at seven o'clock or she would call us.
7. Manuel loves to travel but he has little money.
8. You are a good friend but you annoy me sometimes.
9. There was no milk in the refrigerator nor was there any yogurt.
10. You may want to take algebra or you might enjoy history.

Commas with Introductory Clauses, Phrases, and Words

Rule: **If an *adverb clause* begins a sentence, set it off with a comma.**

Examples: <u>If you do not study for the test</u>, you may fail it.
              <u>When the rain finally started</u>, we all ran home.

Remember that the difference between a clause and a phrase is that a clause has a subject and a verb, while a phrase does not.

Rule: When a *prepositional phrase* used as an adverb is at the beginning of a sentence, set it off with commas. If more than one adverbial phrase is at the beginning of a sentence, place a comma after each phrase.

Examples: Before the wedding, Angela was nervous.

Off in the distance, deep in the forest, we heard the sound of drums.

Rule: When *yes* or *no* is the first word in a sentence, set it off with a comma.

Examples: Yes, I will go with you.
No, you cannot have another apple.

Rule: An *interjection* is a word that expresses a feeling strongly. When an interjection is the first word of a sentence, set it off with a comma.

Examples: Look, I want you to do a good job!
Well, we will think about it.

Skills Activity 4   **Commas with Introductory Clauses, Phrases, and Words**

On a separate sheet of paper, write the following sentences and insert commas in the correct places.

1. After the movie why don't you come to my house?
2. When you write me a letter it makes me very happy.
3. No Anthony may not leave the room.
4. Next to the table there is a chair.
5. Well what do you have to say for yourself?
6. While you were away the daffodils bloomed.
7. Off to the north high in the sky dark clouds were forming.
8. Really I don't know how to thank you!
9. Since Holly insists upon playing soccer Joanna will have to play too.
10. During the summer Dale injured his foot.

Commas and Participial Phrases

Rule: A *participial phrase* acts as an adjective and modifies a noun or a pronoun. If a participial phrase introduces a sentence, set it off with a comma.

Examples: <u>Caught in the rain</u>, we were drenched.
               <u>Accepting the gift</u>, Mr. Sato was deeply moved.

Rule: **If a participial phrase occurs elsewhere in the sentence and is *nonrestrictive*, set it off with commas.**

Examples: Emily, <u>surprised by the visitors</u>, blushed.
               Carl, <u>waiting for a bus</u>, fell asleep.

   Notice that the *nonrestrictive participial phrases* in the examples give more information about the nouns they modify, but they are not necessary to the sentence for the meaning to be clear. If you omit the participial phrases, you have:

   Emily blushed. (the main idea)

   Carl fell asleep. (the main idea)

   Think of *nonrestrictive participial phrases* as helpful, but not essential, to the meaning of the sentence.

Rule: **If the participial phrase is *restrictive*, it is not set off with commas. The *restrictive* participial phrase is essential for the meaning of the sentence to be clear.**

Examples: The boy <u>walking the dog</u> is very cheerful.
               The clown <u>swinging on the trapeze</u> is a fine entertainer.

   In both of these examples, the *restrictive participial phrase* makes the noun in each case definite and specific, eliminating any confusion in relation to other clowns or boys who might be in the area.

Skills Activity 5   **Commas with Participial Phrases**

On a separate sheet of paper, write the following sentences and insert commas in the correct places.

1. Tormented by flies the swimmers left the beach.
2. Dolores enchanted by the music smiled and sighed.
3. Attacking the problem Mario and Francesca soon solved it.
4. Dashing out of the house Tom forgot his lunch.
5. The girl playing the guitar is my sister.
6. Shouting with joy Akira showed his mother the fish he had caught.
7. Julian laughing at the joke almost fell off his chair.
8. The girl sitting next to Leo seems to like him.
9. The woman painting the fence seems bored with her work.
10. The cat purring with pleasure ate its food.

Commas and Transitional Words and Phrases

Rule: **The following words and phrases can be used for *transitional* purposes:**

nevertheless	**in fact**
however	**for instance**
on the other hand	**consequently**
of course	**on the contrary**
for example	**therefore**
furthermore	**unfortunately**
in my opinion	**to tell the truth**

Rule: **Use either one comma or two commas to set off the words of transition or phrases of transition in sentences.**

Examples: Your dinner was delicious. <u>For example</u>, the spinach was perfectly cooked.

I enjoy playing tennis. <u>However</u>, I don't have much time to do it.

Skills Activity 6 | **Commas with Transitional Words and Phrases**

On a separate sheet of paper, write the following sentences and insert commas in the correct places.

1. I think that Mr. Kim is quite wrong. Furthermore I think he is jealous.
2. I don't enjoy movies very much. Nevertheless I'll go with you tonight.
3. You insulted my best friend. Therefore you are no friend of mine.
4. The candidate in my opinion does not think straight.
5. You think I don't like Dorothy? On the contrary I think she is lovely.
6. You are studying stalagmites and stalactites? To tell the truth I don't know the difference between them.
7. We will be going to dinner soon. You are of course coming with us.
8. Many senior citizens enjoy gardening. Some for example plant vegetables in community garden plots.
9. I don't read as much as I should. In fact I haven't read a novel for three months.
10. Vegetables are easy to grow in a garden. Peas for instance grow quickly.

Commas and Interrupters

These are some common *interrupters:*

however	you know	nevertheless
I think	consequently	moreover

Rule: **Interrupters are words inserted into the sentence for emphasis or to change the direction of the thought. They should be set off by commas.**

Examples: Elmer, <u>however</u>, has the right idea.
I have been practicing, <u>you know</u>, but I still cannot play well.

Another type of interrupter is an appositive.

Rule: **An *appositive phrase* follows the word or group of words that it explains. The appositive explains more about the noun or pronoun it is next to in the sentence. It is set off by commas.**

Examples: Frank Sinatra, <u>the well-known singer</u>, will be performing tonight.
Arsenic, <u>a deadly poison</u>, should never be stored near small children.

Rule: **When you address another person, one or two commas should be used, depending on the structure of the sentence.**

Examples: <u>Janet</u>, pick up the dishes.
You know, <u>Meechi</u>, that you should study more often.

Skills Activity 7   **Commas with Interrupters**

On a separate sheet of paper, write the following sentences and insert commas in the correct places.

1. This group of athletes I think is the best team we have had.
2. Henry James a famous novelist wrote about high society in England.
3. Harris was nevertheless the winner.
4. Get in your seats Melissa and David and buckle your seat belts.
5. I want to visit my aunt Ella Sanchez before next July.
6. The result of the election consequently was in her favor.
7. Florence Griffith-Joyner the Olympic champion will go down in history as one of the greatest athletes.
8. Alonzo do you have my bicycle?

9. Give Jim the fellow in the yellow shirt another sandwich.

10. Fried ice cream an unusual dessert is found on some menus.

Commas in Dates and Addresses

Rule: **Place a comma between the day's number and the year.**

Example: March 4, 1942

Rule: **If the year's number is not followed by a period, a question mark, or an exclamation point at the end of a sentence, place another comma after the year's number.**

Examples: On March 4, 1942, Claude joined the army.
July 4, 1976, was an Independence Day to remember.
Alberto was born on May 6, 1980.

Rule: **Place a comma after the following:**

1. **The name of a town, village, city, box number, and rural route number.**
2. **The name of a state.**
3. **The name of a country.**

(Remember that this rule does not apply for addresses on envelopes and packages.)

If any of these is at the end of a sentence, place a period or another end mark after it. There is no comma between the state and the ZIP code.

Examples: Rome, Italy
Columbus, Indiana
Rural Route 3, Jonesville, Indiana
Box 2546, Boulder, Colorado 80322-2546
672 Meadow Street, Franklin Center, PA 19091-6060

Rule: **To write an address within a sentence, use a comma in the following places:**

a. **after the street, avenue, etc.**
b. **after the city or town**
c. **after the ZIP code, if the sentence continues**

Example: Our address will be 2520 West Bayview Blvd., Tampa, Florida 33611-1956, after the first of next year.

Skills Activity 8   **Commas in Dates and Addresses**

On a separate sheet of paper, write the following sentences and insert commas where they belong.

1. Ella went to Houston on June 15 1989.
2. Did you know that January 8 1990 was the day we bought our new car?
3. October 31 1978 was the first Halloween I can remember.
4. My graduation day was June 16 1984.
5. On April 9 1998 I will be twenty-one.
6. You can write to Tia Rosa at 742 Vine Street Houston Texas 77092-8668.
7. Juan can be reached at Box 846 Chicago Illinois 60602-0846.
8. If you want to reach me, I'll be staying at 1400 Page Mill Road Palo Alto California.
9. Amos Jones lives on his farm at Rural Route 2 St. Paul Minnesota 55182-9184.
10. Williams Drive Ramsey New Jersey 17466-1324 is the address of my brother.

Other Punctuation

Four other punctuation marks that you will find useful are *semicolons, colons, dashes,* and *parentheses.*

Semicolons

Rule: **Semicolons act as conjunctions when joining related independent clauses; they also are used to join an independent clause with a clause beginning with transition words such as *however* or *nevertheless.* See page 294 for a list of transition words.**

Examples: Henri was the best soccer player that Lincoln High School ever had; later, in college, he became a champion swimmer.

A sound body is a must for an athlete; moreover, a quick mind is a definite asset.

Note: Do not use semicolons excessively as substitutes for conjunctions. Sentences can become much too lengthy and complicated if semicolons appear too often as connectors. Breaking a long sentence into two sentences often may be a better way to express two related thoughts clearly.

Rule:	**Semicolons should be used in a series of items when commas are included in one or more items.**

Examples: Some great black musicians influenced the playing of jazz instruments: Jay Jay Johnson, the trombone; Louis Armstrong, the trumpet; Thelonius Monk, the piano; and John Coltrane, the tenor saxophone.

Fine tennis players from the past include Henri Cochet, from France; Margaret Court, from England; and Jack Kramer, from America.

Colons

Rule:	**The colon can emphasize explanatory words that follow it.**

Examples: These are citrus fruits: lemons, oranges, and grapefruits.

Juan is an expert in several sports: Ping-Pong, tennis, and swimming.

Rule:	**The colon separates an explanatory list from the statement that introduces the list. Words such as *follows* signal the reader that an important explanation follows the colon.**

Examples: Ned is attracted to women with the following hair colorings: blonde, black, brown, or red.

The Puritans held the following virtues in high regard: faith, hope, and charity.

Rule:	**Colons are used to separate the following: the salutation in a business letter; the hour and minutes when writing the time; and chapter and verse in the Bible.**

Examples: It is now 5:25 P.M.
Dear Sir:
Dear Mary Jones:
Exodus 2:14

Dashes

The dash is similar to a colon, but it has a less formal, more familiar effect than the colon does with most readers.

Rule:	**The dash gives special emphasis to explanatory words that follow it. It can set off explanatory words from the preceding thought or thoughts.**

Example: Tennis, badminton, and Ping-Pong—those are great net sports!

Rule: **A quick change in the direction of thinking or thought is indicated by a dash.**

Examples: "The day seems to be going smoothly—Oh, no! It's raining!"

The collie circled the chair and finally lay down—suddenly barked and bounded forward—then sniffed, lay down again under the table—growled amiably, almost like a mutter—and went to sleep.

Parentheses

Rule: **Parentheses break the thought in a sentence to give the reader information that may be helpful but is not essential to the sentence.**

Examples: Mary's composition (her first) received an average grade.

Bill (Harry's uncle) came to visit us yesterday.

Skills Activity 9   **Using Semicolons, Colons, Dashes, and Parentheses**

On a separate sheet of paper, write the following sentences and insert semicolons, colons, dashes, and parentheses as needed to make the sentences read more clearly.

1. Amanda likes chocolate brownies and cinnamon rolls Tony likes apple pie and peanut-butter cookies.
2. The letter said Dear Mr. Hargrove You can expect to receive from us next week the following items a set of encyclopedias, two training manuals and a contract.
3. They wanted to go never mind that they weren't invited.
4. Along the way we saw the Delta Queen a luxury steamboat five sailboats evidently racing and two houseboats each being pulled by a tug.
5. When the clock showed 8 45 sharp Monica called in her contest entry to the radio station.
6. Deep in his heart he felt sorry for Tori however he knew he'd better not tell her so.
7. I'll call when I get home oh I just remembered I won't be home until after midnight.
8. Some things such as old heartaches are best forgotten about.
9. The qualities necessary for succeeding in anything are as follows a positive attitude determination and high self-esteem.
10. I am interested in numerous hobbies stamp collecting singing roller skating racquetball and dancing to name just a few.

Skill Test **Punctuation**

Rewrite the following sentences and add any needed punctuation to each of them.

1. Alonzo do you have my bicycle
2. I really enjoy Mr. Ortiz the debate coach
3. Throughout the bitter winter we tried to keep warm
4. Gosh was I embarrassed
5. If Natasha wants to come to the party she is certainly welcome
6. On July 20 1982 Harry went to camp for the first time
7. Yes I promise to call Juan tonight
8. because the sun was so hot the tomato plants wilted
9. I want you to move the bed and then I want you to paint the room
10. Aunt Harriet ran into the room grabbed the cage and took our parakeet to the vet
11. There won't of course be enough blankets to keep everyone warm
12. you must study the following verbs ride burst catch and drink
13. Is there a way to make amends unfortunately I don't think so
14. A valentine such as the ones they used to send at the turn of the century can easily be made by hand
15. Anthony I need some help quick
16. Mark Twain the wonderful humorist gave us many memorable sayings
17. August 14 was marked as the day for the rally however it rained too hard to hold it
18. why do they keep changing prime-time shows on TV
19. I know I should eat liver parsley and spinach but I hate all three of these foods
20. please Maria stop acting so sulky and before you know it you'll feel happy again

Chapter 22

USING APOSTROPHES AND QUOTATIONS

Apostrophes and quotations are two punctuation marks that serve several different uses.

Apostrophes

Possession or Ownership

These two sentences have almost the same meaning.

The dispute was over the employee's benefits.

The dispute was over the employees' benefits.

The s on <u>benefits</u> shows that there is more than one benefit. Does the s on <u>employees</u> give you the same information? It doesn't because the word has an *apostrophe*. The apostrophe is the key.

In the first sentence, the apostrophe is *before* the s. That means there is *one* employee.

In the second sentence, the apostrophe is *after* the s. That means there is *more than one* employee. Indeed, the meaning of the whole sentence hangs on one little mark—the apostrophe.

Rule: **To indicate ownership by one person, place, or thing, place an apostrophe before the *s*.**

To indicate ownership by more than one person, place, or thing, add an apostrophe after the *s*.

To use the apostrophe to show possession or ownership do the following:

Singular (one person or thing)

Examples:

employee	Chris	Mr. Jones
Kim	Ms. Harris	Mrs. Johnson

Rule: **Write the noun or name and add the apostrophe and s.**

Examples: employee's benefits   Ms. Harris's office
                Kim's house   Mr. Jones's office
                Chris's house   Mrs. Johnson's office

Rule: **For names that end in two s sounds or a z and s sound, add
              the apostrophe only.**

Examples: University of Kansas' winning team
                Texas' impressive growth
                Francis' house
                Alexis' idea

To add another *s* would make these names awkward to pronounce.

Plural (more than one person or thing)

Examples: employees   teachers   children   women

Rule: **If the plural noun already ends in s, add the apostrophe only.**

Examples: employees' benefits   teachers' association

Rule: **If the plural noun does *not* end in s, add the apostrophe
              and s.**

Examples: children's department   women's jobs

Skills Activity 1   **Singular and Plural Possessives**

Some of the following words are singular and some are plural.
Write the possessive form of each word on your paper.

> *Example:* penny, penny's

1. city   6. phone
2. cities   7. hero
3. Morris   8. Ms. Willis
4. mice   9. child
5. chief   10. children

Skills Activity 2   **Placing Apostrophes Correctly**

Each of the following word groups needs an apostrophe to show possession. On a separate sheet of paper, write each word group and put in the apostrophe correctly.

Example: two cents worth, two cents' worth

1. a babys cry
2. a dollars worth
3. womens shoe sizes
4. the citys taxes
5. a womans shoe size

6. a knifes blade
7. all the knives blades
8. one radios speakers
9. several speakers volume
10. last evenings newscasts

Skills Activity 3   **Showing Possession**

Each of the following word groups can be written another way to show possession using the apostrophe. Rewrite each word group on a separate sheet of paper. Begin with the final noun; use the apostrophe or the apostrophe and *s* to show possession. Then add the word that says what it possesses.

Example: the performance that belongs to Miss Dennis
Miss Dennis'<u>s</u> performance

1. the team that belongs to Kansas City
2. the clothing store that belongs to the men
3. the beauty that belongs to a woman
4. the French Quarter that belongs to New Orleans
5. the car that belongs to Ms. Wallace
6. the programs that belong to the children
7. the forms that belong to the personnel director
8. the drama that belongs to ancient Greece
9. the rules that belong to the club members
10. the costumes that belong to the actress

Contractions

Compare the key words in these sentences:

Examples: <u>They have</u> planned the art fair so that it <u>cannot</u> be postponed even if the weather <u>does not</u> cooperate.

<u>They've</u> planned the art fair so that it <u>can't</u> be postponed even if the weather <u>doesn't</u> cooperate.

The key words in the first sentence are shortened to form the *contractions* in the second sentence. (*Contract* means "shorten" or "make smaller.")

Rule: **Use the *apostrophe* to replace the letters left out of a contraction.**

Examples: we are = we're   do not = don't
             they have = they've   cannot = can't
             she will = she'll   he is = he's

Skills Activity 4   **Forming Contractions**

Each of the following word groups can be shortened to form a contraction. Write the contraction for each word group on your paper.

> *Example:* you will, you'll

1. she will   6. I am
2. he is   7. cannot
3. have not   8. does not
4. do not   9. I have
5. you are   10. they are

Skills Activity 5   **Adding Contractions**

Rewrite the following sentences and add apostrophes where necessary to form correct contractions.

1. Youve seen whats in style for the coming season.
2. Shouldnt that stereo volume be turned down?
3. Its my opinion that you werent on the right track.
4. Werent those committee meetings much too long?
5. Theyve found that Chicago isnt as windy as many other cities.
6. Youll find that girls and boys wont agree on what to play.
7. Dont assume that what hasnt worked cant eventually work.
8. Weve heard your excuses, and they dont make any sense.
9. That doesnt mean you couldnt hit on some bright ideas.
10. I hope youre telling me the truth when you say shell be here soon.

Quotations

Repeating a person's *exact* words is called "quoting." *Quotation marks* (" ") are needed along with other punctuation and capitalization. Find the quotation marks in the example.

Examples: "What are you doing with that lion?" asked Stephanie. "You should take him to a zoo."

"I did take him to a zoo," Jerry replied.

Stephanie asked, "Then what is he doing here?"

"He had such a good time that now we're going to a movie!" Jerry exclaimed.

To write someone's exact words, do the following:

Rule: **Use a capital to begin the first word spoken. Use quotation marks before and after the words spoken.**

Example: "What are you doing with that lion?" asked Stephanie.

Rule: **Name the speaker either before or after the words spoken.**

Example: **Before:** Stephanie asked, "Then what is he doing here?"
After: "I did take him to a zoo," Jerry replied.

Rule: **When the speaker is named before the words, use a comma between the speaker's name and the quotation marks.**

Example: Stephanie asked, "Then what is he doing here?"

When the speaker is named after the words:

Rule: **Put the end punctuation mark between the last spoken word and the quotation mark.**

Example: ". . . doing with that lion?" asked Stephanie.

Rule: **Where the end punctuation mark would normally be a period, use a comma.**

Example: "I did take him to a zoo," Jerry replied.

Rule: **Begin a new paragraph each time the speaker changes.**

Example: "What are you doing with that lion?" asked Stephanie. "You should take him to a zoo."
"I did take him to a zoo," Jerry replied.

Rule: **If appropriate, you may split the quotation and put the speaker's name in the middle of a sentence, using commas and quotation marks.**

Example: "He had such a good time," Jerry exclaimed, "now we're going to a movie!"

Skills Activity 6   **Punctuating Quotations**

The sentences below contain quotations and the source. Some capitals and punctuation marks are missing. Write each sentence, putting in the needed capitals and punctuation marks. Use a separate sheet of paper.

> *Examples:* Max asked   when does vacation start
> Max asked, "When does vacation start?"
>
> when does vacation start   asked Max.
> "When does vacation start?" asked Max.

1. The steward said   please have your boarding passes ready
2. The sign said   this way out
3. the fall semester begins after Labor Day   said the announcement
4. why can't vacations last longer   complained the tourists
5. The sign flashed   don't walk
6. The weather report warned   cloudy with a chance of rain
7. what a terrible show   shouted the TV viewers
8. give me a roast beef on rye   said the customer
9. do you want to sit in the nonsmoking section   asked the ticket agent
10. how high can prices get   exclaimed the shopper

Skills Activity 7   **Creating Direct Quotations**

Each of the following sentences tells about a quotation, but it doesn't give the exact words. On your own paper rewrite each sentence so that it contains a quotation. Change words as needed, and put in the correct capitals and punctuation marks.

> *Examples:* The sign said that the store hours are 9:00 to 6:00.
> The sign said, "The store hours are 9:00 to 6:00."
>
> A shopper asked when the sale would begin.
> A shopper asked, "When will the sale begin?"

1. The operator said that the number had been changed.
2. The pilot suggested that we keep our seatbelts fastened.
3. The weather service repeated that the tornado warnings had been cancelled.
4. The paper said that the transit fare would go up again.
5. The TV announcer repeated that the station is having operating difficulties.
6. The customer asked where the best seats are.

7. The answering machine said to give your message at the beep sound.

8. The ad shouted to buy America's favorite cleanser.

9. The clerk explained that a computer breakdown lost the order.

10. The woman asked when she could see a replay of the special events tape.

Skills Activity 8　　Punctuating Dialogue

Capitals and punctuation marks are missing from the following jokes. On your own paper rewrite each joke, putting in the needed capitals and punctuation marks.

1. what are you going to pay me for this work　　asked Milt

   I'll pay you what you're worth　　replied his boss

   I'd rather have some money　　said Milt

2. the guest said　　I want to leave a 6:00 call

   we're all out of 6:00 calls　　replied the hotel clerk

   then call me twice at 3:00　　exclaimed the guest

3. I've lost my wallet　　shouted Max

   where did you lose it　　asked Gilda

   over there　　replied Max

   then why are you looking for it over here　　asked Gilda

   there's more light over here　　explained Max

Skills Activity 9　　Writing Dialogue

Write your own joke or a brief dialogue between two people. Include two speakers and at least three quotations. Put in the correct capitals and punctuation marks. Don't forget to start a new paragraph each time the speaker changes.

Skill Test　　Apostrophes and Quotations

Rewrite the following sentences and add apostrophes and quotation marks where needed for correct punctuation.

1. Some of the worlds fastest trains arent in the United States but in Japan and France.

2. Dallass huge airport is one of Texas great showplaces, according to the promotional brochure.

3. Wasnt *Hello Dolly* based on Thornton Wilders *The Matchmaker?*

4. Shell come when shes good and ready.

5. Some womens organizations have changed many peoples way of thinking.

6. They say that one persons meat is anothers poison.

7. One persons meat is anothers poison my aunt Ida used to say to her brothers when they argued politics.

8. That movies ending cant be as good as its beginning.

9. Arent the childrens programs shown on Saturday morning?

10. Everyones hope was to get the stars autograph.

11. Maurice yelled thief thief even though the man hadnt yet tried to steal anything.

12. Youll find that a fools money is foolishly spent.

13. A fools money is foolishly spent Judy exclaimed when Tonys sister asked her to buy some raffle tickets.

14. Why cant everyones favorite program be on at the right time?

15. Its a shame that Martins watch hasnt worked right since he bought it.

16. Shouldnt the new cars mileage be better than the old?

17. The sign said this way out but they didnt pay attention and got lost.

18. Atlantas rapid transit system isnt the countrys largest but its the newest.

19. Candices best idea wasnt even heard before the groups president adjourned the meeting.

20. When we entered the theatre the usher said the plays already started. Youll have to wait until intermission to be seated.

Chapter 23

CAPITALIZATION AND ABBREVIATION

Capitalization

This section gives you a review of when and how to use capital letters in *proper nouns*, *titles*, and *names*.

Proper Nouns

Notice the key words in these two examples:

Examples: We drove from the <u>city</u> to the <u>beach</u> in our new <u>car</u> along the crowded <u>parkway</u>.

We drove from <u>New York City</u> to <u>Jones Beach</u> in our new <u>Chevrolet</u> along the crowded <u>Southern State Parkway</u>.

The underlined words in the first sentence do not tell you which city, beach, car, or parkway. For example, the city could be New York, Detroit, Chicago, Houston, or Los Angeles. In the second sentence, the underlined words give readers more specific information. The words in the first sentence do not begin with capitals. In the second sentence, the underlined words do begin with capitals. These are *proper nouns*. Here is how to tell whether to capitalize a noun:

Rule: **Use capitals to begin names of specific places, persons, or things *(proper nouns)*.**

Examples:

New York City	Empire State Building
Jones Beach	University of Texas
Chevrolet	Leathern Suntan Lotion
Southern State Parkway	Canada

Rule: **Do not use capitals to begin words that do not name specific persons, places, or things *(common nouns)*.**

Examples:

city	building
beach	university
car	product
parkway	country

Rule:　**Use capitals for words formed from *proper nouns.***

Examples:　Canadian dollars　　　Chinese cooking
　　　　　　French bread　　　　　English muffins

　　　　Notice how a word is used before deciding on a capital. (Sometimes a word may be either a proper noun or a common noun.)

Examples:　**Common:**　The <u>city</u> is crowded.
　　　　　　Proper:　Let's see a show in New York <u>City</u>.

　　　　　　Common:　Take the next exit off the <u>freeway</u>.
　　　　　　Proper:　Take the Santa Monica <u>Freeway</u>.

Rule:　**Use capitals for words that name historical events, historical periods, special events, and holidays.**

Examples:

Historical Events	**Historical Periods**
French Revolution	Middle Ages
Korean Conflict	Dark Ages
Yalta Conference	Renaissance
World War II	Restoration

Special Events	**Holidays**
World Series	Memorial Day
Junior Prom	Thanksgiving Day
Book Week	Labor Day
Superbowl	Independence Day

Skills Activity 1　　**Capitalizing Proper Nouns**

Read each sentence and find the proper noun. Then, on your own paper, rewrite the sentence, putting in capitals where they belong.

　　Example:　An older building that was the world's tallest is the woolworth building.

　　　　　　An older building that was the world's tallest is the <u>W</u>oolworth <u>B</u>uilding.

1. Many companies have kept their family name, such as the pillsbury company.
2. The atlantic ocean can be treacherously stormy.
3. Where is the campus of florida state university?
4. The eiffel tower was once the tallest structure in the world.
5. One of our most picturesque cities is san antonio.
6. For some reason, chinese cooking is becoming more popular.
7. One holiday that occurs in the fall is columbus day.

8. I have always wanted to attend a world series game.
9. You must be familiar with many of the english writers of the renaissance.
10. The battle of the coral sea occurred during stormy weather.

Skills Activity 2	**Common Nouns and Proper Nouns**

Each item below is a common noun. Write a proper noun that is appropriate for each common noun.

Example: day, Tuesday

1. day
2. month
3. TV personality
4. movie theater
5. lake
6. state
7. country
8. U.S. city
9. European city
10. river
11. ocean
12. street
13. school
14. town, suburb
15. county
16. neighborhood store, market
17. large department store
18. car

Titles

Titles are proper nouns because they are names of exact things such as books, magazines, recordings, songs, movies, and TV shows. Titles either are underlined or set off with quotation marks.

Examples:

The Grapes of Wrath	**Book**
Newsweek	**Magazine**
Greatest Hits Live	**Recording**
"America the Beautiful"	**Song**
It's a Wonderful Life	**Movie**
"Sesame Street"	**TV Show**

To capitalize and punctuate different kinds of titles, do the following:

Rule: **Capitalize the first and all important words. Do not capitalize *a, an, the,* and short words (fewer than five letters) that connect or point out, such as:**

and	in	onto	from
at	into	or	on
by	of	out	with
for	off	to	

Examples: <u>Tunnel in the Sky</u>
              <u>The Yearling</u>
              (*The* is capitalized because it is the first word in the title.)

Rule: **Underline long or major works.**

Book: <u>The Grapes of Wrath</u>
Magazine: <u>Time</u>
Newspaper: <u>Houston Chronicle</u>
Record Album: <u>Sinatra's Greatest Hits</u>
Movie, Play: <u>Raiders of the Lost Ark</u>

Rule: **Use quotation marks for shorter works.**

Short Story: "The Gift of the Magi"
Chapter: "How to Save Energy"
Song: "The Star-Spangled Banner"
Poem: "I Never Saw a Moor"
Article: "Crisis in the Control Towers"
TV Show: "Home Improvement"

Skills Activity 3   **Capitalizing Titles**

The title in each sentence is written without capitals. Copy each sentence, putting in capitals where they belong. Use a separate sheet of paper.

Example: Norman Mailer's <u>the naked and the dead</u> is a well-known World War II novel.

             Norman Mailer's <u>The Naked and the Dead</u> is a well-known World War II novel.

1. James Jones's <u>from here to eternity</u> is another World War II novel.
2. "once by the pacific" is a poem by Robert Frost.
3. The James Dean movie, <u>rebel without a cause</u>, is a classic.
4. Robert Louis Stevenson's "a lodging for the night" is a good short story.
5. <u>road and track</u> is a favorite magazine for car buffs.
6. The chapter, "food for thought," tells how to eat wisely.
7. <u>wind, sand, and stars</u> is an unusual book about the early days of flying.
8. The atlanta <u>constitution</u> is an influential newspaper in the South.
9. Songs like "body and soul" never seem out of date.
10. T. S. Eliot's "the waste land" is a famous modern poem.

Skills Activity 4   **Punctuating Titles**

The title in each sentence is written without punctuation. On a separate sheet of paper, write the sentence, putting in the correct punctuation for the title.

Example: Michael Crichton's The Andromeda Strain is a gripping science fiction novel.

Michael Crichton's <u>The Andromeda Strain</u> is a gripping science fiction novel.

1. The novel Tender Is the Night is one of Fitzgerald's best.
2. Emily Dickinson's poem I Never Saw a Moor is probably her most famous.
3. One of the great TV successes is the show Sesame Street.
4. The Washington Post has outstanding reporting.
5. Poe's The Tell-Tale Heart is a chilling short story.
6. A movie like Raiders of the Lost Ark is shown again and again.
7. I Got Rhythm is a favorite old song.
8. Read the article How Cigarettes Kill.
9. The novel All the King's Men is about politics.
10. The short story The Cask of Amontillado is Poe at his best.

Names

Most people are known by their first names or first and last names.

| *Examples:* | Thomas | Tom | Thomas Katsoulis |
| | Beverly | Bev | Beverly Bianka |

Also, often included with names are titles and initials.

Examples:	Mr. Thomas J. Katsoulis	Miss Beverly Bianka
	Dr. T. J. Katsoulis	Ms. Beverly C. Bianka
	Prof. Thomas J. Katsoulis	Dr. B. C. Bianka

To write names of people, do the following:

Rule: **Use *capital letters* to begin names of people.**

| *Examples:* | <u>M</u>ichele, <u>S</u>helley | <u>J</u>ohn, <u>J</u>ack |
| | <u>M</u>ichele <u>M</u>iller | <u>J</u>ohn <u>M</u>orris |

Rule:	**Use *capital letters* and *periods* for abbreviated titles and initials.**

Examples: <u>Mrs</u><u>.</u> Michele Miller   <u>Mr</u><u>.</u> John Morris
                <u>Ms</u><u>.</u> Beverly <u>C</u><u>.</u> Bianka   <u>Dr</u><u>.</u> <u>T</u><u>.</u> <u>J</u><u>.</u> Katsoulis

Rule:	**Do *not* use a period for a title that is not an abbreviation.**

Examples: Miss Burns (<u>Miss</u> is not an abbreviation.)
                Aunt Beverly (<u>Aunt</u> is not an abbreviation.)
                Uncle John (<u>Uncle</u> is not an abbreviation.)

Skills Activity 5 **Punctuating and Capitalizing Names**

The names in each sentence below are written without capitals and periods. Read each sentence and decide where the capitals and periods belong. Then, write each sentence, putting in the capitals and periods. Use a separate sheet of paper.

> *Example:*   mrs j d parente and mr h p homes headed the committee.
>
>   Mrs. J. D. Parente and Mr. H. P. Homes headed the committee.

1. Both dentists, dr j l brace and dr kathleen d bridges, attended.
2. mayor alvarez asked for more city funds from gov dahler.
3. mrs harris goes to the hair stylist, mr stiles.
4. bruce katz works part time at the animal hospital for dr setter.
5. Two Washington regulars are sen willis quick and rep j b nimble.
6. It didn't take long for mr gil t persons to call his lawyer, ms i m lawless.
7. The new tennis stars are jane court and buddy racket.
8. prof h v braines and prof o b smart are coauthors of a textbook.
9. Did sen m t tung or rep constance noyes speak at the rally?
10. On exhibit were paintings by ms dabble and mr brush.

Abbreviations

This section reviews the correct uses of abbreviations in *titles, terms, organizations, addresses,* and *dates.*

Standard Abbreviations

Here is a bulletin board announcement:

WHAT:	Boy Scouts of America Awards
WHERE:	Public Broadcasting Service
WHEN:	Wednesday, February 16

Several standard abbreviations could help save space in the announcement.

WHAT:	BSA awards
WHERE:	PBS
WHEN:	Wed., Feb. 16

Abbreviations, or shortened forms, save space and make writing simpler.

Rule: **To write standard abbreviations, do the following: Use *capitals* and *periods* for most familiar abbreviations, such as titles of people, initials, months, days, and time and address items.**

Examples: Mrs. Gale F. Harris

Jan.	Ave.	A.M.
Feb.	St.	P.M.
Mar.	Blvd.	Fla. (or FL)
Mon.	Dr.	Ill. (or IL)
Tues.	Mr.	Nev. (or NV)
Wed.	Ms.	

Rule: **When abbreviating state names, the Postal Service suggests two-letter abbreviations. Use capitals and *no* periods.**

AL Alabama	IN Indiana	NV Nevada	SC South Carolina
AK Alaska	IA Iowa	NH New	SD South Dakota
AZ Arizona	KS Kansas	Hampshire	TN Tennessee
AR Arkansas	KY Kentucky	NJ New Jersey	TX Texas
CA California	LA Louisiana	NM New Mexico	UT Utah
CO Colorado	ME Maine	NY New York	VT Vermont
CT Connecticut	MD Maryland	NC North Carolina	VA Virginia
DE Delaware	MA Massachusetts	ND North Dakota	WA Washington
DC Dist. of Col.	MI Michigan	OH Ohio	WV West Virginia
FL Florida	MN Minnesota	OK Oklahoma	WI Wisconsin
GA Georgia	MO Missouri	OR Oregon	WY Wyoming
HI Hawaii	MS Mississippi	PA Pennsylvania	
ID Idaho	MT Montana	PR Puerto Rico	
IL Illinois	NE Nebraska	RI Rhode Island	

Rule: Use capitals *only* for certain abbreviations, such as companies, organizations, and systems.

PBS	TWA	NOW	HBO
GM	UN	ZIP code	WHO
CORE	AM/FM	NBC	NATO
TV	ABC	GE	ROM
CBS	IBM	CD	VCR

Rule: Use small letters and periods for most standard measures.

in.	tbsp.	mi.	gal.
tsp.	yd.	qt.	oz.
ft.	pt.	mph.	lb.

Rule: Use small letters and *no* periods for most metric measures.

cm (centimeter)	m (meter)	km (kilometer)
g (gram)	kg (kilogram)	l (liter)

The exception is *Celsius* (C).

Skills Activity 6   **Using Standard Abbreviations**

Read each word or group of words. Then write the correct abbreviation.

Example: gallon, gal.

1. pound
2. Celsius
3. Colorado
4. Connecticut
5. Arkansas
6. Arizona
7. Maine
8. Maryland
9. Massachusetts
10. frequency modulation
11. quart
12. mile
13. kilometer
14. centimeter
15. kilogram
16. liter

Skills Activity 7   **Writing Correct Abbreviations**

Two abbreviations in each of the following sentences are incorrectly written. Find the abbreviations and copy each sentence, writing the abbreviations correctly. Use a separate sheet of paper.

Example: Was the letter received by dec 31 in Chicago, Il?

Was the letter received by Dec. 31 in Chicago, IL?

1. First-run movies are at 9:00 pm on hbo.
2. It is 2190 Km., or 1111 Mi, between Dallas and Miami.
3. Many of the n.a.t.o. nations are also in the Eec.
4. In the eastern time zone, 8:00 to 11:00 p.m. is t.v. prime time.
5. Does the recipe call for a Tsp or a Tbsp of curry powder?
6. I learned that 60 Mi is nearly the same as 100 Km.
7. Was Hallmark or i.b.m. the sponsor of the holiday special on cbs?
8. The stakeout was at a ninth ave address on sept. 12.
9. A body temperature of 37° c. is normal, while 38° C. is feverish.
10. Soft drinks are sold by the L., but the Qt is still the usual size for milk.

Writing Addresses Correctly

Rule: **In addresses clearly write or print all items, especially numbers.**

1. Keep a straight margin at the left.
2. Capitalize each word or abbreviation.
3. Write the city or town, state, and ZIP code directly below the street address.
4. Use the Postal Service's two-letter abbreviation, as given on page 315.
5. Write the ZIP code after the state name. Do not place a comma between the state and the ZIP code.

Example: Anna Lopez
2520 West Bayview Blvd.
Tampa, FL 33611-2883

Remember that on envelopes and packages you do *not* use punctuation.

Skills Activity 8   **Writing Addresses Correctly**

On your own paper write each of the following addresses, inserting capital letters. Assume these addresses are for envelopes.

Example: 7255 cascade pkwy portland or 97214-1704

7255 Cascade Pkwy
Portland OR 97214-1704

1. 11530 milam avenue houston tx 77090-2449
2. 5220 valley blvd phoenix az 85033-6487

3. 72 palisade terr san diego ca 92117-1179

4. 4950 ringling drive sarasota florida 33582-4894

5. 7825 lee avenue atlanta georgia 30312-4520

6. 3915 boulder ave denver colorado 80211-9131

7. 5935 oakland pkwy houston texas 75231-0055

8. 3550 country club lane kansas city mo 64112-2416

9. 6212 riverview blvd alexandria va 22317-2301

10. 33 ogden avenue hinsdale il 60521-6989

Writing Dates Correctly

Many practical items have the date on them, such as receipts or sales slips, letters, checks, and order forms. The date gives a record of when something was ordered, bought, paid for, or delivered. The date can be written different ways:

Numbers only:

Examples: 5/9/97   2/17/99

Abbreviations and numbers:

Examples: Oct. 18, 1998   Sat., Oct. 18, 1998

Words and numbers:

Examples: October 13, 1997   Saturday, October 13, 1997

For any business document, such as a record of payment, it's a good idea to use words—or abbreviations—and numbers, rather than numbers only.

To write the date, do the following:

Rule: **Use a *capital* to begin each word in a date.**

Examples: July 6, 1998   Monday, July 6, 1998

Rule: **Use a *comma* between the day (if included) and month and between the month and year.**

Examples: July 6, 1998   Monday, July 6, 1998

Rule: **For a date in a sentence, use a comma after the complete date (with or without the year) if the sentence goes on.**

Examples: The fireworks were postponed until Monday, July 6, because of rain.

July 6, 1936, holds the record for the hottest day.

Rule: **Use capitals and periods in abbreviations. (You may need abbreviations if space is limited, as on an entry blank or other form.)**

Examples: Nov. 11, 1999   Mon., Feb. 12, 1998

Day		**Month**		**Month**	
Sunday	Sun.	January	Jan.	August	Aug.
Monday	Mon.	February	Feb.	September	Sept.
Tuesday	Tues.	March	Mar.	October	Oct.
Wednesday	Wed.	April	Apr.	November	Nov.
Thursday	Thurs.	May	—	December	Dec.
Friday	Fri.	June	—		
Saturday	Sat.	July	—		

Skills Activity 9   **Writing Dates Correctly**

On a separate sheet of paper, write each of the following sentences, correctly inserting capital letters or punctuation marks as necessary.

1. The next Kentucky Derby will take place on saturday may 4 1998.
2. Our nation's birthday is july 4 1776.
3. june 6 1944 was the beginning of the greatest military invasion in history.
4. jan 8 is my brother's birthday
5. The date on the letter, 81495, was not clearly written.
6. On february 25 1924 Montuda became a citizen of the United States.
7. I believe that particular event took place in april 1978.
8. When tues september 5 arrives, we'll be in New York City.
9. Their wedding is set for sunday June 18 1998.
10. Dates such as november 27 1960 and december 23 1957 stick in my mind.

Skill Test   **Using Capitals and Abbreviations**

Rewrite each of the following sentences, correctly inserting capitals and abbreviations where needed:

1. aunt cynthia wrote a letter to ms alvarez on my behalf.
2. "The outcasts of poker flat" by brett hart was a good story.
3. She plans to attend washington state university in september 1998.

4. The population of new jersey is about the same as that of japan.

5. The senator wanted to see dr molnar right away.

6. Does the public broadcasting system get any funding from the general public?

7. There is both a portland maine and a portland oregon.

8. Don't drive over 65 miles per hour on the jefferson freeway.

9. Do you like italian or french dressing on your salad?

10. Before you know it, monday september 5 will be here.

11. The library doesn't subscribe to <u>reader's digest</u> any longer.

12. Have you read that great article "how to make a fortune in the stock market"?

13. They called mrs helen k russell to the stand.

14. Which is the world's longest river, the nile or the amazon?

15. They took an apartment at 516 riverside drive in manhattan.

16. The songwriter, jerome kern, wrote "smoke gets in your eyes."

17. Let's go to the orpheum theater and see <u>mash</u>.

18. Is this the week for the superbowl or the world series?

19. prof thomas schuller lectured at the annual may day program.

20. Neither los angeles nor san francisco is the capital of california.

INDEX